Identities

Identities

The Impact of Ethnicity on Canadian Society

EDITED BY

Wsevolod Isajiw

Canadian Ethnic
Studies Association
Volume V

PETER MARTIN ASSOCIATES LIMITED

Canadian Cataloguing in Publication Data

Main entry under title:

Identities

(Canadian Ethnic Studies Association series ; v.5)

A selection of papers presented to the second biennial Canadian Ethnic Studies Association conference held in Toronto, 1973.

Includes index.

ISBN 0-88778-146-2 bd. ISBN 0-88778-154-3 pa.

1. Canada – Foreign population – Congresses. 2. Ethnology – Canada – Congresses. 3. Ethnicity – Congresses. I. Isajiw, Wsevolod W., 1933–   II. Series: Canadian Ethnic Studies Association. Canadian Ethnic Studies Association series ; v.5.

FC104.I34   301.45'0971   C76-017181-5
F1035.A1I34

Design: Michael Solomon

PETER MARTIN ASSOCIATES LIMITED
35 Britain Street, Toronto, Canada M5A 1R7

United Kingdom: Books Canada, 1 Bedford Road, London N2, England.
United States: Books Canada, 33 East Tupper St., Buffalo, N.Y. 14203.

Contents

ix   Preface

Cornelius J. Jaenen   xi   Ethnic Studies: An Integral Part
of Canadian Studies

1   Ethnicity in the Emergence of Canadian Society

J.E. Rea   3   "My main line is the kiddies . . .
make them good Christians and good
Canadians, which is the same thing"

Marian McKenna   11   Commentary

D.H. Avery   15   The Immigrant Industrial Worker in
Canada 1896-1930: The Vertical
Mosaic as an Historical Reality

Marian McKenna   33   Commentary

2   Ethnicity as a Factor in the Development of Canadian Arts

Istvan Anhalt   39   About One's Place and Voice

William Kurelek   46   The Development of Ethnic Consciousness in a Canadian Artist

Eli Mandel   57   Ethnic Voice in Canadian Writing

3 Quebec: Politics and Change

Réjean Landry 71 The Political Development of Quebec: A Strategic Interpretation

Michael B. Stein 85 The Dynamics of Contemporary Party Movements in Quebec: Some Comparative Aspects of Créditisme and Indépendantisme

4 Ethnicity: Power, Commitment or Segregation?

Donald G. Baker 109 Ethnicity, Development and Power: Canada in Comparative Perspective

John Goldlust and 132 Factors Associated with Commitment
Anthony Richmond to and Identification with Canada

Sally M. Weaver 154 Segregation and the Indian Act: The Dialogue of "Equality" vs. "Special Status"

Alexander Matejko 162 Commentary on Section 4

5 Research on Ethnicity in Canada

Howard Palmer 167 History and Present State of Ethnic Studies in Canada

Jerzy Zubrzycki 184 Research on Ethnicity in Australia and Canada

6 Canadian Culture and Ethnic Groups: an Analysis

Raymond Breton, 191 The Impact of Ethnic Groups on
Jean Burnet, Canadian Society: Research Issues
Norbert Hartmann,
Wsevolod W. Isajiw and
Jos Lennards

214 Publications of the Canadian
Ethnic Studies Association

215 Index

PREFACE

This book represents selections from the proceedings of the second biennial conference of the Canadian Ethnic Studies Association which took place in Toronto on October 26 and 27, 1973. When I undertook the organization of the conference, I intended to focus the symposium on the theme of the developing Canadian culture. If we can assume that Canadian culture is something unique to Canada and something relatively unified but still in the process of development, what influence, if any, does ethnic diversity have on it? By the term culture I mean not only the "finer" aspects of life—art, philosophy, manners—but the total way of life, the ways and patterns of behaviour which are familiar to most people in society.

I have discussed this theme with the chairmen of the sessions and asked the participants to keep it in mind when preparing their papers. Each participant approached the problem from the vantage point of his or her discipline. Some, like those who discuss the arts, have dealt with it directly, others more indirectly.

Explicitly or implicitly the papers suggest several dimensions of the problem. These dimensions can be stated in the form of questions. To what extent do the creators of the fine culture choose between the elements of the various Canadian ethnic experiences in the process of artistic creation? To what extent do they rely on aspects of their own ethnic experience? Do elements of their ethnic experience psychologically necessitate certain artistic expressions or forms?

The papers given by the historians raise an antecedent question. To understand the place of ethnicity in the Canadian way of life, one first has to understand the structure of social relationships between the majority and the minority ethnic groups. This can be done by going back into history and using certain events as characteristic of this relationship. Although I did not plan it this way, it is perhaps no accident that those who spoke on the general topic of the emergence of the Canadian culture and society chose the history of the Prairies to make their point. It may very well be that a uniquely Canadian way of life was forged in the west, and that the Prairies offer the best test case of Canadian intergroup relations.

Another dimension of the general theme can be expressed in the following questions. Before we can speak of any integrated way of life, should we not first examine the extent to which various ethnic groups have power in the total society? To what extent are they committed to the total society?

And inversely, does commitment and power erode the basis on which many ethnic groups develop and maintain their unique values and patterns. Do they need a degree of segregation from the total society?

What about Quebec? With Quebec's significant reach for power, politics and political process seem to have become a major part of the province's way of life. What happens when a culture becomes politicized? Is politics a way of rationalizing the traditional, or is it a way of rebelling against it? How has the rest of Canada adjusted its way of life to the recent political processes in Quebec?

One session at the conference was dedicated to stock-taking, to reviewing research on ethnicity in Canada and comparing it with that in other countries, particularly Australia. There are many similarities between Australia and Canada. But have ethnic groups posed similar or different questions for the two societies?

When it was over, a group of sociologists decided to get together to discuss the issues raised at the conference as well as the issues which the conference failed to raise. The last chapter, an analysis of the conference, is the result of their discussions. It was first published as an article in the *Canadian Review of Sociology and Anthropology* and is reprinted here with the permission of the editor.

Studying ethnicity in Canada is studying Canadian society. That is what this book is about. It was also the theme of the presidential address at the conference and as such it acts as a fitting introduction to the volume. I trust that *Identities* will further our insights into Canadian society.

I would like to take this opportunity to thank all those who have helped to make *Identities* possible. Thanks are due to the Department of the Secretary of State in Ottawa for their generous assistance and special thanks to Mr. Steve Yaworsky. Ms. Valerie Wyatt's careful and expeditious editing of the manuscript is especially appreciated.

Wsevolod W. Isajiw
University of Toronto
July 1975

INTRODUCTION

Ethnic Studies: An Integral Part of Canadian Studies

Cornelius J. Jaenen

We are all ethnics. I am reminded of a recent cartoon in a popular magazine. A worried-looking father paternalistically looked at his recently engaged daughter and then turned to his prospective son-in-law and said, "And your children will be ethnics, I suppose!" Yes, we are all ethnics. We all have an *ethnos*. The English, Scots, Irish, Welsh, Québécois and Acadians are as ethnic as the Serbs, Danes, Ukrainians, Portuguese or Chinese.

The proposition I want to advance is that, given the multi-ethnic nature of this country, its vast and as yet largely untapped and undeveloped reservoir of rich human and cultural diversity, Canadian studies must necessarily incorporate a large and substantial component of ethnic studies.

What precisely is meant by ethnic studies? Is it limited to the study of obscure ethnic communities, to racial ghettos, to quaint folkways, to unassimilated cultural backwaters? I would like to suggest, while not excluding these areas, that the general area of ethnic studies is far more comprehensive than is generally recognized.

If ethnic studies is a comprehensive area, it can be presumed that it encompasses several distinct topics or fields, and that it overflows the traditional disciplinary boundaries. To my mind this is definitely the case. I would include within the compass of ethnic studies such socially discernible and historically documented experiences as immigration history, intergroup relations, race relations, aboriginal history as well as the study of individual ethnic groups. It flows over into the disciplines of sociology, political science, Slavic studies, linguistics, demography, psychology, human geography, ethnology, anthropology, law and the fine arts. It is evident that in a new country of recent development (in historical terms) all history is tied in some way to ethnicity. Our history begins with explorers and exploiters, merchants and missionaries. It rapidly becomes dominated by the theme of the transplantation and the gradual transformation of immigrant institutions. As the immigrant groups become more varied, a new theme—that of intergroup or interracial relations—takes on significance. With the emergence of a number of recognizable minorities, the study of minority groups, defined in linguistic, racial or religious terms, becomes an important part of national history.

In our day such minority group studies have taken on special emphases: for example, black studies, Indian studies, English-French relations and human rights. Every university calendar and every public school curriculum takes some of these areas into consideration. Indeed, the recognition of minorities as a third component in relation to the two dominant cultures or host societies in Canada has consecrated a new terminology—multiculturalism and ethno-cultural communities.

Let me illustrate from the traditional themes of Canadian history how ethnic studies are an integral part of national development. Let us begin with the French regime, an area of Canadian studies that is greatly neglected in many regions of this country, although it offers an explanation of the "French fact" in terms of both origins and characteristics.

The story of New France begins with a transfer of western European institutions and a migration of Renaissance European habits of thought to the New World. To be understood, this colonial beginning must be approached in terms of the impact which the New World and its aboriginal inhabitants made on metropolitan Frenchmen. Introduction to a new world and to new peoples provided challenges to cherished European ideas and ideals and, in very general terms, resulted in a confirmation in European minds of their superiority in technological, cultural and religious matters. Significantly, the French somatic norm image of their cultural superiority over the Amerindian cultures they encountered in New France did not include a racial component. Very rapidly the development of French colonies in Acadia, Newfoundland and Canada in the seventeenth century and in the "upper country" of Canada, the Illinois country, the far west and Louisiana in the eighteenth century was inextricably bound to aboriginal relationships. The French thought of themselves as the host society; the Catholic church promoted evangelization of the tribesmen, and the French state encouraged assimilation of the natives, giving them full citizenship rights by law as early as 1627. But the social realities ran counter to the ideological objectives. The Amerindians perceived their cultures as inherently superior to the French on a number of counts. French-Indian relations continued to be a dominant theme in colonial development.

The French responded to the processes and pressures of cultural contact with policies and "solutions". These ranged from acceptance of cultural pluralism, such as when the French minority (composed largely of traders, garrison troops and missionaries) lived in "Indian country" and depended on the aboriginal peoples' way of life, to a more assertive assimilationist position characterized by the homogeneous French seigneuries and towns of

xii

the St. Lawrence lowlands in which were located a few reservations of converted, domiciled, francisized Indians. The reservation, or *réserve*, had been inaugurated as early as 1637 to encourage isolated cells of converted aborigines to abandon their nomadism and animism and take up a settled agricultural life in a Catholic environment. This "solution" to problems of cultural contact, occasioned by the confrontation between a seventeenth-century French-Catholic technological civilization and an Amerindian aboriginal culture, was introduced both to integrate Indians into an alien European way of life, and to protect them from opposition in their traditional pagan society and from the evil effects of certain features of French society. Problems such as alcohol addiction, cultural disorientation, counter-innovative techniques in Indian societies and undercurrents of prejudicial group discrimination were in evidence even during this seemingly golden age of white-red relations. It is interesting and significant that the chief characteristics of European-aboriginal cultural contact were already delineated, and "solutions" to problems were advanced as early as the seventeenth century. These became the enduring features of this aspect of intergroup relations in Canada and persist to this very day. Unfortunately the current vision of the north differs little from the Talon vision of the west: recent administrations have made little progress beyond the Frontenac administration; the Department of Indian Affairs has come up with few "solutions" that Colbert's Ministry of the Marine had not already proposed 300 years ago.

Other aspects of our past, such as the growing tensions between the colony and the motherland and the existence of small minorities within New France, have continued to the present. All of these qualities of colonial life have persisted in some form to the present day, thanks to periodic renewal and fresh inputs. All may properly be considered as being within the domain of ethnic studies.

French immigration was never very extensive. At most only 10,000 immigrated over a 200-year period. Therefore a predominantly Canadian-born population soon emerged and reacted to later eighteenth-century French immigration, to the presence of French troops and to the dominant role of French administrators and entrepreneurs. This social and potentially political cleavage between French and Canadian was obvious by the mid-eighteenth century. The development of a colonial identity was not exclusively a Canadian phenomenon; an Acadian identity also asserted itself, especially after the conquest of 1713 and the brutal expulsion of 1755. The Articles of Capitulation in 1759 recognized these colonial identities as social realities and provided distinctive terms of settlement for the French, the Canadians and the Acadians.

Furthermore it is wrong to think of New France as a colony of homogeneous Norman-Catholic settlement. Other minorities in New France demanded recognition. The foundations of the fishing and trading enterprises were laid by the Huguenots, the French-Protestant minority which was often aided financially by foreign (e.g. Dutch) Protestant and Jewish investors. There were Huguenot merchants in the colony prior to the revocation of the Edict of Nantes in 1685, Huguenot soldiers in almost every contingent sent to America, and a significant increase in the number of French Protestants immigrating to Canada in the decade before the British conquest as toleration gained political ground in Enlightenment France. The origins of the French-Catholic population can be traced to almost every region of France, although most came from the north-western Atlantic region. The numbers of non-French people—Scots, Irish, Germans, Basques, Italians, Jews, New Englanders—assimilated into the original French-Canadian community is remarkable. In addition 230 Anglo-Americans, mostly captives of the Indians and prisoners of war, are known to have been assimilated by the French-Catholic colony. There was some interracial marriage between French men and Indian women, but the more significant miscegenation occurred outside the bonds of sacramental marriage. Demographers know very little about the numerous offspring of Indian women and French traders and soldiers. All this, of course, is the warp and woof of ethnic studies.

And what of the conquest and the cession of 1763? Approximately one-third of our population today is part of Canada by virtue of military conquest and diplomatic cession. That conquered component was Canadian before the conquest, Canadian at the cession, and remained Canadian after it became British. This elementary observation is a basic historical and sociological fact which large numbers of people in our generation have failed to grasp. It took a royal commission to bring this social reality into public prominence. And after the royal commission had thought its findings complete, there emerged yet another social reality which could not be ignored. Not only was Canada dualistic and bilingual, it was also a multi-ethnic nation.

But let us return to our colonial origins. The conquest experience was undoubtedly traumatic both for the French and the Canadians and for many British administrators. Some Canadians "never had it so good", to employ a popular expression, as when the British came; others were ruined, their economic or social position having been undermined. The Huguenot minority, for example, enjoyed a brief moment of prominence. But the old British Empire, of which Canada became a part, would never be quite the same again. How would Protestant Britain rule a French-speaking Catholic colony situated on the doorstep of restive Anglo-American colonies? Even the intro-duction of such traditional British procedures and rights as trial by jury and elected legislature necessitated a recognition of human rights and political privileges as yet unknown in Britain. Jury service and political office when instituted in Canada (or Quebec, as the British preferred to call it) involved some recognition of the civil rights of Roman Catholics, the use of the French language and ultimately the recognition of Canadian civil law and customs. This was a traumatic experience and a significant concession on the part of the British. From whatever perspective the conquest experience is approached (and there are many interesting avenues of investigation), it does seem to be well within the domain of ethnic studies.

To be fully understood, Canada's history as a British colony must be seen from the viewpoint of ethnic studies. One example of this is the arrival of the Loyalists during the American Revolution. The Loyalists created a new problem of dualism at the popular level which was intensified by demands for representative government and English common law. The answer was separatism, and the Loyalists became our first separatists. They successfully agitated for the division of Canada into upper and lower sections to reflect the fact that there were two races, two languages, two cultures and two sets of institutions in Canada. The Loyalist migration created new provinces in the Maritimes. It also introduced new balances among the various social, religious and ethnic communities which in turn influenced the development of responsible government, free common schools and, eventually, political union.

A second example is the French presence. The French forced recognition of the fact that to be British, one did not need to become English. This re-pudiation of assimilation, though not universally or willingly accepted by all British North Americans, was to have important implications in future decades for minority groups in Canada. The War of 1812 reminded French Canadians that, if to be British they did not need to become English, it was equally true that they could remain French Canadian precisely because they were British and not American.

And so one might proceed through our history. Take, for example, the beginnings of western Canada. How does one explain the Nor' West-Hudson Bay rivalry and the trials of the Selkirk settlers? How did the dual French-Catholic and English-Protestant support base for Louis Riel develop? Can the Red River resistance of 1869-70 and the creation of the province of Manitoba be understood apart from the approach of ethnic studies? The history of western Canada is basically a tale of aboriginal rights, intergroup relations and, most importantly, of immigration. Just as the populating of eastern Canada is associated with the great migration of 1815-1850, so the populating of western Canada is associated with the Laurier-Sifton immigration of 1896-1914. Canadian history—seen as social change and the economic and political consequences that resulted from it—is basically immigration history.

I submit that our history since 1867 can, and must be studied from the social viewpoint. The building of the C.P.R., for example, may be presented in the political framework of Confederation for British Columbia, the Pacific scandal, and Macdonald's nation-building. But to be understood completely, it has to be seen as massive state support of private enterprise and studied in terms of European immigration, western settlement, eastern industrial development and so on. It should be studied not merely as an investment by British and American financiers in Canada's future and their own fortunes, but also in the context of the labour of hundreds and thousands of men, many of them eastern European immigrants. The Slav settler helped build the C.P.R., and the Ukrainians provided much of the railway maintenance in succeeding decades. The western settler was brought out on the railway, and he remained economically tied to it whether he was a city labourer, a railway worker or a farmer. Similarly, if one looks at the development of mining in Canada, one cannot ignore the contribution of immigrant ethnic communities.

There is little point in wearying the reader with examples. To ignore ethnicity when studying such important national events as the Confederation debates, the National Policy, the New Brunswick and Manitoba Schools Questions, the immigration policies, the conscription debates of two World Wars and the "war hysteria" of the First World War, the emergence of national public schools, the Winnipeg General Strike and every federal election since 1896 is to rob these events of meaning.

Let us look at some of the leading Canadian-based news stories of the past few years—the James Bay development controversy, bilingualism in the federal civil service, the Gendron report in Quebec, the South Indian Lake controversy in Manitoba, the Cornwall and Elliott Lake school problems, the question of aboriginal rights and the Quebec provincial election. These news stories centre on ethnic studies. Can the issues raised by these events be identified without some reference to, and knowledge of Canada's immigration history, intergroup relations, cultural pluralism, diversity, minority rights and human rights? Obviously it is impossible to understand the social currents of the day without recognizing the importance of these issues. But in the past, the importance of ethnic studies has been ignored. It is a never-ending source of amazement to me that Amerindians are not mentioned in

xvi

our history texts after the period of the early French fur trade and the settlement of the west, that immigrants are almost totally ignored and that the role of the French Canadians is negligible. Our history has been largely the history of an elitist minority or dominant group, probably because we have written political history rather than social history.

By removing those areas of ethnic studies from Canadian Studies programmes, we remove what is characteristically and uniquely Canadian. But by emphasizing the elements I have mentioned, we can give Canadian Studies programmes themes and elements that more fully explain our national development in terms which have significance both for the Canadian experience and for other national experiences. Immigration, the development of a national consciousness, frontierism, decolonization—to my mind, these Canadian studies are in significant ways inescapably ethnic studies.

1 Ethnicity in the Emergence of Canadian Society

J.E. Rea   3   "My main line is the kiddies . . . make them good Christians and good Canadians, which is the same thing"

Marian McKenna   11   Commentary

D.H. Avery   15   The Immigrant Industrial Worker in Canada 1896-1930: The Vertical Mosaic as an Historical Reality

Marian McKenna   33   Commentary

"My main line is the kiddies . . . make them good Christians and good Canadians, which is the same thing"

J.E. Rea

There are two points of reference for this discursive paper. The first is the act of the Legislative Assembly of Manitoba passed in 1916 which established a unilingual system of public education, thus ending a bilingual system in theory and a multilingual system in practice. The second point is the reception given to the Royal Commission on Bilingualism and Biculturalism by the ethnic minority groups of the prairie west. Many people were surprised, indeed shocked, by the vehemence with which these groups objected to the alleged pretensions of francophone Canadians.

Others were struck by the irony of the situation. The ethnic groups which protested most vociferously about such irrelevancies as "having French forced down their throats" were also the very groups seeking most ardently the development of a multicultural Dominion. What hope would there be for their cultures if the French could not survive and flourish after more than three hundred years of struggle? Put this way, the attitude of prairie ethnic groups could be interpreted as one of spiteful resentment. But this interpretation fails to understand the ethnic groups and, more importantly, fails to appreciate the nature of prairie society which has evolved in the past sixty or seventy years. The greatest error, in my opinion, is to accept completely the proposition that the western ethnic groups are neither English nor French, despite their own claims.

This heretical observation is one historian's view of prairie cultural development and supports my thesis that the reaction of the ethnic minorities to Quebec, or more specifically to the recent policy of the federal government, may be partly explained by examining events which occurred during and after World War I. The extended title of this paper — "My main line is the kiddies . . . make them good Christians and good Canadians, which is the same thing" — is not intended to be taken facetiously. It is a quotation from the novel, *The Foreigner,* written by Winnipeg author Ralph Connor in 1909. It represents the settled conviction that the new immigrants, if they were not to threaten the social fabric, must be taught English and assimilated. The agents of assimilation were to be the Protestant churches and the public schools, especially the latter. The urgency resulted from the

3

fact that the prairie west was not a secure society with social institutions that could withstand the shock of a relatively massive immigration of people alien in language, religion and culture. The west was too new, too unformed, too fluid.

Modern prairie history dates only from 1870, the time of the creation of the Province of Manitoba and the Northwest Territories. The population of Manitoba was then evenly divided between Protestant anglophones and Catholic francophones. Their society was not unharmonious; it was perhaps Canada's only successful experiment in bicultural living. But it was not to last. Ontario had seen in Confederation the opportunity to make the prairie west a hinterland and to create there a society in its own image. So the Ontario migrants came in the thousands in the 1870s and 1880s, disrupting the cultural balance of the Red River community. They put their own stamp on Manitoba through what W.L. Morton has called "The Triumph of Ontario Democracy" and the creation of "A British and Canadian Province".

The political and administrative manifestations of cultural duality were thrust aside by Grit egalitarianism; the French language lost its official status and the dual school system was abolished. What became known as the Manitoba School Question was simply the last step in consolidating the desires of the new majority. The final, face-saving event in this chain was the Laurier-Greenway Compromise of 1897. Manitoba, it was then felt, would be free to develop according to the majority impulse. But one clause in the legislative embodiment of the Compromise was to have great repercussions.

Clause 258 of the amended Public Schools Act of Manitoba stated that, "when 10 of the pupils in any school speak the French language, or any language other than English, as their native language, the teaching of such pupils shall be conducted in French, or such other language, and English upon the bilingual system". The wording was carefully designed to placate both the Quebec Liberals and the Orangemen, who would object to any special privilege for the French alone. It was assumed that with the increase in Manitoba's English-speaking majority, the clause would very likely become a dead letter. As a result no attempt was made to define what was meant by "bilingual", and no provision was taken to prepare teachers in languages other than English.

The most obvious test of the cultural and social strength and integrity of any society is its capacity to absorb immigrants. Manitoba's challenge began just as the uproar over the School Question was quieting in the wake of the 1897 Compromise. One of the great migrations of the world was gathering strength in the late 1890s. Millions of people abandoned Europe to seek new lives in North America and Australasia. Hundreds of thousands streamed through Winnipeg to participate in the great enterprise of settling the Prairies. Ironically, Clifford Sifton, who had negotiated the Compromise for Greenway's government, encouraged and abetted this migration as Minister of the Interior in Laurier's cabinet. Sifton did not foresee the social problems which would result. To him, these sturdy peasants were the labour factor which would finally complete the great equation of the National Policy.

Not surprisingly, in their loneliness and apprehension the newcomers settled in groups, often encouraged by the policies of government and the avarice of land companies and railroads. Who could blame them for seeking to preserve what was left of their familiar world through any means open to them? They soon discovered the loophole in the Manitoba Public Schools Act that allowed them to have their children educated, at least partially, in their own language. Not all new immigrant groups took such advantage; but very quickly German, Ukrainian and Polish, in addition to French public schools were set up under the bilingual system permitted by the Schools Act. The Manitoba Government was even belatedly compelled to set up a teacher training programme for non-English teachers. The Ruthenian Training School located in Brandon attempted to cope with the difficulty of providing at least minimally prepared teachers. This development, of course, had been quite unforeseen when the 1897 Compromise had been adopted.

The ethnic minority groups had been welcomed at first for the economic contribution they could make to the development of western Canada in general and the Winnipeg business community in particular. But as their numbers increased and as they began to avail themselves of the opportunity presented by the Public Schools Act, a reaction set in. The attack was led by John W. Dafoe of the *Manitoba Free Press*. It would be absurd to accuse Dafoe of fomenting ill feeling against the minority groups or to blame him for the result. But his newspaper was a powerful instrument, and he became one of the most articulate opponents of clause 258. Between 1910 and 1914 the *Free Press* carried sixty-eight special articles and over a hundred editorials on the question of the public schools of the province. More and more Dafoe's concern focused on the language issue.

This was not unexpected. Dafoe's opinion had begun to shift as early as 1908 when he wrote:

> In a country like ours where so many nationalities are settling in our midst, it is imperative that the children of these different nationalities should be taught the same language, the same aspirations,

the same ideals of citizenship as our natural-born Canadians.[1]

Virtually the same argument was used by Connor the following year in *The Foreigner*. "These people here exist as an undigested foreign mass," he wrote. "They must be digested and absorbed into the body politic. They must be taught our ways of thinking and living, or it will be a mighty bad thing for us here in Western Canada."[2] The concensus for change was forming.

For Dafoe and those who followed his lead, the issue of bilingualism in the west was a contest between disruptive alien nationalism and unifying Canadian nationalism. The latter is not necessarily an ignoble ideal. But its legacy could have had an unfortunate effect. Dafoe objected to the operation of the bilingual clause because, he asserted, "it is dotting Manitoba with hotbeds for the propagation of foreign racial prejudice".[3] Throughout his campaign there was an unwavering assumption of the superiority of English. "This is an English-speaking province," he claimed, "and it is the duty of the government to see that every pupil of the public schools is given a sufficient education in English to equip him, in part at least, for the business of life."[4] His argument for the utility of the English language may be accepted. But over these years he insisted on referring to non-English schools as racial schools,[5] implying that only English schools were Canadian schools. As he put the issue in his characteristically direct manner, "We must Canadianize this generation of foreign-born settlers, or this will cease to be a Canadian country in any real sense of the term."[6]

Enough has been said to indicate the attitude forming in the majority group. By the outbreak of World War I the ethnic minorities were considered a threat to the cultural future of the prairie west. They must not be allowed to speak their own language, to be led by priests of their own faith or to read newspapers in their own language. They must be Canadianized.

> Is it not a profoundly significant thing that we must wait till our non-English-speaking population begin to give cause for apprehension before we awaken to the real problem involved in a situation where twenty-five per cent of the population are non-British.[7]

More and more the proposition was forced on the minority groups that to be accepted as Canadians, they must become English.

The emotion and hysteria of the war years intensified the majority group's determination to undo the mistake of 1897. In view of our present concern with multiculturalism, it seems ironical that the strongest objection came from Henri Bourassa. From his office in *Le Devoir*, he warned that "the anglicizers of the West will not be disarmed as long as they are not conquered. And they will be conquered . . . only by the union of all the non-English groups which do not intend to allow themselves to be Saxonized."[8]

In the Manitoba provincial election of 1914 T.C. Norris' Liberal Party adopted unilingual, compulsory education as part of its programme. The Liberals did not specifically attack bilingualism, but they deplored the growing multilingual character of the public schools. The Conservative government of Sir Rodmond Roblin toppled the following year after a sensational scandal. The Liberals were confirmed by a large majority in a subsequent election and were then free to implement their programme.

In the autumn of 1915 the new Minister of Education, R.S. Thornton, launched an investigation into bilingual schools. The inquiry was undertaken by Charles K. Newcombe, Superintendent of Schools, and the regular school inspectors. In the 1916 spring session of the Manitoba Legislature, the bilingual system was abolished. The traditional interpretation by anglophone historians has been that the bilingual system had failed to provide adequate instruction in English, and that the extension of the system to several language groups had brought the province to the edge of linguistic chaos.[9] Thus explained, the introduction of compulsory, unilingual education was justified in order to rectify the chaotic condition of the schools and, secondarily, to satisfy the chauvinism generated by the war.

I would like to pause briefly to examine this contention. Thornton's entire case for abolition rests on the Newcombe Report and the statement attributed to Robert Fletcher, the Deputy Minister of Education, that "the situation was nearly out of hand".[10] In the Report of the Department of Education for 1913-14 prepared by Fletcher and Newcombe, the following summation appears:

> One of the most difficult problems with which the Department
> has to deal is the question of bilingual teaching.
> The outlook, however, has never been so hopeful as it is at the
> present time. Our own secondary schools are beginning to furnish
> French, German, and Ruthenian students who are able not only
> to give efficient instruction in two languages, but to inculcate the
> true spirit of Canadian patriotism.[11]

Their report for 1914-15 scarcely mentions the matter of bilingualism.[12]

After he retired in 1951, Fletcher addressed the Manitoba Historical Society on the subject, "The Language Problem in Manitoba Schools". Nowhere in this paper did Fletcher claim that the situation in Manitoba in 1916 was "getting out of hand". He did assert that:

> The Department endeavoured to maintain a sympathetic attitude
> to all the groups while insisting on instruction in the schools
> being carried on in the English language as required by law. It

was a case of make "haste slowly"; but improvement on the whole was steady.[13]

In other words there does not appear to be any direct and adequate evidence to support Thornton's assertion that his deputy minister was expecting disaster.

The Newcombe Report, the result of Thornton's request for an enquiry into bilingual schools, has received almost no critical assessment. A careful reading reveals that both the newspapers of the day and Thornton grossly distorted the report.[14] Newcombe, in fact, did not recommend the abolition of bilingual schools. Instead, he pointed out certain "administrative difficulties" which could have been removed by legislation or regulation without repealing clause 258 of the Public Schools Act. But in the House Premier Norris insisted that Thornton's bill proceeded directly from Newcombe's report. "The Government had to take notice of the report. It would have been a crime against the citizenship of the province not to have done so."[15] This brings us, obviously, to the Hon. R.S. Thornton, Minister of Education.

Thornton's ideas and ideals may be found in his speeches to the Manitoba Educational Association conventions from 1916 to 1920 and his addresses to various teachers' groups. Two examples will suffice.

> The immigrant children are the raw material of Canadian citizenship. They will grow up to carry the burden of responsibility of Canadian citizenship . . . the sooner we understand this the quicker they will assimilate themselves to our conditions and the admixture we all desire will take place. We shall build up a Canadian nationality under the British flag, carrying on British justice, freedom and democracy.[16]

And again.

> In the past we have not been careful of whom we admitted, but have taken in all classes from Germany, Russia, Italy, Austria and given to them the privileges of citizenship. . . . To those who come determined to be one hundred per cent Canadian, who come prepared to identify themselves with this country, we will bid welcome. But if they come determined to stay German, to stay Ruthenian, we want them turned back.[17]

To sum it up, Thornton conceived of Canadian nationality as based on the English language and the traditions of the British Empire. The immigrants must be made to conform to this ideal through the agency of "national schools" as Thornton called them, and he argued:

> We must thrust down the selfish boundaries of the various

provinces. We must become one country from east to west.
A teacher should be a teacher, not for one province only,
but for all Canada. Our schools should not be Manitoba
schools, but Canadian schools situated in Manitoba.[18]

A better prescription for a melting pot would be hard to imagine.

It is interesting to note that the *Western School Journal,* the organ of
the teaching profession, never advocated abolition and indeed almost
studiously avoided the whole subject of bilingualism. However Thornton
did draw support from the Manitoba School Trustees Association. The
repeal of bilingualism was, therefore, the accomplishment of a limited group
of English-speaking extremists led by Thornton and the newspapers, and had
the acquiescence, if not the enthusiastic support of the English-speaking
community. They could rationalize their decision as being the only common
sense solution to a thorny problem and take comfort in the argument that
the end of bilingual schools was good not only for Manitoba, but for the
immigrants as well.

The point of this digression is not to heap blame on Thornton, but to
shed some additional light on a complex situation and to question the easy
explanations of the past. In the context of prairie society and wartime
psychology Thornton's actions are at least understandable. The difficult
question to answer is, what did it all mean to the ethnic minority groups?
Since we do not as yet have adequate information from the immigrant
groups themselves, all attempts to draw conclusions are at best conjectural.
What effect, for example, did the threat to their language posed by the
abolition of bilingualism have on the decision of several thousand Mennonites to leave Manitoba? It is not at all clear yet.

However some observations may be ventured. There is no mistaking the
implication in Dafoe's remark that the "Ukraine is the proper place for
Ukrainians. If there is such a Country as Canada-Ukraine, we do not know
of it."[19] The immigrant's natural hunger for acceptance could only be
satisfied if he shed the external manifestations of his cultural differences.
If, for example, the genteel Methodist ceremony was the proper standard
for a wedding, the Ukrainian joyous celebration became culturally suspect.
Any identification with the beer-swilling, garlic-eating caricature of the
Galician was to be shunned. But these were externals only. If his standard
of acceptable public behaviour was "what would the English think", would
he be any less Jewish or less Polish?

The real work of acculturation was accomplished by the school and the
church. Any rough survey of educational materials used in the Manitoba
schools from 1910 through the 1920s reveals that the values being emphasized were British-Canadian nationalism, individualism, the Protestant work

ethic, materialism and so on. It is a truism, of course, to state that a public school system reflects the values of those who control it. In Manitoba's case, after 1916 those who devised curricula, selected textbooks and directed patriotic observances were committed to the use of the schools as an assimilative agent. The adult immigrant population could be, and was ignored, and all efforts bent to the Canadianization of the children. The communal values of the immigrant groups had great difficulty in the face of this onslaught.

The church also had a role to play. Was it the doctrinal attraction alone of the United Church which drew people of Orthodox and Eastern Catholic background or the badge of social acceptance that membership might confer? I do not mean to make judgments on the sincerity and hopes of men like Thornton, Dafoe or Ralph Connor. Rather, I mean to point out only that actions prompt reactions.

The reaction of the ethnic minority groups of the Prairies to the Royal Commission on Bilingualism and Biculturalism still remains to be fully explained. Is it enough to say that the price they paid for acceptance in the prairies was enforced conformity, and that this explains their paradoxical attitude toward French Canadians who have maintained a full and vigorous cultural life? Somehow I doubt this is enough. Perhaps Thornton and his fellows wrought much better than they knew, and the public schools succeeded in moulding a regional outlook both insular and homogeneous, especially as it concerns French-English relations.

The prairie definition of Canadianism has been patterned on an Ontario model now somewhat obsolete in central Canada. It is still very serviceable in the west, however, and has led many of our legislators to such paranoid displays as the vote on the Official Languages Bill. After the prairie experience should we really expect western minority groups to treat French-Canadian aspirations sympathetically? Perhaps. But I am inclined to think that our schools may have done their job far too well — that western minority groups may have become old style Ontario Grits in funny costumes.

J.E. Rea is an associate professor of History at St. Paul's College, University of Manitoba.

NOTES

1 *Manitoba Free Press*, 1908.

2 Ralph Connor, *The Foreigner* (Toronto, 1909), p. 255.

3 *Manitoba Free Press*, 7 August 1912.

4 *Ibid.,* 21 October 1910.

5 See, for example, *ibid.,* 10 August 1915.

6 Cited in Ramsay Cook, *The Politics of John W. Dafoe and the Free Press* (Toronto, 1963), p. 55.

7 *Manitoba Free Press,* 6 October 1917.

8 *Ibid.,* 10 August 1915.

9 See, for example, W.L. Morton, *Manitoba: A History* (Toronto, 1967), p. 351; C.B. Sissons, *Bilingual Schools in Canada* (Toronto, 1917), p. 125.

10 Morton, *Manitoba,* p. 351.

11 Manitoba, Department of Education, *Report of the Department of Education, 1913-1914* (Winnipeg, 1914), p. 19.

12 Manitoba, Department of Education, *Report of the Department of Education, 1914-1915* (Winnipeg, 1915).

13 Robert Fletcher, "The Language Problem in Manitoba Schools", *Historical and Scientific Society of Manitoba,* Vol. III, 6 (1951).

14 Manitoba, Department of Education, *Special Report on Bilingual Schools* (Winnipeg, 1915).

15 *Manitoba Free Press,* 1 March 1916.

16 *Western School Journal,* May (1916), p. 186.

17 *Ibid.,* June (1919), p. 207.

18 *Ibid.,* May (1920), p. 177.

19 Cited in M. Donnelly, *Dafoe of the Free Press* (Toronto, 1968), p. 73.

Commentary

Marian McKenna

Evidently Professor Rea intends to raise more questions than he means to answer and to provoke discussion on what is at present a controversial issue. It is my feeling that provoking debate is a legitimate use of these kinds of meetings, and one which ought to be employed by scholars more often than it is.

After tracing the evolution of the Legislative Act of 1916, undoubtedly intended to be the focus of his paper, Professor Rea leaves some key questions unresolved and then moves far ahead in time for his second point of reference, the *Report of the Royal Commission on Bilingualism and Biculturalism.* In doing so he draws our attention to the widespread and largely unfavourable reaction to its inquiries on the Prairies. But we are told nothing about intervening developments in bilingualism in Manitoba during the period between 1916 and the 1970s. In my opinion treating two such widely disparate time periods with no reference to the fifty years separating them makes it virtually impossible to find answers to the questions arising from the material presented.

However some important questions are answered. For example, we now have a clearer understanding of why the bilingual schools arrangement in Manitoba was overturned. For the first time we are given a scholarly analysis of the motives and political manoeuvering behind the Thornton request for an enquiry into the teaching of languages in Manitoba schools, an analysis of the Newcombe Report which arose out of that enquiry, and of the legislative enactment which supposedly ended bilingualism as it had been known in that province's school system since the Laurier-Greenway Compromise of 1897.

Anglo-conformity, as Milton Gordon has described it in his study of assimilation in American society, was apparently an ingredient in western Canadian life. As described by Professor Rea, it was a matter of an overwhelmingly Anglo-Canadian hostility to the idea of allowing immigrant children to enjoy instruction, even for a small part of the school day, in their native language in the public schools. It would be possible, in expanding this theme, to go beyond the well-known Anglo-Saxon bias in such organs of opinion as the *Manitoba Free Press* for expressions of a desire for Anglo-conformity. One such spokesman, a well-known figure in Manitoba religious and social development, was J. S. Woodsworth, then actively engaged in doing settlement work among the immigrants in the North End ghetto. He opposed the idea of instruction in any but the English language. In the school conducted by his All People's Mission, which may have serviced more immigrant children than the public schools in the years between 1907 and 1914, an attempt was made to begin instruction in the children's native tongue. But the announced aim was to transform the schoolroom as quickly as possible into an English-speaking one. This was equally true of the Mission's adult evening school, which was also actively engaged in teaching English to foreigners.

In his bibliography Professor Rea cites a *Report of the Department of Education for Manitoba, 1913-14* as one of the sources for his conclusions on the manner in which the Legislative Act of 1916 was produced. I wonder if a series of consecutive reports was published by this department annually, and, if so, where the researcher can find them.

With reference to the immigrant groups' reaction to the Manitoba government's reversal of policy, one can only sympathize with Professor Rea's statement that we do not as yet have adequate sources from the immigrant groups themselves to explain their reaction. Anyone who has tried to uncover primary materials on social history by searching provincial records will understand the limitations on research progress. In a survey of existing sources from the ethnic press, for example, it was found that there were only two or three Ukrainian or other foreign language newspapers in Manitoba during this early period, although the numbers across Canada increased to six or seven by 1931. Even if material from ethnic presses for this period was available, it might not reflect reactions from rural ethnic groups so much as the urban immigrants. But given the present state of source materials, it seems almost impossible to find any concensus. However there is the untapped source of vocal and literate ethnic group leaders of the present generation whose memories might serve a useful purpose in scholarly research.

If difficulties exist in arriving at satisfactory answers to some of the questions relating to the act of 1916 and reaction to it, the methodological problem of explaining the adverse reactions of the various prairie ethnic groups to the work of the B. and B. Commission is much more complex. Here, of course, there is no dearth of sources. On the contrary, the social researcher is inundated with conflicting, controversial and often emotion-charged opinion. An enormous amount of data on public reaction can be gathered and analysed, perhaps even computerized; indeed, the process may already be underway. On this question I would like to make only two observations. First, it seems important that some attempt be made to distinguish between the opinions of rural and urban ethnic groups. In fact opinion polls might have to be broken down to distinguish between the various ethnic groups within these two broader groupings. One cannot assume that the life experience, adjustment to Canadian society and reactions to controversial public issues of one group will be the same as that of others. There is a factor of diversity here. Professor Rea's analysis and assessment of reactions might profit greatly if his sources permitted him to distinguish between immigrants in rural and urban settings and along inter-ethnic lines. Jews and other eastern European groups do not react to language retention issues in the same way as Icelanders or Mennonites.

Secondly, adverse reaction to the work and findings of the B. and B. Commission in the Prairie Provinces is by no means exclusively confined to the ethnic minorities. Anglo-Canadians have, and will continue to express themselves with vigour on this troublesome subject. The east-west cleavage is as pronounced as ever, if not more so, and it will persist; with issues such as the national energy policy debate exacerbating it, the split may in time grow more devisive. If Canada is ever to be true to its purpose of being or becoming a bilingual society, it will not only have to convert the "third", "fourth" or "fifth" force, it will also have to convert one of the charter groups. As a touchstone against which contemporary attitudes can be measured, I asked a well-educated, seventy-year-old Anglo-Canadian friend, a retired optometrist, what his reaction was to the recommendations on bilingualism of the B. and B. Commission. He answered, "Why we wouldn't have had any strong objection to it if they hadn't shoved it down our throats

Finally I would like to raise one other issue. In his paper Professor Rea has ignored, perhaps intentionally, any reference to the lack of compulsory school attendance laws on the municipal or provincial level in Manitoba in the years before 1917. There were a number of religious and political tensions operating within the province to obstruct measures of this kind. One cannot help but wonder, though, if the idea never crossed the minds of the Thorntons and Newcombes, not to mention the T.C. Norrises and Roblins, that it didn't really matter what language of instruction was used in the public schools of the province if the immigrant children were not there.

J.S. Woodsworth gives a graphic description of the situation in Winnipeg's North End: hundreds, perhaps thousands of immigrant children wandering about the streets, gathering wood for fuel in the winter, taking on odd jobs throughout the city or working full time in factories. More often than not the immigrant mother went out daily to do cleaning and washing; the children were sent out on the streets as soon as they were old enough to earn a pittance; and the father remained at home, unable to find work. Case after case of this kind is reported by settlement workers in the North End slums. Here is the view of Nellie McClung:

> When the children are big enough to work and earn a little money
> the real difficulty begins, and many a bright boy and girl who
> hungers for an education is taken out of school, and in spite of tears
> and heartbreak, is sent to earn a pittance a week in a factory. The
> kindergarten teacher appeals in vain, she tries to reach the pride of
> the parents by telling how clever Peter is—Peter has a "good brain"—
> "learns fast"—"will earn big money"—but all in vain. There is no
> more education for little Peter. His parents do not care about
> education—our legislators do not care about education—no one
> cares but Peter and the kindergarten teacher, and so Peter falls under
> the wheel and the Union Jack continues to wave over the schools.[1]

From this, the conclusion becomes obvious that what Manitoba really needed, long before it came in 1917, was a compulsory school attendance ordinance and a province-wide child labour law. But what the school and provincial government authorities gave its people was a unilingual school system designed to serve those already fluent in the language of Anglo-conformity.

1 Quoted in James S. Woodsworth, *Thirty Years in the Canadian Northwest* (Toronto, 1917), pp. 253-54.

The Immigrant Industrial Worker in Canada 1896-1919:
The Vertical Mosaic as an Historical Reality

D.H. Avery

The influx of thousands of immigrants from central and eastern Europe between 1896 and 1914 significantly influenced both Canadian society and the immigrant groups.[1] These immigrants entered Canadian society at the lowest occupational level; a disproportionate number of them became unskilled labourers in either the agricultural or industrial sectors of the economy. They did not experience appreciable upward social mobility between 1896 and 1914, but continued to fulfil the function of an agricultural and industrial proletariat.

John Porter in *The Vertical Mosaic* argues that the most important factor in determining entrance status for immigrant groups is "the evaluations of the 'charter' members of the society of the jobs to be filled and the 'right' kind of immigrants to fill them".[2] In the period before World War I the influence that Anglo-Canadian industrialists exerted on the Laurier and Borden administrations was the most important determinant of immigrant status. The attitude of these industrialists was disarmingly simple; immigrants should supply a steady flow of cheap labour.

Although the primary motive for encouraging an "open door" immigration policy was economic and was a product of an entrepreneurial mentality, the Anglo-Canadian public at large also demanded certain standards of cultural acceptability. Hence Orientals, despite their economic utility, were so culturally undesirable that their entry was restricted.[3] No such prohibition was applied to continental Europeans. Although they had some reservations about the cultural characteristics of these immigrants, particularly those of Slavic origin, the Anglo-Canadian community generally believed that continental Europeans could eventually be assimilated.[4] While this assimilation was in progress, the Anglo-Canadian community used such racially stereotyped usages as 'bohunk' or 'Pollack' to exemplify and vindicate the existing ethno-class stratification.[5]

World War I seriously disrupted ethnic relations in many countries with heterogeneous populations. In Canada the increasing intensity of the conflict subjected inter-ethnic relations to tremendous strain. Many central and eastern European immigrants were officially classified as enemy aliens, and their economic rights became a subject of national debate.

15

Between 1914 and 1916 the controversy centred on two main issues. Were enemy aliens to be allowed to hold jobs that deprived Anglo-Canadians and "loyal" aliens of work? Were enemy aliens to be permitted to occupy positions which offered opportunities for subversion? By 1917 the war effort had absorbed all available manpower. This created a new set of questions. Should enemy or allied aliens be allowed to refuse work? Should they be permitted to strike? Finally, in 1917, the Russian Revolution and the spread of Bolshevist ideas within Canada added another variable to an already complex situation. Should Bolshevist aliens be permitted to remain in the country, or should they be forcibly deported?

Canada experienced extensive economic growth between 1896 and 1914: railway mileage doubled, mining production tripled, and wheat production increased ten-fold. Canada also experienced rapid population growth in this era; the census of 1911 showed a 34 percent increase in the nation's population during the preceding decade.[8] Much of this increase can be attributed to immigration, particularly in the Prairie Provinces where the population increased by over a million. In 1911 over 25 percent of the population in Manitoba, Saskatchewan and Alberta were from continental Europe.[9] The influx of continental European immigrants facilitated the settlement of western Canada, especially the development of the less fertile lands of the northern park belt. Many settlers came from countries where inferior land had been cultivated for centuries, and many of them were "willing to make any sacrifice in order to obtain land for themselves and their children".[10] However the difficulties of adapting to the Canadian environment and of securing enough money to survive the initial years of settlement posed a very real problem for many of these immigrants.

A survey of Ukrainian rural settlement in western Canada conducted in 1917 revealed that 50 percent of the 832 families interviewed had no money on arrival in Canada, and another 42 percent had less than $500.[11] Many Ukrainian settlers found it necessary to seek temporary employment in railroad construction, mining, harvesting or lumbering. The initial years of adaptation described by one Ukrainian family in the Vonda district of Saskatchewan was quite typical of the experience of many continental European immigrants:

> When they arrived at Rosthern, Saskatchewan, they had not a cent left. Her husband could not get work on account of a strike of section laborers. Later he managed to obtain farm work for three months from a German farmer near Rosthern. The money thus earned was their means of living for a whole year. They lived after this fashion for three years until they were settled on their own homestead.[12]

The connection between railroad construction and immigration was direct and immediate. The opening up of the Prairies, and the resultant demand for feeder lines and additional transcontinentals to move the bountiful harvests, acted as a tremendous catalyst for railway building.[13] The building of these lines required a pool of cheap labour which was prepared to endure the deplorable conditions of construction camp life. Not surprisingly, the railway companies preferred to employ European settlers in construction, especially since Ukrainians and other groups had proven themselves to be "obedient and industrious" because of their poverty.[14] However this source of labour was insufficient to meet the demands of the railroad contractors, particularly after 1906, when the feverish construction of the Grand Trunk and the Canadian Northern exhausted domestic labour supplies.[15] Through their political leverage, railroad contractors were able to circumvent immigration regulations and to recruit railroad labourers in Europe and the United States. Completion of the two transcontinentals was of such crucial importance to both the Laurier and Borden governments that they were prepared to allow the contractors virtually a free hand.[16]

The Dominion governments — Liberal and Conservative — also seemed prepared to countenance the high accident rates and unsanitary working conditions that existed in many construction camps in order to have the transcontinentals completed. Although 23 percent of industrial accidents in Canada between 1904 and 1911 occurred in railroad construction, there appears to have been little attempt to enforce safety regulations in this industry.[17] It was alleged in labour circles that government inspectors visited the camps only infrequently and that they rarely came into contact with the immigrant navvy.[18] The foreign worker was particularly vulnerable to this type of exploitation; he was often unable to communicate in English, he was frequently manipulated by an "ethnic straw boss", and he often had a basic mistrust of state officials. For the immigrant navvy, the government inspector simply did not offer a viable channel of protest.[19]

Similar trends developed in the mining industry. From the entrepreneurial perspective the greatest advantage to be derived from importing large numbers of continental Europeans for mining work was that they were prepared to work for wages and in conditions that would not be tolerated either by native Canadians or British workers. As one mining authority put it, "Canadians won't work in the mines. They are quite willing to boss the job but they are not going to do the rough work themselves. . . . What we want is brawn and muscle, and we get it."[20] By 1911 over 20 percent of the labour force in the Crows Nest Pass coal mining region and the mining regions of northern Ontario were from continental Europe. Clearly the mining companies were extremely successful at recruiting cheap labour. Within the mines there were gradations of skills, and this stratification was usually reflected in the ethnic composition of the work force. The supervisors, certified miners and skilled mechanics were mainly Anglo-Saxons or Scandinavians. The continental European ethnic groups were found at the other end of the mining spectrum; they were the underground labourers, miners' helpers and surface labourers. It is also significant that the mechanization of the mining industry between 1896 and 1919 increased rather than decreased the demand for the type of labour which these immigrants provided.[22]

The management of the mining industry tended to downgrade safety precautions as long as the supply of unskilled immigrant labour seemed to be inexhaustible. Reports of the Ontario, Alberta and British Columbia mining inspectors throughout the period from 1896 to 1914 were generally critical of high accident rates, especially among the foreign workers.[23] This criticism was most effectively stated in a 1914 report of the Ontario mining inspectors:

> Anyone looking over the list of mining statistics . . . cannot but be struck with the large percentage of names of foreign origin. . . . In part this may be due to unfamiliarity with the English language and the difficulty of comprehending quickly spoken orders in an emergency. Mental traits have also to be reckoned with, and the fact that few of these men were miners before coming to this country. . . .[24]

The report neglected to state that many mine managers were reluctant to maintain costly safety regulations. The apparent lack of solidarity among the mine employees due to ethnic differences reinforced this callous approach. Prior to 1914 many entrepreneurs and industrial managers had realized the advantages of having a labour force with a diverse ethnic composition. This view was clearly stated by Edmund Kirby, manager of the War Eagle Mine in British Columbia: "In all the lower grades of labour and especially in smelter labour it is necessary to have a mixture of races which includes a number of illiterates who are first class workers. They are the strength of the employer, and the weakness of the union."[25]

Although it has been customary to regard Slavic and other European industrial workers as an obstacle to the formation of trade unions, more detailed studies have indicated that once these workers became accustomed to North American economic and social conditions they manifested a pronounced sense of class consciousness. According to the American labour historian Victor Greene, "far from weakening labor organizations, the Polish, Lithuanians, Slovak, and Ukrainian mine workers, and their communities, supported labor protest more enthusiastically than many other groups and were essential to the establishment of unionism permanently in the coal fields".[26] In Canada the involvement of these particular ethnic groups in trade unions such as the United Mine Workers of America (U.M.W.A.) reinforces this image of pronounced union involvement and labour militancy.

The leadership of the U.M.W.A. recognized the importance of the immigrant worker in the mines of the United States and Canada. At the binational conference of 1913, U.M.W.A. President John L. Lewis declared that his union recognized that "the foreign-speaking mine workers have the same interests in the U.M.W.A. as all others who are members. . . . It is our duty to give them reasonable opportunity of understanding the mission of the union."[27] Since it was the duty of the union to educate the foreign-speaking worker, U.M.W.A. literature was translated into Italian, Finnish and the various Slavic languages. By 1914 the U.M.W.A. had a number of foreign-language organizers in its three Canadian districts. Their involvement with foreign workers was particularly significant in District 18, which included the coal fields of Alberta and eastern British Columbia.[28]

The involvement of foreign workers in socialist organizations was also quite pronounced. In part, the alienation experienced by many of these men in the Canadian economic system made them receptive to an ideology which attacked the abuses of capitalism and predicted the inevitability of a proletarian revolution. In part, the formation of socialist organizations such as the Ukrainian, Russian and Finnish Social Democratic parties was a natural extension of Old World institutions. Many of the Slavic and Finnish immigrants who gravitated to Canadian industrial centres had been involved with socialist organizations in industrial communities in the Austro-Hungarian and Russian empires.[29] Many of the founders of the Winnipeg branch of the Ukrainian Social Democratic Party, established in 1907, had been active in the Ukrainian Social Democratic Party of Lviv, in the Austrian province of Galicia.[30] Similarly, Ukrainian socialist newspapers like *The Red Flag* (1906) and *The Toiling People* (1909) advanced European socialist ideas, such as support for the second international advocacy of militant atheism and predictions about the inevitability of class struggle between the proletarian and capitalist classes.[31] Socialist organization among Finnish immigrants was illustrated by the formation of the Finnish Social Democratic Party in 1908. By 1914 it had become a radical force of considerable influence within the Finnish community of Canada, especially in the mining districts of northern Ontario. With the establishment in 1917 of the Finnish socialist newspaper *Vapaus* (*Liberty*),[32] Sudbury became its organizational centre.

The response of the Anglo-Canadian people, especially those associated with labour intensive industries, was quite hostile towards the involvement of immigrant workers in militant trade unions and socialist organizations. During labour disputes it was common for representatives of the industrialists to play on public fears about the presence of alien agitators. These agitators, it was alleged, would incite the illiterate foreign workmen into blind anarchistic riots. Such tactics were employed against the United Mine Work in the 1909 Nova Scotia strike, the 1911 Crow's Nest Pass strike and the 1913 Vancouver Island strike.[33] In the latter case the use of the militia to crush the strike was justified on the grounds that considerable violence had been committed "by members of the I.W.W. chiefly composed of aliens, people without any sense of responsibility or respect for life or property".[34] The charges were false. The International Workers of the World, an American-based, anarcho-syndicalist organization, had not organized a single mining union in British Columbia, and the vast majority of strikers arrested after the Ladysmith riots had been Anglo-Saxons.[35] These allegations reveal the deep concern that many Anglo-Canadian businessmen experienced about the ability of industrial trade unions to incorporate workers of all races and nationalities.[36]

The presence of large numbers of immigrants in cities such as Winnipeg, Fort William and Edmonton also produced a defensive response on the part of the Anglo-Canadian businessmen in these cities. In Winnipeg, for example there was mounting apprehension among Anglo-Canadians between 1900 and 1914 about the growth of socialist doctrines in the North End ethnic ghetto.[37] This fear became particularly pronounced when the famous anarchist Emma Goldman visited the city in 1908. Mayor J.H. Ashdown, a prominent Winnipeg businessman, clearly articulated the views of Winnipeg's elite Anglo-Canadian community when he criticized the Immigration branch for allowing Emma Goldman into the country:

> We have a very large foreign population in this city. . . .
> Many of these people have had trouble in their own country
> with their Governments and have come to the new land to get
> away from it, but have all the undesirable elements in their
> character that created the trouble for them before. They are
> just the crowd for Emma Goldman or persons of her character
> to sow the seeds which are bound to cause most undesirable
> growths in the future. . . .[38]

The coming of war in 1914 exaggerated many of the problems facing the immigrant worker. The immediate effect was the dismissal of large numbers of aliens from their jobs for "patriotic reasons". These dismissals swelled the ranks of the thousands of aliens already unemployed because of the economic depression of 1913-14.[39] At the start of the war prominent businessmen and local government officials agitated for the mass internment of these idle and impoverished aliens, both for humanitarian and security reasons.[40] But the Dominion government was not prepared to implement a mass internment policy, primarily because of the prohibitive cost of operating internment camps.[41] Arthur Meighen articulated the view of the majority of Cabinet members when he argued that, instead of being interned, unemployed aliens should each be granted forty acres of land which could be cultivated under government supervision. He concluded his case with the observation that "these Austrians . . . can live on very little".[42] It is interesting that at the 1915 convention of the Trades and Labor Congress, resolutions suggesting the placement of unemployed central-European workers on homesteads in northern Ontario were favourably received.[43]

By 1917 the role of the alien worker in the Canadian economy had changed considerably. Other sources of labour were now either unavailable or unacceptable. The heavy manpower losses suffered in Europe necessitated the recruitment of thousands of native-born Canadians, thereby removing them from the industrial work force.[44] Moreover, the United States entry into the war substantially reduced the supply of industrial labour from that quarter.[45] Yet suggestions from large employers of labour in both the agricultural and industrial sectors of the economy that Chinese coolies be imported on a temporary basis encountered violent opposition from organized labour.[46] Faced by a growing labour shortage, the Borden government implemented several programmes to mobilize labour from within the country. The powers of the Canadian Registration Board were expanded to provide for the compulsory registration of all men and women over the age of sixteen.[47] In April, 1918, the so-called "anti-loafing law" was enacted. This provided that "every male person residing in the Dominion of Canada should be regularly engaged in some useful occupation".[48] For many Anglo-Canadian businessmen and politicians, the main target of these laws was the alien worker.

Demands for coercive measures against alien workers prevailed throughout 1917 and 1918. The secretary of the Mountain Lumber Manufacturers' Association, I.R. Poole, expressed the view of many Anglo-Canadian businessmen when he demanded action by the Dominion authorities to show "the foreigner[s] . . . that they must not go idle".[49] Even more drastic suggestions were made by coal operators such as W.A. Wood, president of the Vallance Coal Company, who urged Prime Minister Borden to send troops into District 18 in order "to make the foreigners work at the point of a bayonet". The hard line adopted by the coal operators in District 18 can be attributed to the militant stance of the U.M.W.A. It became common for management to charge that the wave of strikes of 1916-18 were symptomatic of changes within the leadership of the mining union:

> The foreign element among the miners preponderatingly outnumber the English-speaking members. Their ideals and methods are not merely different from the notions of the old-time leaders . . . but on war matters are diametrically opposed.[51]

Throughout 1918 an increasing number of reports on the growing radicalism of the alien workers were received by the Borden government.[52] In April 1918, H.S. Clements, a wealthy British Columbia businessman, made a speech in the House of Commons in which he charged that "at least one-third of the total membership of the labour unions of Canada consists of enemy aliens or aliens of neutral countries".[53] What made this situation even more ominous, Clements asserted, was the fact that these aliens "had been taught from their earliest infancy that only by force can they get what they want and I submit that they ought to be controlled by force".[54] Labour unrest in British Columbia, northern Ontario and industrial cities such as Winnipeg during the summer and fall of 1918 intensified the pressure for drastic action by the Dominion authorities against the alien worker. In Winnipeg, for example, the Registrar of Alien Enemies informed the Commissioner of the Dominion Police that industrial unrest in that city was definitely attributable to alien activity. He recommended sending all striking aliens off to an internment camp which had been established at Kapuskasing, Ontario.[55] Even as early as August, 1918, plans were being made to incarcerate and deport alien radicals along with other interned enemy aliens.[56]

The case for a repressive policy was further strengthened in September, 1918 by C.H. Cahan's report on alien radicalism. Based on a series of interviews with security officials in both Canada and the United States, the report pointed out that "Russians, Ukrainians and Finns, who are being employed in the mines, factories and other industries, are now being thoroughly saturated with the Socialistic doctrines which have been proclaimed by the Bolsheviki faction of Russia."[57] Cahan further alleged that "delegates from Bolsheviki organizations in Russia have recently come to the United States, and no doubt to Canada to organize and inflame their comrades in America".[58] On the basis of this assessment the Borden government implemented a series of coercive measures. By two Orders-in-Council (P.C. 2381 and P.C. 2384) the foreign language press was suppressed, and a number of socialist and anarchist organizations were outlawed.[59] Most of these organizations were composed of ethnic workers; the most prominent were the Russian Social Democratic Party, the Ukrainian Social Democratic Party and the Finnish Social Democratic Party.[60] Penalties for possession of prohibited literature or continued membership in one of these outlawed organizations were extremely severe. Fines of up to $5,000 or a maximum prison term of five years could be imposed. In October, 1918, a Public Safety Branch of the Department of Justice was created in order to enforce the legislation. Not unexpectedly, C.H. Cahan was appointed director of the Branch.

In the enforcement of the law the full powers of censorship and police harassment were directed against the alien radical. A case involving Michael Charitinoff, the former editor of *The Toiling People,* clearly revealed this tendency. In October, 1918, Charitinoff was arrested and charged with the possession of prohibited literature. Judge Hugh John Macdonald, a prominent member of Winnipeg's Anglo-Canadian community, sentenced the young Ukrainian socialist to three years imprisonment and a fine of $1,000.[61] What made Charitinoff's case even more interesting was the degree of support he received from Anglo-Canadian socialists not only in Winnipeg, but throughout western Canada. This support illustrates the growing class solidarity that had developed between Anglo-Canadian and alien socialists in western Canada.[62] This trend was clearly evident at the founding convention of the One Big Union in March, 1919. The Union passed a resolution declaring that "the interests of all members of the international working class being identical . . . this body of workers recognize[s] no alien but the capitalist".[63]

The hatred and fear stirred up by World War I did not end with the Armistice of 1918: social tension spread in ever-widening circles. Anglo-Canadians who had learned to despise the Germans and the Austro-Hungarians had little difficulty transferring their hatred to the Bolsheviks. Although the guns were silent on the Western Front, Canadian troops were being sent to Siberia "to strangle the infant Bolshevism in its cradle".[64] Within Canada there was wide-spread agitation against potentially "disloyal" aliens and those involved in socialist organizations. An editorial in the *Winnipeg Telegram* summed up these sentiments: "Let every hostile alien be deported from this country, the privileges of which . . . he does not appreciate."[65]

In the early months of 1919 the Borden government was deluged by a great wave of petitions, particularly from veterans' organizations, demanding the mass deportation of enemy aliens.[66] Inquiries were made by the Dominion government concerning the possible implementation of a policy of mass deportation.[67] But such a policy was rejected as undesirable both because of its likely international repercussions and because of the demands it would make on the country's transportation facilities at a time when Canadian troops were returning from Europe.[68] In the face of continued harassment by returned soldiers and the uncertainty of government policy, a substantial number of Germans and Ukrainians returned to Europe during 1919 of their own accord. One source has placed the number of such migrants as high as 150,000.[69]

The demand for the immediate imposition of discriminatory economic regulations was another element in the anti-alien agitation by the Anglo-Canadian community. It was argued that the returned soldiers deserved the jobs that enemy aliens had secured. One aspect of this issue was the growing fear that the veterans would be radicalized and lured into socialist organizations if industrialists continued to employ large numbers of alien workers.[70] Faced by a hostile public and press, many companies began to dismiss their non-Anglo-Saxon workers. This trend was particularly obvious in British Columbia. By February, 1919, the British Columbia Employers' Association, the British Columbia Manufacturers' Association and the British Columbia Loggers' Association all had announced that their memberships were prepared to offer employment to returned soldiers by dismissing alien enemies.[71] This same pattern prevailed in the mining region of northern Ontario. In the early months of 1919 the International Nickel Company, for instance, dismissed 220 of their 3200 employees. The vast majority of those who lost their jobs were foreigners.[72]

The Dominion government's decision to establish a Royal Commission on Industrial Relations on April 4, 1919, illustrates the government's concern for the status of the alien worker. Between April and June, 1919, the Commission travelled from Victoria to Sydney and held hearings in some twenty-eight industrial centres. The testimony of industrialists showed an ambivalent attitude towards the alien worker. Some industrialists argued that the alien was "usually doing work that white men don't want", and that it would "be a shame to make the returned soldiers work at that job".[73] But in those regions where there was high employment among returned soldiers, and where the alien workers had become entrenched in radical trade unions, management demonstrated a strong tendency to deprecate the utility of the alien labour force. William Henderson, a coal mine operator at Drumheller, Alberta, informed the Commission that the unstable industrial climate of that region could only be reversed by hiring more Anglo-Canadian workers, "men that we could talk to . . . men that would come in with us and co-operate with us".[74] Several mine managers from British Columbia, Alberta and northern Ontario stressed the fact that alien workers could not be expected to respond in a responsible manner since they were "more or less illiterate and not imbued with British values having come from countries

with tyrannical governments".[75] Many mining representatives indicated
that their companies had released large numbers of aliens who had shown
radical tendencies. There were repeated suggestions that these aliens should
not only be removed from the mining districts, but deported from Canada.[76]

The industrialists' concern over the presence of the radical alien coincided with an intensification of the fear, among many Dominion security
officials, about the possibility of an international Bolshevik conspiracy.
Throughout the early months of 1919 Canadian security officials submitted
reports to the Cabinet describing the extent of Bolshevist subversion among
the aliens.[77] They stressed the danger which Bolshevist doctrines presented
to the Anglo-Canadian way of life. It was alleged that personal property,
religious principles and the sanctity of the family unit would all be destroyed
if the Bolsheviks gained power. One widely-circulated report described how
the Bolsheviks in Russia had implemented the practice of nationalizing
women.[78]

The government's gradual withdrawal of some of the more oppressive
security measures, particularly Orders-in-Council P.C. 2381 and P.C. 2385,
further alarmed many security officials.[79] Both C.H. Cahan, the Director
of Public Safety, and Major General Gwatkin, the Chief of the General Staff,
deplored the restoration of civil liberties to "dangerous" individuals and
groups. Gwatkin criticized the politicians for catering to the demands of
organized labour and predicted that "one day they will regret that, adopting
the tactics of the ostrich, they took no measure for their own protection".[80]
The security officials' apprehension was intensified by numerous reports
describing the activities of radical foreign-language organizations such as the
Russian Workers' Union, the Ukrainian Labour Temple Association (U.L.T.A.)
and the Canadian Finnish Organization. It appeared that, from bases in cities
such as Vancouver, Winnipeg and Sudbury, these radical organizations were
creating an elaborate network of intrigue among aliens throughout the mining and agricultural districts of western Canada and northern Ontario.[81]

The reaction of the Anglo-Canadian community towards radical alien
organizations varied. In some cities, such as Fernie, civic officials prevented
U.L.T.A. organizers from holding public meetings.[82] In other cities, notably
Winnipeg and Port Arthur, a substantial element of the Anglo-Canadian
"establishment" began to adopt tactics calculated to intimidate radical
aliens. Attempts were also made to establish Anglo-Canadian vigilante
organizations.[83]

The most blatant example of alien intimidation occurred in Winnipeg in
January, 1919. A mob of returned soldiers attacked scores of foreigners and
wrecked the business establishment of Sam Blumenberg, a prominent alien

socialist. Neither the city police, nor the R.N.W.M.P., nor the military made any attempt to intervene to protect the aliens.[84] *Winnipeg Telegram* reports of the incident reflect the attitude adopted by many Anglo-Canadian residents of the city. The *Telegram* made no apologies for the violence; instead the newspaper contrasted the manly traits of the Anglo-Canadian veterans to the cowardly and furtive behaviour of the aliens. "It was typical of all who were assaulted," the report read, "that they hit out for home or the nearest hiding place after the battle."[85]

The Winnipeg General Strike of May 15 to June 28, 1919, brought the elements of class and ethnic conflict together in a massive confrontation. The sequence of events has been well documented: the breakdown of negotiations between management and labour in the building and metal trades; the decision by the Winnipeg Trades and Labor Council to call a general strike for May 15; the mass support for the strike, with between 25,000 and 30,000 workers leaving their jobs; and the claims on the part of management and a substantial element of the Anglo-Canadian community that the Bolsheviks had seized control of the city.[86]

One of the most persistent themes running through local reporting of the strike (except by the *Western Labor News*) concerned the alleged insidious role assumed by the radical alien. The *Manitoba Free Press,* for example, blamed the crisis on alien workers and a few irresponsible Anglo-Saxon agitators:

> It is through the solid fanatical allegiance of the Germans, Austrians, Huns and Russians in the labour unions that the Red Five—Russell, Veitch, Robinson, Ivens and Winning— have climbed to power in the labor organization.[87]

The *Free Press* strongly urged the Dominion government "to clean the aliens out of this community and ship them back to their happy homes in Europe which vomited them forth a decade ago".[88] Pressure for strong action against the alien radicals also emanated from the Citizens' Committee of One Thousand, an organization that viewed itself as the defender of the Canadian way of life in that city. The involvement of members of this organization in both the ranks of the Special Constables, who replaced the city police on June 9, and in the militia units further heightened ethnic and class tension.[89] Of even greater importance was the influence exerted on the Dominion government by men like A.J. Andrews, a prominent Winnipeg lawyer and a leading member of the Citizens' Committee. As a result of his appointment on May 26 as the Winnipeg representative of the Department of Justice, Andrews assumed an important role in formulating the subsequent strategy of the Dominion government towards the strike. His involvement was particularly noticeable in the decision to make two amendments to Section 41 of the Immigration Act in order to deport both radical aliens and British-born socialists.[90] Andrews was also very much involved in the plan to arrest and deport, presumably without hearings, the key Anglo-Saxon strike leaders and "dangerous" aliens.[91] Although the police raids of June 17 netted six of the prominent Anglo-Saxon socialists and four radical aliens, the pressure of public opinion forced the Dominion government to alter its original plan. Deportation charges against the British-born were dropped, and the four aliens, Michael Charitinoff, Sam Blumenberg, Moses Almazoff and Oscar Schoppelrie, were granted deportation hearings.

The violent confrontation between Winnipeg strikers and the R.N.W.M.P. on June 21 caused an intensification of anti-alien measures. During this clash the Special Constables and the R.N.W.M.P. arrested some thirty-one foreign-speaking "rioters".[93] On July 1, a series of raids were carried out across the country on the homes of known agitators and on the offices of radical organizations such as the Ukrainian Labor Temple Association.[94]

Many of the incarcerated aliens were denied due process. This was not surprising, given the attitude of magistrates such as Hugh John Macdonald, who presided over many of the alien trials in Winnipeg. In a letter to Arthur Meighen dated July 3, 1919, Macdonald emphasized that only an uncompromising attitude towards the radical alien would end the current industrial disorder:

> As Police Magistrate I have seen to what a large extent Bolsheviki ideas are held by the Ruthenian, Russian and Polish people, whom we have in our midst . . . it is absolutely necessary that an example should be made . . . they do not understand generous treatment and consider it is only extended to them because the Government is is afraid of them: indeed, fear is the only agency that can be successfully employed. . . . If the Government persists in the course that it is now adopting the foreign element here will soon be as gentle and easily controlled as a lot of sheep.[95]

It is significant that Arthur Meighen praised Macdonald's "insight . . . as respects the alien population". He also expressed his willingness to co-operate in the restoration of law and order in Winnipeg.[96]

The actions of the Dominion government concerning the radical aliens between July and December, 1919, suggest that Macdonald's advice was basically followed. Most of the aliens who had been sentenced by Macdonald and sent to the Kapuskasing Internment Camp were subsequently deported, despite pleas for writs of *habeas corpus* by lawyers of the Winnipeg Trades and Labor Council.[97] On the other hand, the four aliens arrested in Winnipeg on June 17, Charitinoff, Blumenberg, Almazoff and Schoppelrie, were brought before an Immigration Deportation Board. Their cases provided an important opportunity to test the effectiveness of Section 41 of the Immigration Act as a means of deporting foreign people who belonged to either socialist or anarchist organizations. The result of the trials revealed that Section 41 could not be used indiscriminately; only Schoppelrie was ordered deported, not because of his seditious utterances, but because he had entered the country illegally.[98] This decision was a severe blow to those who wished to effect mass deportations of radical aliens.[99]

But it was still possible to utilize the Immigration Act to exclude from the country certain ethnic groups, such as Ukrainians, Russians and Finns, who were deemed undesirable because of their involvement in socialist and anarchist organizations.[100] Instructions were issued to immigration officers in Great Britain and in Europe to prevent the immigration of Ukrainians, Russians and Finns on the grounds that "the general policy and the application of the regulations tends definitely to keep out of Canada those who cannot be readily assimilated".[101] It is significant that in 1919 even the Canadian Manufacturers' Association, the long-time advocate of the "open door" immigration policy, endorsed the exclusion of continental European immigrants.[102] Temporarily, at least, the ethnic, cultural and ideological differences of these immigrants had become more important than their economic worth. Whether Canada was prepared to accept a slower rate of economic growth in order to ensure its survival as a predominantly Anglo-Canadian nation became one of the crucial questions of the 1920s.

An equally important question was whether Anglo-Canadians would ever be prepared to make an economic and cultural adjustment to foreign immigrants. In 1919 Alfred Fitzpatrick, the Principal of Frontier College, implored the Dominion government to assume greater responsibility for "new" Canadians:

> The foreigner was brought to Canada under a wrong impression if not false pretenses. Canada owes him a clean bed, the privilege of learning the language and of becoming a citizen. . . . I do not think we should listen to those who cry to hell with the 'foreigner' and are not prepared to take his place.[103]

Fitzpatrick's arguments were in vain; neither the Dominion nor the provincial governments assumed responsibility for offering "new" Canadians the full advantages of citizenship during the 1920s.[104] Indeed the "open door" immigration policy which came into effect again after 1925 resulted in the immigration of thousands of unskilled immigrants from central and eastern Europe.[105] These immigrants provided a pool of cheap labour for both the agricultural and industrial sectors of the economy as they had before 1919.

Their presence also made it possible for Anglo-Canadian businessmen to continue to depress the wages of those European immigrants who had arrived prior to 1914. In addition to receiving low wages, the continental European worker remained particularly susceptible to the dangers of unemployment, as the statistics from the Great Depression graphically illustrate. In 1930 the average unemployment period for Ukrainian workers was twenty weeks, while British-born workers were unemployed an average of only nine weeks.[106] The 1930s clearly demonstrated that the immigrant worker was the last to be hired and the first to be fired. The words of Sandor Hunyadi, the fictional character created by John Marlyn in his book *Under the Ribs of Death,* vividly conveys the dilemma of many "new" Canadians:

> The English, he whispered. "Pa, the only people who count are
> the English. Their fathers got all the best jobs. They're the only
> ones nobody ever calls foreigners. Nobody ever makes fun of
> their names or calls them 'bologny-eaters', or laughs at the way
> they dress or talk. Nobody," he concluded bitterly, "cause when
> you're English it's the same as bein' Canadian."[107]

Donald Avery is an assistant professor of History at the University of Western Ontario.

NOTES

1 According to reports for the Immigration Branch between 1900 and 1914, 739,213 European immigrants entered Canada. Canada, *Dominion of Canada Sessional Papers* (hereafter *Sessional Papers*) (Immigration Branch Reports, 1900-1915).

2 John Porter, *The Vertical Mosaic: An Analysis of Social Class and Power in Canada* (Toronto, 1966), p. 60.

3 C.J. Woodsworth, *Canada and the Orient: A Study in International Relations* (Toronto, 1941), pp. 91, 289.

4 John W. Dafoe, *Clifford Sifton in Relation to His Times* (Toronto, 1931), pp. 45-50; Vladimir Kaye, *Early Ukrainian Settlement in Canada, 1896-1900* (Toronto, 1964), pp. 15, 25, 160.

5 Porter, *The Vertical Mosaic*, pp. 67-85.

6 Canada, *Revised Statutes of Canada, 1927*, Vol. IV, Chapter 206, pp. 1-3.

7 O.J. Firestone, *Canada's Economic Development, 1867-1953* (London, 1958), p. 65.

8 *Fifth Census of Canada, 1911*, Vol. II (Ottawa, 1913), pp. 42-44.

9 *Report of the Royal Commission on Bilingualism and Biculturalism*, Book IV (Ottawa, 1968), pp. 238-46.

10 R.W. Murchie, "Agricultural Land Utilization in Western Canada" in W.F.G. Joerg (ed.), *Pioneer Settlement: Comparative Studies by Twenty-Six Authors* (New York, 1932), pp. 17, 22; Manitoba, Bureau of Social Research, *Ukrainian Rural Settlements* (Winnipeg, January 25, 1917), p. 4.

11 *Ukrainian Rural Settlements*, pp. 5-6.

12 *Ibid.*, p. 59.

13 James B. Hedges, *Building the Canadian West: The Land and Colonization Policies of the Canadian Pacific Railway* (New York, 1939), pp. 34, 47, 129-30; G.R. Stevens, *Canadian National Railways,* Vol. II (Toronto, 1963), pp. 12-19, 54-55.

14 Public Archives of Canada, Immigration Branch Records (hereafter referred to as I.B.), File 60868, C.W. Speers, Travelling Immigration Inspector, to Frank Pedley, Superintendent of Immigration, January 24, 1900.

15 G.R. Stevens, *Canadian National Railways,* Vol. II, pp. 159-63, 172-83, 214-17.

16 This theme has been extensively discussed by the author in a paper "Canadian Immigration Policy and the 'Foreign' Navvy, 1896-1914", Canadian Historical Association *Papers* (1972).

17 Statistics were tabulated from *Sessional Papers, 1913* (Report of the Deputy Minister of Labour), No. 36, p. 72.

18 Don Avery, "Canadian Immigration Policy", pp. 20-25.

19 *Ibid.*

20 Arthur Coleman, "Address" in *Empire Club of Canada: Addresses . . . During the Session of 1911-12* (Toronto, 1913), p. 163.

21 Charles McMillan, "Trade Unions in District 18, 1900-1925: A Case Study" (M.A. thesis, University of Alberta, 1969), pp. 80-90; *Census of Canada, 1911,* Vol. II, pp. 162-65, 168-71, 220-30.

22 John Brophy, *A Miner's Life* (Madison, 1964), pp. 6, 16, 20; Rowland Berthoff, *British Immigrants in Industrial America, 1790-1950* (Cambridge, 1953), pp. 29, 55.

23 British Columbia, Department of Mines, *Report of the Minister of Mines, Province of British Columbia, 1901* (Victoria, 1902), p. 1194; *Ibid.*, 1911, p. 232; Paul Phillips, *No Power Greater: A Century of Labour in British Columbia, 1867-1967* (Vancouver, 1967), p. 6; Charles McMillan, "Trade Unions in District 18", pp. 80-90; Ontario, Bureau of Mines, *Report of the Ontario Bureau of Mines, 1909* (Toronto, 1910), p. 78; *Ibid.*, 1914, pp. 86-87.

24 *Report of the Ontario Bureau of Mines, 1914*, pp. 86-87.

25 Cited in Martin Robin, "British Columbia: The Politics of Class Conflict," in Martin Robin (ed.), *Canadian Provincial Politics* (Scarborough, 1972), pp. 29-30.

26 Victor Greene, *The Slavic Community on Strike: Immigrant Labor in Pennsylvania Anthracite* (Notre Dame, 1968), p. 94.

27 John L. Lewis, "Report", *United Mine Workers' Journal,* Vol. 21, No. 35, cited in Charles McMillan, "Trade Unions in District 18", p. 86.

28 *Ibid.*, pp. 84, 86, 190; Phillips, *No Power Greater,* p. 57; *The District Ledger* (Fernie), 18 April 1919.

29 William Maranchuk, *The Ukrainian Canadians* (Winnipeg, 1970), p. 225; William Rodney, *Soldiers of the International: A History of the Communist Party of Canada* (Toronto, 1968), p. 10; Arthur May, *The Hapsburg Monarchy, 1867-1914* (Cambridge, Mass., 1960), pp. 160, 172, 344.

30 Paul Yuzyk, *The Ukrainians in Manitoba* (Toronto, 1953), p. 97.

31 William Rodney, *Soldiers of the International,* p. 10.

32 *Ibid.*, pp. 34-35.

33 The editorials of *The Canadian Mining Journal* illustrate this trend. See, for example, *The Canadian Mining Journal,* 1 March 1909, 15 June 1911, 1 September 1914.

34 Public Archives of Canada, Department of National Defence Papers, File 363-1210, Report of Lt. Col. Hall, Officer in Command, Civic Aid Forces to Vancouver Island, 1913, to District Officer in Command, Military District 11 (British Columbia).

35 Paul Phillips, *No Power Greater,* pp. 52-60.

36 *Ibid.*, p. 61; *British Columbia Federationist* (Vancouver) 8 June 1912; Melvyn Dubofsky, *We Shall Be All: A History of the Industrial Workers of the World* (Chicago, 1969), p. 127.

37 *Canadian Annual Review, 1909* (Toronto, 1910), p. 306.

38 I.B., File 800111, J.H. Ashdown to Frank Oliver, April 8, 1908. The tactics of harassment adopted by the Winnipeg police were sufficient to force Emma Goldman out of the city; *Ibid.,* W.D. Scott, Supt. of Immigration to Frank Oliver, Dec. 15, 1908.

39 *Canadian Annual Review, 1914,* pp. 277-281; *Canadian Annual Review, 1915,* pp. 352-64.

40 Public Archives of Canada, Robert Borden Papers (hereafter Borden Papers), 105935, Thomas Shaughnessy, President of the C.P.R., to Martin Burrell, Minister of Agriculture, Aug. 26, 1914; *Ibid.,* 105962, J.A.M. Aikins to Borden, Nov. 12, 1914.

41 Major-General W.D. Otter, *Internment Operations, 1914-20* (Ottawa, Sept. 30, 1920), pp. 3, 6.

42 Public Archives of Canada, Arthur Meighen Papers (hereafter Meighen Papers), 105995, Arthur Meighen to Prime Minister Borden, September 4, 1914.

43 *Proceedings of the Thirty-first Annual Session of the Trades and Labor Congress of Canada* (1915), pp. 16-17.

44 I.B., File 29490, J. Bruce Walker, Commissioner of Immigration in Winnipeg, to W.D. Scott, Superintendent of Immigration, July 24, 1916.

45 *Canadian Annual Review, 1918,* p. 330.

46 *British Columbia Federationist,* 25 January 1918; Public Archives of Canada, Diary of Robert Borden, Jan. 21, 1918.

47 *Canadian Annual Review, 1918,* pp. 490-99.

48 *Ibid.,* p. 491; *Statutes of Canada,* 9-10, Geo V, p. xciii.

49 Borden Papers, 56588, I.R. Poole to Borden, Feb. 11, 1918.

50 *Ibid.,* 120351, W.A. Wood to Borden, May 16, 1917.

51 *Ibid.,* 120421, Meighen to Borden, Feb. 9, 1918, enclosed anonymous report sent to Meighen, Dec. 31, 1917.
52 Public Archives of Canada, Department of National Defence Records (hereafter Defense Records), C-2102.

53 *Debates of the House of Commons of the Dominion of Canada* (hereafter *Debates*), 1918, pp. 976-79.

54 *Ibid.*

55 Defence Records, C-2665, Major-General Ketchen, G.O.C., M.D. No. 10, to Secretary of the Militia Council, July 7, 1917.

56 Public Archives of Canada, Secretary of State Records, Internment Operation Files, File 6712, Major-General Otter to Arthur Meighen, the Acting Minister of Justice, December 19, 1918.

57 Borden Papers, 56668, C.H. Cahan to Borden, Sept. 14, 1918.

58 *Ibid.*

59 *Statutes of Canada* (1919), 9-10, Geo. V, pp. lxxi-lxxiii, lxxvii-lxxx.

60 *Ibid.* The Finnish Social Democratic Party was not initially prohibited; it was added to the list in November, 1918. Rodney, *Soldiers of the International,* p. 18.

61 Public Archives of Canada, Secretary of State Records, Chief Press Censor Files, File 144-A-1, to Colonel E.J. Chambers, the Chief Press Censor, to Major-General Ketchen, Oct. 3, 1918; *The Western Labor News,* 5 October 1918.

62 R.C.M.P. Archives, Ottawa, Royal Canadian Mounted Police Records, Headquarter Files on the Winnipeg Strike, Vol. 7, R.B. Russell to Joseph Knight, December, 1918; Chief Press Censor Files, 144-A-1, Vol. 27, Fred Livesay, Western Press Censor, to Col. Chambers, April 17, 1919.

63 Chief Press Censor Files, 279-12, Vol. 125. Excerpt memorandum prepared for Colonel Chambers, April 22, 1919.

64 James Eayrs, *In Defence of Canada: From the Great War to the Great Depression* (Toronto, 1967), p. 30.

65 *Winnipeg Telegram,* 28 January 1919.

66 Borden Papers, Series OCA, File 252.

67 Borden Papers, 83164, Sir Thomas White to Borden, Feb. 3, 1919; *Ibid.,* 83152, White to Borden, Feb. 11, 1919; *Ibid.,* 83073, Borden to White.

68 On February 28, 1919, the German Government lodged an official complaint with the British authorities over "the reported plan of the Canadian government to deport all Germans from Canada". In forceful tones the German Government warned that such action "would prove a serious menace to a lasting peace of reconciliation". *Ibid.,* 83101, George Perley, Canadian High Commissioner, to White, March 17, 1919; I.B. File 912971, Swiss Ambassador, London, England, to Lord Curzon, Feb. 28, 1919, enclosed memorandum.

69 I.B. File 963419, W.D. Scott to James A. Calder, Minister of Immigration and Colonization, Dec. 11, 1919; Toronto *Telegram,* 1 April 1920.

70 Defence Records, C-2817(2), Secret monthly report, Comptroller, R.N.W.M.P., to Lt. Col. Davis, April 7, 1919.

71 *Vancouver Sun,* 26 March 1919.

72 Canadian Department of Labour Library, Ottawa, Mathers Royal Commission on Industrial Relations, 'Evidence', Sudbury Hearings, May 27, 1919, Testimony of J.L. Fortin, p. 1923.

73 *Ibid.,* Victoria Hearings, April 28, 1919, Testimony of J.O. Cameron, President of the Victoria Board of Trade, p. 75.

74 *Ibid.,* Calgary Hearings, May 3, 1919, Testimony of W. Henderson, p. 100.

75 *Ibid.,* Testimony of Mortimer Morrow, Manager of the Canmore Coal Mines, p. 142.

76 *Op. cit.,* Sudbury Hearings, May 27, 1919, Testimony of J.L. Agnew, Vice-Presicent of the International Nickel Company, p. 1942.

77 Chief Press Censor Files, 292, Vol. 125, C.H. Cahan, Director of the Public Safety Branch, to Sir Thomas White, Jan. 7, 1919.

78 Chief Press Censor Files, 292, Vol. 125.

79 Martin Robin, *Radical Politics and Canadian Labour* (Kingston, 1968), pp. 174-77.

80 Defence Records, C-2051, Major-General Gwatkin to C.H. Cahan, Jan. 4, 1919.

81 *Ibid.,* C-2665, Agents' Report to Commisioner Perry, R.N.W.M.P., March 22, 1919.

82 *The District Ledger,* 12 September 1918.

83 Defence Records, C-2665, Agent's Report to Commissioner Perry, March 22, 1919.

84 *Western Labor News,* 31 January 1919; R.C.M.P. Archives, Ottawa, Deportation Board of Enquiry Hearings, the Sam Blumenberg Enquiry, Aug. 1, 1919, Testimony of L. Goldstein.

85 *Winnipeg Telegram,* 29 January 1919, p. 1.

86 D.C. Masters, *The Winnipeg General Strike* (Toronto, 1950).

87 *Manitoba Free Press,* 22 May 1919, p. 1.

88 *Ibid.* p. 1.

89 Royal Canadian Mounted Police Files on the Winnipeg Strike, Major-General Ketchen to Secretary of the Milita Council, May 21, 1919; Masters, *The Winnipeg Strike,* pp. 95-97.

90 Borden Papers, 61838, A.J. Andrews to Arthur Meighen, June 6, 1919.

91 R.C.M.P. Files 22/4, Vol. 70, Commissioner Perry to Comptroller A. McLean, June 16, 1919.

92 *Manitoba Free Press,* 18 June 1919; Borden Papers, 62012, A.J. Andrews to Arthur Meighen, June 18, 1919.

93 *Manitoba Free Press,* 22 June 1919; *Winnipeg Tribune,* 30 June 1919.

94 R.C.M.P. Files, Vol. 2, Commissioner Perry to Comptroller McLean, July 6, 1919.

95 Meighen Papers, 002537, Hugh John Macdonald to Meighen, July 3, 1919.

96 *Ibid.,* Meighen to Macdonald, July 11, 1919.

97 Public Archives of Canada, Department of Justice Records, 1919, File 1960, T.J. Murray to J.A. Calder, October 30, 1919.

98 The transcript of the Deportation Hearings are in the R.C.M.P. Files on the Winnipeg Strike.

99 I.B., File 563236, Department of Justice, Memorandum for J.A. Calder, July 22, 1919.

100 "An Act to amend an Act of the Present Session entitled An Act to amend the Immigration Act", *Statutes of Canada,* 1919, Geo. V, Chapter 26, s. 41.

101 I.B., File 2183, J. Obed. Smith, Superintendent of Emigration, London, England, to F.C. Blair, Secretary of Immigration and Colonization, Ottawa, Feb. 28, 1921.

102 W.J. Bulman, President of the Canadian Manufacturers' Association, cited in *Industrial Canada* (Toronto), July, 1919, pp. 120-22.

103 Public Archives of Canada, Frontier College Papers, 1919, Alfred Fitzpatrick to J.D. Reid, Minister of Railways and Canals, Dec. 17, 1919.

104 A Dominion programme for citizenship training was not implemented until 1946.

105 I.B., File 216882, W.J. Egan, Deputy Minister of Immigration and Colonization, to Edward Beatty, President of the C.P.R., July 29, 1925.

106 W. Burton Hurd, *Racial Origins and Nativity of the Canadian People,* Census Monograph No. 4 (Ottawa, 1937), pp. 716-79.

107 John Marlyn, *Under the Ribs of Death* (Toronto, 1964), p. 24.

Commentary

Marian McKenna

In his opening paragraphs Professor Avery states his thesis and the theme around which he builds his argument. He suggests that between 1896 and 1919 the influence exerted by Anglo-Canadian industrialists on the Laurier and Borden administrations was the most important determinant of the low status held by immigrant workers from eastern and central Europe. According to Professor Avery these immigrants did not enjoy any appreciable upward social or economic mobility during the period studied. He then goes on to show the kinds of tensions and strains which World War I created for immigrant adjustment and inter-ethnic relations. His research further reveals the degree to which these immigrants, suddenly finding themselves classified as alien enemies, were subjected to intimidation, harassment and serious enfringement of their rights.

I question the appropriateness of the title of this impressive research paper, "The Immigrant Industrial Worker in Canada 1896-1919: The Vertical Mosaic as a Historical Reality". Aside from the first two pages, in which some reference is made to those determinants used by John Porter in his study of the vertical mobility of new Canadians, Avery's study does not deal with the usual indices of social and economic mobility, nor does it deal with mobility as such. Avery focuses on the experience of industrial workers, particularly in railroad construction and mining, in an exploitive capitalistic society where the industrialists have the leverage to influence provincial and federal officials and to secure special privileges and the relaxation of federal immigration policy. I suggest that a paper dealing in large measure with radicalism, union response and the multiple restrictions imposed during wartime might better be titled "The Red Scare in Canada" or some variation on that theme. It might be added that no good, bad or indifferent study of that subject has yet appeared in monograph form and in investigating such a promising subject, Professor Avery is plowing virgin ground.

The material on wartime hysteria and peacetime exploitation is based on a solid foundation of exhaustive research mainly in primary sources. Avery presents a masterful survey of the plight of immigrants faced with the strange new world of the Canadian labour force characterized by downgrading, repression, denigration, tenuous job security and disdain for union activity.

Of the two peacetime industries studied, Avery gives a better idea of anti-alien and anti-union attitudes among mining interests than among the railroad builders. Perhaps this is because it is more difficult to gain access to records relating to railroad personnel and hiring policies. However the outward manifestations of exploitation appear to be similar to those documented in the mining industry. Although it is difficult to find statistics on the railroad industry, accident rates appear to be similar to those of mining. Numerous isolated instances of shop injuries and track accidents connected with the C.P.R. are reported in the pages of the *Winnipeg Free Press.* Seldom did the railroad companies pay compensation for injuries, even serious ones such as the loss of a leg.

Any survey of immigrant literature in Canada during the period covered in Professor Avery's paper reveals that the emphasis is on the experiences of rural immigrants and agricultural labourers. While there are studies of block settlements, communal ethnic groups, homesteaders and harvest labourers, little, if any, attention has been paid to the urban immigrants, a large part of whom formed a base of industrial workers. Here again the Avery study must be considered a pioneer work.

Many questions arise out of his comprehensive treatment of a complex subject. How can Professor Avery explain the relatively large numbers of unskilled immigrants found in the ranks of industrialized labour when the immigration policy advanced by Sifton and Laurier favoured agricultural labourers? Officials in the Interior Department were outspoken in their opposition to recruiting unskilled labourers who might compete for jobs with native workers in the slowly developing industrial economy. Canada needed homesteaders to settle the prairie lands and harvesters to bring in the wheat crop and other agricultural produce. How did those Slavic workers who were unskilled or unsuited for prairie farming get past the federal immigration authorities and their designates in the provinces? Did some of them drift across the border from the United States? Were the specified limitations on an "open door" policy a mere technicality, violated with impunity by a group of high-ranking federal officials influenced by mining operators and railroad builders? What percentage of the industrial labour force did immigrants form during this period?

From this and other evidence, one might well question Professor Avery's assertion that "no prohibition was applied to continental Europeans" coming to Canada after 1896. In addition to exclusion on the basis of poor health, mental instability, and so on, there were financial requirements designed to discourage impecunious immigrants from entering the country and becoming the responsibility of the state. Aside from the standards imposed by federal immigration policy, there were numerous and vehement expressions of Anglo-Canadian resentment towards unlimited immigration from central and eastern Europe; groups often singled out for these vehement denunciations were the Ruthenians, Bukovinians, Galicians (all of them Ukrainians!) and above all others, the Doukhobors. In some influential circles these groups were considered incapable of being assimilated into Canadian society. Editorial opinion in Anglo-Canadian prairie newspapers favoured refusing these Slavic groups at ports of entry and expressed open resentment to their "non-conforming habits" after they came in. This nativist hostility and anti-immigrant sentiment bore a close resemblance to attitudes in the United States toward the so-called "new immigration" from south and central Europe after 1890.

Parallels can be drawn between U.S. and Canadian treatment of alien enemies and suspected subversives among the labouring classes during World War I and in the postwar era. The same forms of restriction and intimidation practiced in Canada were used in the U.S. but on a larger scale and in a more vehement way. Radicals and anarchists were arrested, jailed, tried on sometimes false charges, deported or imprisoned for long periods, and civil liberties among alien enemies were suspended. Aliens in both countries were interned and their property confiscated. Only a limited part of this property was returned or compensated for after revelations of gross irregularities in the Alien Property Custodian's Office in Washington, D.C.

In the U.S. fully 4,000 persons, many of them American citizens or otherwise loyal subjects, were hurried off to jails and bull pens in thirty-three major cities in twenty-three states. Persons trying to visit these "criminals" in one centre, Hartford, Connecticut, were also arrested on the grounds that they too must be Communists! Eventually, one-third of all these victims were released for lack of evidence. But 556 aliens allegedly proven to be members of the Communist party were deported.

If, in the face of widespread resentment to radicals infiltrating the trade union movement in Canada, there was an unprecedented wave of hysteria and anti-alien feeling similar in its manifestations to the "red scare" in the U.S. after 1917, how can Professor Avery account for the abrupt reversal in federal immigration policy after 1925 and a return to the "open door"? Why, just when restrictive leagues and rigid immigration laws were being formed in the U.S., did Canada adopt "a progressive immigration policy" and make every effort to attract more immigrants? Admittedly, these questions extend beyond the time period his paper covers, but since Professor Avery himself has mentioned this trend near the end of his discussion, one hopes that he will comment on these and other questions which this commentary has raised.

Marian McKenna is a professor of History at the University of Calgary.

2 Ethnicity as a Factor in the Development of Canadian Arts

Istvan Anhalt   39   About One's Place and Voice

William Kurelek   46   The Development of Ethnic Consciousness in a Canadian Artist

Eli Mandel   57   Ethnic Voice in Canadian Writing

About One's Place and Voice
Istvan Anhalt

I

At its simplest ethnicity in music may manifest itself through the use of folksong, a characteristic intonation curve or a preferred rhythm, but it may also come to life in a way that takes a deeper kind of perception to bring it to the surface of consciousness.

The point I shall try to make, and it is a truism, is that there is no formula that predictably defines how a man composes by using his place of birth and residence as firm indicators. While there are numerous cases where correlations between country and idiom are demonstrable, there are also many cases where there seems to be no correlation. The roots that bring up the creative juices often reach far down in a multitude of intricate patterns of intertwining threads.

Are John Cage, Jasper Johns and Roy Lichtenstein American? I do believe they are. Are Varèse or Yves Tanguy French or American, are they both or neither? Varèse is both and much more besides. For me, Tanguy is just Yves Tanguy, one of those artists who make the concept of ethnicity irrelevant. What about Jean Tanguily, the maker of the self-destroying machine? Well, he is "ethnic" in the sense of sharing a stratum that cuts across nations and continents and which is inhabited by people who are served by, abused, and at times smothered by contemporary technology.

The Estonian-born Canadian composer Udo Kasemets is probably the most knowledgeable and sympathetic protagonist of the aesthetics of John Cage in Canada as well as a highly talented experimental composer. He may be considered Canadian in the sense that this was the place where he could, unimpeded by flag-waving nationalism, develop his complex, syncretistic artistic personality.

The same holds true for the German-Canadian Otto Joachim, the composer of the first indeterminate composition written in Canada. He came here after a lengthy sojourn in China, where he made a living in music and also in electronics. It was in Canada that he was able to combine these fields and become one of the most creative composers of electronic music in the country.

39

II

I shall now turn to the work of five Canadian composers and to their orientation in the 1960s and 1970s. I have chosen to discuss music which uses the human voice, because this seems a good medium for testing the feasibility of moving toward a definition of ethnicity in contemporary Canadian musical composition.

First I will discuss a composer who possesses what I believe to be the strongest and most clearly identifiable Canadian voice. He is John Beckwith, who for over twenty years has kept his ear closely attuned to the sound and emotive world of rural and small-town English Canada of today and yesteryear. His scope expanded a while ago, and he gave voice also to the sounds and dynamics of the great city. Now his interest ranges from one end of the country to the other.

Beckwith respects, and what counts more, is fond of decent and unostentatious people. He sees them in the flesh and also in the flow of history. He wants to depict their emotions, but, like some of his models, he considers emotive excess bad form. When pathos impends, he often suddenly withdraws with tact, with understatement and, at times, with humour.

An example of this and also of his social consciousness is *Gas*, a relatively short piece for a speaking chorus based on inscriptions found on various municipal and provincial traffic signs in south-central Ontario. The text ends with "Dead End". What a double-entendre! But he does not want to overdo it: no "Ode to Ecology" for him. Instead he tells the performers that this "ending should not be made *too* deep".

Beckwith is an excellent maker of musical collages, one of the first in Canada. An example of this is his long trilogy, *Canada Dot—Canada Dash,* composed for the Centennial. In the first part, *The Line Across,* he begins in the Maritimes and progresses westward. In the overture one almost senses the salty air and the blunt, warm, earthy personalities of the Maritimers, wrapped in hauling groans and sweeps of sea-shanties. Then comes a nineteenth-century Quebec, depicted through the sounds of an opera comique, with a Grand Galop on the theme of, of all things, Caliza Lavalle. Brio, verve, joie de vivre—all are here. It should be noted that Beckwith elected not to interpret the seething moods of some groups in east-end Montreal at the time of Expo 67. He tactfully and wisely left this for other people to do.

Beckwith can be, as he is in this work, Walt Whitmanesque, but he is more similar in spirit to the painter J.E. Hughes. His music has a surface quality that attracts most listeners. This surface quality is at various times deceptively simple, outspokenly complex, sweet sounding, or raw and forceful. His modulations from mood to mood, from idiom to idiom and between styles are his very own. Whether smooth or abrupt, the modulation is dictated by a sophisticated perception of reality and its artistic potential. But what really matters lies below these surface qualities. It is the voice of the deep stratum, the sub-text, the inward searching glance, the groping for roots. An example of this is his beautiful *Sharon Fragments,* in which he tried to recreate the spiritual world of David Willson, the founder and patriarch of the Children of Peace sect, who lived with his followers in Sharon, Ontario in the mid-nineteenth century.

In almost all of his works Beckwith digs deep into the land and taps the mind and the historical roots of his people. In these sources he finds universal value. This aspiration, or vision if you wish, finds a clear expression in the words of Margaret Atwood, whom Beckwith admires. She wrote the following lines for the libretto of *The Trumpets of Summer,* one of Beckwith's most eloquent works:

Around us is a ring of chairs
Around us is a ring of walls
Around us is a ring of green lawns
Around us is a ring of rivers and white swans
and a ring of houses and a ring of towns
and a ring of land and sea and empty air see:
the round world around is out there.
This chair is the centre
This chair holds the earth and the skies . . .

III

Serge Garant is one of the most dynamic figures in modern French-Canadian music. Conductor, pianist, composer—he excels in all of these areas. While, like most composers in French Canada, he seems to favour the instrumental media, he has also written a number of works in which the voice has a significant role.

Anerca, a work for a solo soprano with eight instruments, is one of these. The text he chose is in Eskimo, but he elected to labour under the handicap of an English translation. Aesthetically the work belongs to the Boulezian world of the *Marteau sans Maitre.* It is timbrally refined, brittle, nervous, subtle, in a special, seemingly hardly Eskimo way. But after hearing it repeatedly, one begins to discern a certain angularity, a certain starkness, a certain feeling of isolation that makes one revise first impressions. The text of the first song suggests a solitary voice in a vast landscape that is free of man-made screens and into which man and thought blend as a matter of common occurrence:

I arise from rest
with the beat of raven's wings.

I arise to meet the day
My eyes turn from the night
to gaze at the dawn now whitening.

The piece dates from 1961. A few years later in the mid-60s Garant composed *Phrases II,* a powerful work for full symphony orchestra, in which the players themselves are called upon to speak, murmur, shout and whisper from time to time. The words are chosen from texts by Che Guevara. The orchestra plays a dramatic, often violent kind of music. Most of the time the voices are muffled and inarticulate. This combination is evocative of repression and pent-up rage. It may remind those who lived in Montreal in the mid-60s of the mood of the city as a result of certain conditions, certain events and certain reactions to these. The piece is, in this sense, a truthful statement, and it is also a work of art of power and sophistication.

Garant's works show a consistent striving toward a combination of dramatic and musical imagination with an inner need to express ideas through a carefully-calculated blueprint. His language has evolved toward a synthesis in which swarms of note-clouds live in harmony with brusque percussive attacks, expressive chromatic cantilenas, and with a counterpoint fashioned from masses of medium density. His is one of the strongest and most individual voices in French-Canadian composition today; a voice that is thoroughly cosmopolitan, but one that nevertheless has the undertones of his own land and society.

IV

Harry Somers has a deep attachment to the voice. One need only recall his opera, *Louis Riel,* a major work that resulted from the burst of creativity engendered by Canada's Centennial. It was a great undertaking, and parts of it, for example Riel's long unaccompanied soliloquy, remain in memory as strong, personal statements.

Somers is on a sustained search for what is Canadian in the total human mix, and to find what he is looking for he explores other cultures as well. His *12 Miniatures,* composed in 1966, is a very lean, sharply-etched piece in moods resembling some Japanese expressions, which is fitting since the texts are haiku poems. The key to this expression is economy of means, intelligibility of text, sharp focus on details and an intimate feel for nature, human as well as physical.

In contrast, his most recent choral work, *Kyrie,* is a statement made on a very large scale. It seems to address itself to all humanity. It is a gripping and moving work in many hues, of which even the darkest show considerable variety of colour of carefully balanced sonorities. There is nothing hurried here, nothing intimating theatrical excess, no local colour. Instead Somers makes what seems to be a long-gestated universal appeal, or cry from the deep, and a passionate warning to all.

V

Murray Schafer is another Canadian-born composer who searches far and wide, both intellectually and geographically, for musical expression. He is one of the most interesting and important composers in the country today: a mind of wide interest, a remarkable musical sense, a feel for the topical and the essential and a prodigious worker.

His travels took him to Europe, to the East, to Australia. Name it, and he has likely been there. He thinks big and makes the world's business his own in education, sonic ecology and in other fields as well. It is challenging to keep up with Murray's interests and programmes. I cannot say much here about his valuable work in the education of the young through awareness of the sonic environment. A passing remark will have to suffice: after considerable preliminaries, he now is busy mapping, with a small band of associates, what he calls "the music of the environment".

In his thinking and compositions R.M. Schafer is a descendant of Freud, Jung, Ezra Pound, E.T.A. Hoffman, Machaut, Monteverdi, Debussy and Cage. His work is also related to that of Stockhausen, Berio and Lutoslawski, especially to the latter two.

His oeuvres show a number of major concerns. The first of these is for the individual psyche, making some of his works a sort of musical-psychiatric quest. The pieces *"Toi-Loving"* (his first opera), *Requiems for the Party Girl* and *Dream Passage,* among others, belong to this stratum.

His second concern involves a quest for peace, for new life-patterns for the individual and the group, and for an understanding of the mystical. This induced him to study non-Western cultures, such as those he observed in India, Turkey and Iran. This orientation and the Eastern influence are evident in a number of pieces: *Gita* (1966) for chorus, brasses and tape uses fragments from the *Bhagavad Gita* in the original Sanskrit; *From the Tibetan Book of the Dead* (1968) for voices, instruments and tape uses inflections resembling the tone-glides of the original Tibetan; *In Search of Zoroaster* (1971) uses words from a number of Zoroastrian sources, both in the original and in translation. The last is a long, drawn-out contemplative piece for voices and for percussion instruments played by the members of the chorus.

Schafer's third concern is of a socio-political nature. An example of this is *Threnody,* composed in 1966. The text of this work, intended to be performed by young performers, is derived from two sources. One is eye-witness accounts of children and young people after the atomic bombing of Nagasaki. The other derives from comments and telegrams sent to and from the Potsdam Conference in July, 1945, concerning the United States' first successful test explosion of the atomic bomb. The work has a harrowing quality and great emotive power.

Schafer aspires to be a citizen of the world, and he is well on the way to achieving this. The porousness of Canada's geographical, political, economical and cultural boundaries allow, and even facilitate this development. Canadians have a tradition of listening to the other fellow's point of view, perhaps more so than other nationalities. Schafer is a world-trader in ideas— ethical, aesthetic and political. That he was able to develop this in such a short career may attest not only to his great talent, but to an evolved attribute that is a characteristic of the place where he was born and works.

VI

My own *Foci* is a composition for voices and instruments in nine sections to be performed in a planned visual environment. As the title suggests, *Foci* is a series of views of life, glimpses of contemporary existence and glimpses of situations from the past. Some of these views suggest perceptions of exterior events, spaces and aural and visual images, however most of them are concerned with the inner spaces of the mind/heart.

The most important single idea permeating *Foci* is the thought that each person's uniqueness is embodied in his or her voice as it speaks, sings, whispers, laughs, moans and sighs, and that it transmits itself through these and the many other forms of vocal expression. The work consists of soliloquies, duos (together or with the participants not relating to each other), as well as groups of vocal sounds in English, French, Italian, German, Yiddish, Aramaic, Greek, Hungarian and Creole, accompanied by instruments. The words come from diverse sources: a dictionary of psychology, the New Testament, the Genevan Psalter, the Zohar, the Ishtar legend, *The Odyssey,* voodoo texts, legal formulae, newspapers and elsewhere. I shall comment on only one of its movements.

Section 3 of the work, entitled *Icons,* is to a large extent autobiographical. It tells of certain thoughts and feelings I came to develop about the city of Geneva. The first one of these is my fondness, dating back many years, for the tunes of the Genevan Psalter. These are pure and gentle in contrast to so much in music and life generally. In 1968 it was my good fortune to visit Geneva. It was my first stay there and, although a brief one, I came to sense strongly and be enchanted by the spirit of that city. One of the strong impressions I gathered there came from an exhibition of Greek icons from Swiss collections in the Musée Rath. Among them was one by the seventeenth-century painter Demetrios portraying Elijah ascending into heaven in a chariot of fire. This icon fused, in some manner I cannot explain, Calvin's Geneva with Byzantium in my mind. In a flash I became conscious of the iconic quality of the words and melodies of the Genevan Psalter and, consequently, of their affinity to the pictorial icon from that other world, the seventeenth-century Greek echo of Byzantium. The principal languages used in this section are French and Greek, and there is a single phrase in English.

The soundspace of this piece may be likened to intersecting, multidimensional hierarchies, realized through a variety of texts, languages, individual vocal timbres and expressions, as well as through vocal and instrumental group textures and timbres implying vast architectural spaces.

In this work as well as in others (*Cento,* for example) I was, and continue to be influenced by a great number of things Canadian and by other blends. I sense that I function as a composer almost as a receptacle, changeable in shape to be sure, but giving an outline to that which accumulates. A long time ago I came to the realization that I could do this better in Canada than anywhere else I have ever lived. And for this I am grateful.

VII

I would like to conclude by reaffirming the belief that there is no formula for predictably defining how a man writes by using his geographical and family origins as firm and sole indicators. His birthplace and ancestry may be of great or little consequence, or they may appear to have no direct influence. Who knows for sure? Perhaps it is what one picks up from the road that counts most. But it seems safe to say that only the whole man counts—who he is, how he got to be who he is and his secret aspirations for the future, both for himself and for those people who are close to him. There are no short-cuts to finding this identity: all the details matter. One has to look at, and listen to everything that seems important in the process.

Istvan Anhalt is a composer and Chairman of the Department of Music, Queen's University.

Development of Ethnic Consciousness in a Canadian Painter
William Kurelek

When I was asked by Professor Isajiw to give this paper, I didn't consider myself qualified. For one thing I'm not a scholar in any sense, and as a painter I'm a loner. I don't get involved in artists' discussions, movements or associations, and I can't speak for others from practical experience with them. Nevertheless it is true that I am an ethnic painter. So when Professor Isajiw asked me to present this paper, even if strictly from a personal standpoint, I agreed. I decided to do it in the hope that one man's story might be of some help to other individuals or even groups. However I'd like to point out to my readers that they are free to pick and choose what they think applicable to the subject under discussion. They will have to anyway because my approach is rather simple and rambling.

I first became conscious of being "ethnic" and of being an "artist" at the age of seven. Those of you who may have already read my autobiography[1] know the two incidents to which I am referring, but I will cite them for those who don't. In the first, I found out the hard way that Ukrainian was not to be spoken in public:

> It was about the second day of school. As I sat in my little grade one desk I spotted a fly on the window. "Mookha, Mookha!" I exclaimed pointing to it. It was probably the first fly of the season. John even got up to catch it. The teacher stared icily, and the classroom roared with laughter as we sank red-faced back into our seats.

The second had to do with my scholastic rivalry with a boy in my grade in the first years of public school:

> The two of us were standing by the school. "I bet I can draw a better train than you!" I said. "I bet you can't. I can," he shot back. So in we went and drew our respective trains. I don't really recall what the drawings were like, or if in fact mine *was* better. The important thing was that I realized I could draw. I also soon realized that this talent drew attention and admiration, and I was starved for both.

However at that stage these two awarenesses were still two separate entities. They did come together for a few years in my late teens and early twenties but parted again for a good ten to fifteen years before totally new circumstances allowed a reunion. And this time I think it is a permanent one.

That first union wasn't actually very healthy and, on hind sight, I see it was just as well that it failed. It's hard to know where to draw the line on the influences that brought it about. My father's was by far the biggest adverse influence then. But he in turn could blame others.

At the time my father arrived in Canada, a semi-literate son of Ukrainian peasants, there was virulent Ku Klux Klan movement in western Canada, and a strong feeling against "foreigners", that is, those who weren't W.A.S.P. He must have had some bad experiences from that source because ever since I can remember he was anti-English. He didn't want to learn the English language and sneered at the absurdity of its spelling. Nevertheless it's rather difficult to be anti-something all the time without being pro-something. So, for example, the Kurelek family continued to celebrate Ukrainian Christmas on January 7 and even considered it a worthwhile sacrifice to lose a perfect attendance record at school if the 7th fell on a week day. During the war father was pro-German simply because he was anti-establishment. It was only after the war was over that we learned to our dismay what a bad mistake we'd made in the placing of our sympathies. Yes, I'm ashamed to say that there were brief periods in those formative teens when I was a Nazi sympathizer. Actually I vacillated, and I did so because I had ambivalent feelings toward my father. It's natural for a son to identify with his father—to look up to him as a hero. But mine was so unapproachable because he despised me for my timid, sensitive nature. He had no use for my artistic inclination either, and I was scolded and threatened in an effort to make me give it up. My Anglo-Saxon teachers, however, were kind and tolerant and even congratulatory in their detached English way.

I went through the public school years wondering whether I was Ukrainian or English Canadian until father sent my brother and me to high school in Winnipeg. He also sent us to evening schools, one of which was a Ukrainian class. There I fell under the influence of Father Mayewsky, a teacher and dedicated Ukrainian nationalist. When I say "fell", I mean just that. At last I had found someone who was a man, a teacher and a Ukrainian, and I considered him a father figure. He taught us the history of the Ukraine, with its brief moments of glory followed by centuries of suffering under various foreign occupying powers. I was at last clear in my mind (or so it seemed to me) that I was a Ukrainian, not a Canadian. I dreamed of doing great things for the cause of Ukrainian liberation, and I idealized the Ukrainian countryside, people and culture, although I had never been there. I couldn't of course visit the Ukraine even if I'd had the wherewithal because the Iron Curtain was shut good and tight.

Father Mayewsky also took note of my natural artistic talent and gave me some art work to do for the Orthodox church where he was the priest. And so it was that one of my dreams of dedicating myself to the Ukrainian cause came to take the form of an epic illustration of the whole of Ukrainian history. Some of my readers might want to point to that time as my coming to maturity as an ethnic artist. I don't think so, and I'll soon explain why. At this time Father M. also had a talk with my father. Finally, after all those years of angry opposition, I won his grudging recognition that art might have some prestige value. However he insisted (and I had to admit it even to myself) that there was no financial future in it. I don't think there was a single Canadian painter at that time who lived by his paintings. The big change in Canadian society that gave artists a chance to make a living and more has come only in the last few phenomenal years.

Therefore to satisfy my father and to insure his financial support for my education, I played along with his worldly ambition for prestige and security. I said I'd be a teacher, and I actually meant it at first. But the university turned me into a rebel. I fell under the influence of several books we studied or that I read myself: Joyce's *Portrait of the Artist as a Young Man,* Butler's *The Way of All Flesh* and Stone's *Lust for Life.* All of these are atheistic. My father had always ridiculed religion, and I wasn't sure what I believed. But Father M.'s influence had made me give it a try. The books' influence proved stronger. That meant that Father M.'s nationalistic influence was waning. Having lost respect for official religion of which he was a representative, I could come no closer to him and in fact had to avoid him. Secondly, it meant rebellion against family loyalties (and the family *was* Ukrainian) and turning instead toward self-discovery and development. Finally, despite the good influence of contacts with displaced persons who were coming over in large numbers and telling the truth about Soviet society, I came under the counter influence of leftist rebels. I simply had no leg to stand on in political discussions with them at the university and at art school.

It is true that in my wanderings across western Canada, Mexico and Europe I would return to Ukrainian subject matter from time to time. Sometimes one might even say that my art was nationalistic as is, for example a large painting illustrating Gogol's *Taras Bulba.* But primarily my emphasis was on "social consciousness"—that is, the solid virtues of working people and peasants. Eventually I ended up in a psychiatric hospital in England and my days as an "ethnic artist" seemed to be over. The English peoples' gentlemanly kindness, tolerance and hospitality to me in a time of need prompted me to settle and remain in England. I threw over the influence of my father's prejudices, not knowing that he was mellowing back home and making English friends at last.

And then came the big turning point in my life, my conversion to the Christian faith. It is because of this conversion that I am today an ethnic artist and writing a paper on the subject. I had reached such a low point that I was finished no matter how you looked at me, as a Canadian, a Ukrainian, an artist or even just a human being. The irony from the point of view of this paper is that I was pulled back from the brink of suicide by an Anglo-Saxon, Margaret Smith. She helped me by practicing her Catholic Christian faith and by setting a good example. Readers of this paper may object that these facts are not pertinent to the subject since my experience was not typical. I grant that the lives of other ethnic artists may not be as dramatic or violent or whatever you wish to label it. But I was asked to do this paper even if it presented a purely personal experience, and I can do it no other way. To me, being a genuinely religious person is inextricably tied in with being an ethnic artist. I'll explain this by showing the series of steps by which I came full circle back to ethnic art. And this time I became an ethnic artist not merely in conviction, but in actual practice. It started out with getting rock-bottom answers to rock-bottom questions.

First, is life worth living for any human being, regardless of his origin? In the earth's long history nations and races have come and gone, but man has remained. Life certainly seemed to be worth living once I realized that it is a good God who created us, and that He has prepared a happy ending for each of us. This life is but an exciting time of trial to prove ourselves worthy of that happy ending.

I found the Catholic faith to be a world religion, embracing members of all nations and races. So in the two years I stayed on in England and for a few more on my return to Canada in 1959, I prided myself on being a world citizen. This means that men should not be ashamed of, or disloyal to their nationality. It also means that men must respect people of other origins and, when possible, share their heritage: taste each others' food, enjoy each others' music, learn each others' language and literature. Strange to say this made me happier with my own background. For as long as I had tried to be loyal only to the Ukrainian cause, I was bound to be disillusioned. Ukrainians, whether as individuals or as a group, cannot be idealized. They are human beings and as such are just as prone to weaknesses as all other descendants of the first man.

My work took somewhat the same course. When I did resume painting after my recuperation and conversion, I had given up specifically Ukrainian, Canadian or leftist subject matter. It is true that many of those elements were still evident, but my over-riding ambition was to do religious art. My old ambition to do an epic work had turned into a decision to illustrate the

Bible. Before this my life's work had looked like an unfinished puzzle. I remember saying to myself, when I realized that everything had clicked into place, "But of course, this is what I was heading for all these years." And so it was that I produced the Passion according to St. Matthew, sentence by sentence, one painting a week for three years—160 in all. This was strictly an act of love for God for His great mercy to me. I visualized the pictures being made into a slide film for Bible instruction in the missions. By helping spread His Gospel, I would share with others the good thing I had found

It was an act of faith too, for in worldly eyes I was a failure. I was thirty-three years old, unmarried, jobless and cooped up in a small bed-sitting room on Huron Street in Toronto with only a few dollars of my savings left I had given up the idea of being an artist by profession several years before and had trained for two years in England as a picture frame maker. But that was no help either, for I'd already spent six months searching in vain for employment, and no one would give me money to start a business of my own. I had even tried to go into teaching, a decision which naturally delighted my family. But teachers' college decided I was unsuitable after a few days trial. However no sooner did I begin the actual paintings for the St. Matthew series, when near miraculous things began to happen.

God is not to be outdone in generosity. As it is written in the New Testament by St. Luke, "Give and it shall be given unto you, good measure, pressed down and shaken together and running over, shall men give into your bosom." I was given a one-man show by the Isaacs Gallery in Toronto, and it was a success. After ten years of searching in vain for acceptance by galleries and critics, the breakthrough had come. But I still refused to believe my good fortune or to think of myself as a full-fledged artist. I said I was a picture framer and an illustrator, a religious propagandist. For God had given me the job in picture framing too, at the Isaacs Gallery.

Here was yet another lesson in the healthy development of an ethnic artist. For the person instrumental in the second biggest break in my life (after Margaret Smith) was also a non-Ukrainian. Mr. Isaacs is of Jewish origin, and most of the buyers at my first few shows and the critics who acclaimed my work were either Jewish or Anglo-Saxon. My second show at the Isaacs Gallery, entitled "Memories of Farm and Bush Life", established me as a "farm" painter, one who relates the history of pioneering people developing the new lands of western Canada. It was brought to my attention that I spoke for all ethnic groups not just the Ukrainians. In my third show I returned to works of religious propaganda and unveiled a series which I called "Experiments in Didactic Art". These paintings were not as popular with the public or with Av Isaacs, but they were a revelation none the less as fa as my development was concerned. On the strength of previous shows, people still came and looked. This prompted me to follow the advice of a new and saintly Catholic friend of mine, Mrs. Helen Cannon: "Paint both kinds of pictures, ethnic and didactic. Both give glory to God in their own way."

There was still more of the "pressed down and overflowing" to come. Much more. With each overflow I found myself getting further into so-called ethnic art. As I prepared for another exhibition of farm paintings, it occurred to me that perhaps there *was* a way of harnessing even the farm paintings to a religious purpose. What about honouring my father with a series of paintings about him? As a practicing Christian I was bound to observe the third commandment, "Honour your father and your mother." It was true that I had suffered a great deal under him, but that was no excuse for I was now bound to return good for evil. Nor was there any excuse in the fact that my father did not believe and in fact ridiculed religion. So was born my fourth show at Isaacs Gallery, a series of twenty paintings titled "An Immigrant Farms in Western Canada". It told my father's story, from his leaving the old country to, after many struggles, his life farming the land in this new country. The show was a near sellout.

Several other things happened. I use the word "happened" because I don't for a minute doubt that God's hand was in it. One of these things was that the first Ukrainian Canadian made a purchase at a one-man show of my works. It was a night scene of a Ukrainian Easter vigil in Alberta to which I could remember going with my parents. It also had a Ukrainian carved frame which I had made, being naturally drawn to Ukrainian crafts. The most obviously Ukrainian subject, that of a Bukovinian straw-thatched house before which my father bids farewell to his parents, was purchased by an English company for their board room. There were very obvious signs that the Ukrainian community was interested in my work, even though few paintings were actually bought by Ukrainians. Av Isaacs explained that, as far as buying, they had to be given more time: they had had a hard struggle and were just beginning to become financially secure. He suggested that they had to go through a period of material acquisition before they would feel secure enough to begin adorning their homes with less material things like art.

Isaacs' explanation made me better able to understand John Sims' troubles with another ethnic art project inspired by my show. John Sims, a young Ukrainian-Canadian writer and song composer, was so moved by "An Immigrant Farms in Western Canada" that he interviewed my father and wrote his story. He presented the story to various Ukrainian groups and tried to convince them either to make a film of it themselves or to financially back some one else to make it. But he failed. Finally he approached the National Film Board which, with its talented people and fine equipment, produced a little masterpiece for Canada's Centennial celebrations. My father had always liked telling his life story to anyone who cared to listen. But neither he nor I had visualized, even in our wildest dreams, that his story might be broadcast right across Canada in movie theatres, on television and in school courses. I myself have seen the film shown to Eskimos in the far north and to my father's countrymen in major cities of the Ukraine. I had the pleasure of introducing him to Mrs. Pearson, the prime minister's wife, when both of them appeared at the opening of "An Immigrant Farms".

Another development of that exhibition led me into an even deeper commitment to the Ukrainian community. When the exhibition ended, four executive members of the Ukrainian Women's Committee of Canada approached me with a request to depict the part of the Ukrainian woman in the development of western Canada. They promised that they would persuade their group to acquire the series. With my acceptance of that commission I was only one or two steps away from total awareness of the ethnic role that had been cut out for me.

The four women gave me moral support as my research—interviews, photographs and a three-week trip to western museums—and the actual pairing progressed. Unfortunately they failed to communicate their vision and enthusiasm to the rank-and-file members of their group and so they bought only one-third of the series. This didn't bother me because, with Av Isaacs' salesmanship, it was a sellout anyway. By far the most important thing was that I had managed to give the series a religious direction, not only in the prophetic note at the end, but in my observance of the third commandment. The predominant figure was my own mother, and the spirit of the show was in praise of her virtues.

After my fifth show the Ukrainian community began to buy in earnest. As if in confirmation of Isaacs' evaluation of the community's progression of values, the greater number of those who bought proved to be new Canadians. They had arrived after the last war practically destitute. Yet in an amazingly few years they had acquired money. Since most had educated an cultured backgrounds in the Ukraine, they spent a considerable portion of their wealth on art. I bring up the matter of patronage because I follow the rather simple view of art held in the Middle Ages, that art is not something esoteric and sacrosanct, but a craft and a commodity. As a craftsman the artist produced what he was commissioned to do or what was saleable for that was his livelihood. Like the medieval artist, I rely on, and try to satisfy my customers in subject matter, size and medium. The result is that since

I now have a large number of Ukrainian buyers who often buy Ukrainian themes, I automatically find myself producing ethnic art. It's as simple as that. About four or five years ago another two new Canadians entered my life to further cement my position in the Ukrainian-Canadian community. They are gallery owners Mykola and Olga KolianKiwsky. For a long time I could not have any business dealings with them because I was morally bound by my business tie with the Isaacs Gallery. Then to my amazement the Kolian-Kiwskys bought the whole St. Matthew series and planned to use it as a permanent backbone exhibit for their new museum in Niagara Falls. That same year they led a cultural group tour of the Ukraine, and I went along. This visit helped me to answer the question I'd put to myself some twenty-five years earlier: "Am I Ukrainian or Canadian?" In my case the answer was not to be found in the cities where the Soviet authorities led us to see the showpieces of Ukrainian Art. It lay in the small villages.

Fortunately, with the help of the KolianKiwskys, I obtained permission to visit my father's village. Although this visit lasted a mere four hours, I felt that it was well worth putting up with the ennui of the three-week-long conducted tour. In those four hours I saw, however fleetingly, the houses in which the peasants lived, ate the food they ate, photographed the village pond and talked the language of my forebears. It was like living a lifetime in one day. Here were my ultimate roots. For these hard-working, simple (you might almost say naïve) people reminded me so much of the Ukrainian farm people I knew in Alberta. This was the real Ukraine, not the attenuated vision I had worshipped in my nationalistic days in Winnipeg. And it excited me as Van Gogh's *Potato Eaters* excites me but Van Dyck's portraits do not.

One of the Soviet guides for our group was a Kiev journalist whom we suspected of being an unofficial "ear"—a spy. She had overheard me declare that I hoped to "find myself" on the tour, and in a journalistic interview with me on our last day in Kiev she asked, "Well, have you found out if you're Canadian or Ukrainian?" I replied that in all honesty I hadn't found out but that I now knew how to find the answer. "Ask your government to give me permission to come back and paint for three weeks in my father's village," I said. "And the following year give me three more in the village of Vasyl Stephanyk. Then I'll be able to answer both of us." Many think that Stephanyk was the Ukraine's greatest prose writer. He interested me because he portrayed the common people's feelings about emigrating to the New World. Although the journalist assured me that I would be welcome in both villages, I'm still trying to obtain a work visa three years later. Had my efforts been successful, I would be sitting over a drawing board in the village of Borwitsi at this very moment.

The proposed work trip was to have been an integral part of my plan to produce a Ukrainian-Canadian epic in the form of a mural. I have already done two years of research for it here in Canada, and the Old Country part of the research was to take another two years. I felt I had to go to the Ukraine so that I could better comprehend the emigration of my people to foreign lands. What was it that gave them the drive and the courage to face a terrifying ocean journey, homesickness and the dangers and hardships of homesteading in virgin wilderness? One day this giant mural series will be centred in Ottawa so that all Canadians and visitors from abroad can see the story of Ukrainian settlement and development. As I said at the beginning of this paper, I have come nearly full circle back to the dreams of my Winnipeg days, but my dreams are healthier this time.

Before I conclude this paper I should mention one last important factor in my development—my wife and family. I think my experience is especially pertinent to this paper because it reflects a common concern of ethnic group in Canada today. While ethnic groups are becoming more aware of their own virtues and values, they are also in the process of being assimilated, and one factor of assimilation is intermarriage.

When I finally married at the age of thirty-five, I married a Canadian girl of British origin. I recall wondering during our courtship if the difference between our heritages would present problems. But I believed that my wife would learn the Ukrainian language and gradually the rest of my culture— dress, cooking, music, literature and so on—as I had learned hers.

But this was not to be. And I began to realize that in all probability my children would not learn my language or culture either. This would mean that approximately one-quarter to one-third of my cultural background would remain strange, foreign, unshared. I felt that I was at a crossroads, and finally I decided I must hold onto my own heritage, rather than be assimilated into the general milieu of Anglo-Saxon North American culture.

For as my fame spred I observed that the Ukrainian community came into our home more than ever before. They came to buy, to get advice, to invite me to address their organizations or simply to talk. I found that the more I tasted that culture, the more I came to love it. Some of my happiest moments were, and still are spent listening to Ukrainian music as I paint. I was getting closer to my heritage and further from my wife and family for the simple reason that they did not share my interest in the Ukrainian heritage— I mean an interest that would spontaneously draw them to it, to taste and be nourished by it.

In a strange way my disappointment has helped me. I have become more keenly aware of the differences between the two cultures and better able to represent that difference in my painting. Secondly, I have become more sympathetic with the émigré Ukrainian's concern over the Russification of his motherland. Finally, my experience has helped me to appreciate how fortunate I and other people of various origins are to be living in Canada. Although we cannot always share our heritage, we can at least express it in freedom.

This then is the story of one man's odyssey toward ethnic awareness. As I said in the beginning of this paper, each reader is free to extract his or her own set of conclusions, but I venture to offer my own conclusions in the hope that self-analysis may be of value.

1. Ethnicity cannot be manufactured any more than morality can be legislated. It is there by birth or experience and can only be uncovered or nurtured.

2. I would advise the ethnic artist not to feel sorry for himself and not to wait until his people have organized to give him practical assistance. If help is offered, accept it and be grateful and use that assistance honestly. If not, go to the government or any ethnic or public-spirited groups willing and interested in helping.

3. There is no longer any excuse for anyone in this country to be ashamed of his cultural background. Canada has a multicultural society. The days of Anglo-Saxon domination are gone, or nearly gone. The English have their own virtues and culture. We must not forget those virtues, for in the days of their domination they gave our ethnic culture at least a breathing chance.

4. Harbouring bitterness toward individuals or groups who deny you development or expression is a mistake. Bitterness poisons the soul and does little, if any hurt to the oppressor. If at all possible, go somewhere where you do have opportunity for development and do your thing for your people there.

5. Art is not the most important thing in the world, neither are race or nationality. Human beings—individual human souls—are the most important. The prime activity of each individual, whether he be talented or ordinary, is saving his soul and helping others save theirs. The reason is elementary: we have only a few short years here, but all eternity in the next life.

6. Put God first and your nationality or ethnic origin second. If you really practice this priority, He will be more than generous in helping you in your work for your people.

7. Give love and energy towards some work for the whole family of man, whether it be for individuals or less fortunate groups.

8. Just as it is wise to know yourself and to face up to your own weakness so it is also wise to recognize the deplorable faults of your race. But don't dwell on those weaknesses: it is better to work at eradicating them. As for th opposite mistake—worshipping or attributing ideal qualities to your race or country—it should be fairly obvious that no such ideal people exist!

Having had his formal education cut short by the misfortune of war, my father was a great believer in real life experience as a teacher. He loved telling about his education from the Book of Experience. I have taken a leaf from that book in presenting this paper. I'm sure that some of you who have come to expect more academic papers will find my approach and conclusions rather odd. All I can do is echo what Professor Maas said in the foreword to my autobiography:

> It is for certain that many readers will take issue with Bill's religious convictions. However the factual material is vividly presented and the reader is therefore able to draw his own conclusions. This is as it should be in a valuable learning experience.

William Kurelek is an internationally-known Canadian artist now living in Toronto.

NOTE

1. *Someone With Me* (Ithaca: Cornell University Press, 1973).

Ethnic Voice in Canadian Writing
Eli Mandel

I

Let me begin with a dilemma. Any entry into the sociology of writing offers genuine theoretical difficulties, and yet the subject to which I have been asked to address myself calls for just such an entry. Of course, you might ask, "Why not simply be satisfied with description and simple categorization?" The answer is that the subject of ethnicity generates pressures that do not permit anything like the remoteness suggested by an easy survey. At this point the real alternatives become clear: the material before me, the subject itself, is either fictional or not. I mean precisely to question the subject itself and to ask where is the source of this deep-rooted and troublesome sense that somehow it is always evading us, slipping away. Let me illustrate.

"The true meaning of *immigrant* is . . . to be dispossessed of the culture even if one is born into it," remarks Elizabeth Janeway.[1] We are all immigrants to this place," says Margaret Atwood.[2] "Well, yes," we say. But when she adds that we're all mental patients too, we may not agree so readily. Quite possibly it is only Atwood's habit of mind that leads her to see the spirit of this country as a ghostly mad old woman on a St. Clair streetcar. And perhaps it is her habit of mind too that moves her to work out all the implications in the image of alien: to feel in that word not only a sense of otherness—of being apart from, foreign—but even more, a sense of the unnatural in the science-fiction sense of the word. Or could it be that a disturbing, dislocating quality enters the discussion the moment we place concepts of social class, cultural definition or group structure at the forefront? It is not only that as strangers we find ourselves in a strange land, but with the burden upon us as well, to paraphrase a remark of M.L. Lautt's, of living simultaneously within the influences of our own and another's culture.[3] To live in doubleness is difficult enough. To articulate that doubleness simply intensifies the pressure, the burden. But there is a further step in which what Atwood calls "inescapable doubleness" turns into duplicity, a strategy for cultural identification that I take to be the ethnic strategy and the "voice" I'm trying to identify in these remarks. The sense in which I am using the term "duplicitous" is perhaps special, though I hope it will become clear enough from the examples I have chosen, as well as from a general comment on the senses in which we can speak of the "self" as deceptive. The comment is R.D. Laing's. The examples from what we usually call ethnic writing are not extensive. The questions which they pose will be dealt with after I have said what I can about the writers and their works.

To begin, then, with Laing's comment:

> Heidegger has contrasted the natural scientific concept of truth with a notion of truth which has its origins in pre-Socratic thinking. Whereas in natural science, truth consists in a correspondence, an adequatio, between what goes on *in intellect* and what goes on *in re*, between the structure of a symbol system 'in the mind' and the structure of events 'in the world', there is another concept of truth which is to be found in the Greek word *Aletheia*. In this concept, truth is literally that which is without secrecy, what discloses itself without being veiled. . . . When one sees actions of the other in the light of a form of truth or falsehood, one says that a man is truthful or 'true to himself' when one 'feels' that he means what he says, or is saying what he means. . . . Between such 'truth' and a lie there is room for the most curious and subtle ambiguities and complexities in the person's disclosure/concealment of himself. . . . What has been revealed, what concealed, and to whom, in the Gioconda simile, in the 'twixt earnest and jest of Blake's angel, in the infinite pathos—or is it apathy—of a Harlequin of Picasso. The liar (he deceives others without deceiving himself), the hysteric (his deception of himself is anterior to his deception of others), the actor (*his* actions are not 'him'), the hypocrite, the impostor (like Thomas Mann's Felix Krull, absorbed into the parts he plays), are at the one time the exploiters and victims of the almost unlimited possibilities in the self's relation to its own acts, and of the lack of final assurance that one can attribute correctly the other's relation to his actions.[4]

The landscape we enter into through ethnic culture, then, is not so much social as psychological, that problematic and perplexing place where we confront "the almost unlimited possibilities in the self's relation to its own acts". And the reason for this is surely not entirely mysterious. As soon as a question of ethnicity is raised, the question of identity appears along with it. A psychologist like Laing sees identity questions in phenomenological terms. And he sees too the accompanying paradox: while definitions abstract the boundary-less world is schizophrenic. As Gloria Onley argues, Laing "seems to believe that schizophrenia is a form of psychic anarchy—a usually involuntary attempt by the self to free itself from a repressive social reality".[5] In critical and literary terms this means what is only too evident in Canadian writing: to raise the question of identity is virtually to assure that it cannot be answered. I don't think it has been observed that part of the extraordinary power of Atwood's *Survival*—and perhaps one reason for its enormous success—lies in her perception that the problem of identity can only be answered in fictional terms, that is, by turning it into a story. *Survival* is a ghost story disguised as politics and criticism. The victor/victim pattern enables Atwood to work out as Canada's identity a sado-masochistic sexual fantasy that is at the basis of gothic tales. Or to put this point another way, as another of our novelists, Robert Kroetsch, does, "In a sense we haven't got an identity until somebody tells our story, the fiction makes us real."[6] As with the nation, then, so with its mosaic, its cultural identities, the ethnic voices to which I now turn.

II

I begin with Jewish writers: Mordecai Richler, Leonard Cohen and Irving Layton. Later I will extend these remarks to include John Marlyn and F.P. Grove and a number of poets whose work has been translated into English. I suppose that much of what I have to say here and elsewhere in this paper is essentially an elaborate footnote to George Woodcock's comments in his fine book on Richler and particularly to this remark: "It might be a metaphorical exaggeration to describe Canada as a land of invisible ghettoes, but certainly it is, both historically and geographically, a country of minorities that have never achieved assimilation."[7] Whatever one makes of Richler's development from realism through farce to a peculiarly grotesque satiric mode, it is clear that thematically his concerns have remained constant. If there is a development, it involves simply a growing and deepening sense of what the question of identity implies or, more specifically, what is implied in the attempt to escape from the ghetto. In practice this works out as a series of choices in the novels, each novel moving toward a choice which then creates the situation for the next. "Choices" is perhaps the wrong word. Closer would be Sartre's "whirligig", an opposition in which the opposing forces endlessly turn into one another and in which an endless oscillation between them appears to be the only mode of existence for the individual so trapped.

As often as not, Richler's whirligigs involve paradoxical inversions of identities: the Jew who is a goy and the goy who is a Jew, for example. In turn these can be satirically or comically complicated by a reflexive series, such as the one that transforms a gentile into an anti-semitic Jew whose Jewishness is affirmed by the very vehemence of his denial of Jewishness. But there is a more sinister form as well—the man who is a monster, the monster who is a man—and a whole series of related whirligigs spinning off from, and commenting on the main ones: films creating reality; reality imitating films; barbarians who are civilized; cultivated barbarians, and so on. The generating force of the whirligigs is the structure of illusions that, for Richler, constitutes the ghetto or community. It is interesting to note how often such a community is culturally defined not by ethnicity, but by "creativity", that is, as a community of artists, filmmakers or writers, those who both manipulate illusion and who feed on social snobbishness. Richler's argument seems to me to be based on his conviction that class values, defined as economically determined positions, are more important to an individual's sense of self than are traditional values, and on his belief that economic rather than cultural forces define relationships and that stereotype are not only illusory but immoral.[8]

In practice this argument, if it is one, dissolves into the forms and images of Richler's novels. But at the same time it does help to explain some of the apparently gratuitous aspects of Richler's satire—he is never simply random or brutal—and it is the intellectual equivalent of the startling vision we now confront. *Son of a Smaller Hero,* for example, sets up what appears to be a resolution to an almost unbearable dilemma. If life in the ghetto is impossible because illusory, but to leave it is to be an "other" and to deny one's own existence, where then is home. How is authentic human existence possible? Noah's decision not to define himself in opposition, but by remaking himself—not by being a goy, but a man—appears heroic, although everything that follows in Richler's work suggests it may be sinister. For the dialectic of self and other may generate not humanity, but monstrousness. Duddy Kravitz's ferocious energy turns him into Wonder-Boy, his own model of escape from the ghetto; Dingleman, and who *he* is, we see in a moment. Richler presents the dialectic of *The Apprenticeship of Duddy Kravitz* to us in Uncle Benjy's letter. A great and terrible cry wells up in Benjy: "Experience doesn't teach; it deforms." But there is a footnote: "Be a Mensch."[9] The opposition surely is right. We now know what the choices are: deformity or menschlichkeit, the grotesque or the human. But Richler does not allow easy resolutions. He takes the self-made man, the re-made man, with terrifying literalness. He becomes the Star-Maker, the man with spare parts, plastic man, transplanted man, unnatural man, alien man, inhuman, androgynous, in George Woodcock's words, "a figure of nightmare, the monster lurching out of dreams and demanding to be clothed in modern guise who inhabits almost every Richler novel".[10]

"Be a Mensch" means re-make yourself. At the psychological level that can mean, disastrously, to act like someone else, to turn into someone else. But in socio-cultural terms, the choice is scarcely better: the ghetto's conservatism opposed to society's liberalism, progress as physical transformation, transplantation. In moral terms the great cry still is, as in Rilke, "There is no place that does not see you. You must change your life."[11] But at least in Richler, the opposites, grotesque or human, resolve themselves monstrously. These choices obviously have been vigorously rejected by the Jewish community which regards Richler as a Jewish anti-semite. But the images he uses may be finally less horrifying then at first sight they appear. In the binary oppositions of myth Edmund R. Leach proposes that the discriminations between, say, "human/superhuman, mortal/immortal, male/female, legitimate/illegitimate, good/bad" despite "all variations of theology" remain constant and are "followed by a 'mediation' of the paired categories thus distinguished".[12] He goes on to say:

> 'Mediation' (in this sense) is always achieved by introducing a third category which is 'abnormal' or 'anomalous' in terms of ordinary 'rational' categories. Thus myths are full of fabulous monsters, incarnate gods, virgin mothers. This middle ground is abnormal, non-natural, holy. It is typically the focus of all taboo and ritual observance.[13]

How can you be a Jew in a goyisha land? Be a monster. It is not so extraordinary, though perhaps it is difficult to live with. The numinous figure *is* the resolution to an impossible situation, the situation of the ghetto, of ethnicity. To say this is to say that we are in the presence of a myth and all its duplicities. Leach, in the article from which I have quoted, argues, for example, that the two major common characteristics of myth are redundancy and a markedly binary aspect; myths tell the same story over and over again and always involve a dualism resolved by a monstrous or holy third. In the language of systems engineers, "a high level of redundancy makes it easy to correct errors introduced by noise", or as Leach says, "in the mind of the believer, myth does indeed convey messages which are the Word of God".[14] God as systems engineer or computer operator resolves dualities and reassures us daily, as Richler does, by telling again and again the same story of self, other and monster.

My argument that the voice of ethnicity in literature is duplicitous begins to look suspiciously like a form of structuralism. If so, it is only so to enable me to say, as Levi-Strauss does in the introduction to *The Raw and the Cooked,* that we can only handle myths critically by writing them, and that stories of identity, though presented as social analyses and political propaganda, are ghost stories or forms haunting our restless imagination. Ethnicity, I would argue, sets into motion for the writer a whirligig or duality that can only be resolved in a myth, a restructured self, a fictional being.

Take as another example Leonard Cohen's *Beautiful Losers.* Many have remarked on Cohen's preference for style over conviction, religiosity rather than religion. It is that quality which enabled a Montreal Jewish boy, as Pre-Raphaelite pretending to be medieval Catholic, to convince a whole generation of readers of the spirituality of his essentially perverse reading of Christianity. It is fairly evident now that *Beautiful Losers* works out the whirligigs of male-female or female-male by producing the monstrous tree-hermit Christ, a pederast, who turns into a movie. In Cohen's poetry the sadomasochistic sense of sexuality prevails, coloured by a special elegance of phrase that does not conceal the profound polarity—Jewish/Christian, master/slave—that impels his work towards its fated end. By no accident his latest book of poems appeals to us with another sexual version of ethnicity, *The Energy of Slaves*. Like William Burroughs, Cohen constructs or reconstructs selves in a sad narcotic exercise for numbing pain.

Layton's version of this myth essentially inverts that of both Cohen and Richler, attempting to insist that the other is monstrous and the self, authentic. Layton's self, of course, is defined as identical to poet. Two observations here will suffice to take us through his version of ethnicity. One concerns his equating of poet with Jew. He places the Judaic-prophet-poet in opposition to the WASP professor, Presbyterian morality, Christian ethics, vision and Canadian society in its puritanical and lifeless routine. Nowhere does he do this to better effect than in the stunning conclusion to his homage to "Osip Mandelshtam (1891-1940)":

I know my fellow-Canadians, Osip;
they forgot your name and fate as swiftly
as they learned them, switching off
the contorted image of pain with their sets,
choosing a glass darkness to one which starting
in the mind covers the earth in permanent eclipse;
so they chew branflakes and crabmeat gossip make love
take out insurance against fires and death
while our poetesses explore their depressions
in delicate complaints regular as menstruation
or eviscerate a dead god for metaphors;
the men-poets displaying codpieces of wampum,
the safer legends of prairie Indian and Eskimo

Under a sour and birdless heaven
TV crosses stretch across a flat Calvary
and plaza storewindows give me
the blank expressionless stare of imbeciles:
this is Toronto, not St. Petersburg on the Neva;
though seas death and silent decades separate us
we yet speak to each other, brother to brother;
your forgotten martyrdom has taught me scorn
for hassidic world-savers without guns and tanks:
they are mankind's gold and ivory toilet bowls
where brute or dictator relieves himself
when reading their grave messages to posterity
— let us be the rapturous eye of the hurricane
flashing the Jew's will, his mocking contempt for slaves[15]

The other observation concerns his sense of a male-female dialectic that constantly demands his assertion of masculinity and the recurring image of a self threatened by castration or engulfment. Both are versions of a dialectic, sometimes cast in Nietzschean terms, sometimes simply as a mythicized version of the holy family of St. Urbain street, that requires the poet to create himself daily. An apocalyptic-romantic version of ethnicity, then, Layton's story first turns him into the poet who dies, is reborn and dies again: the self makes itself over daily. And secondly it turns him into the monster who rages through suburbanite closets and bedrooms; the man from the ghetto remade; Duddy Kravitz as poet-prophet:

> And if in August joiners and bricklayers
>   are thick as flies around us
> building expensive bungalows for those
> who do not need them, unless they release
>   me roaring from their moth-proofed cupboards
> their buyers will have no joy, no ease.

> I could extend their rooms for them without cost
>   and give them crazy sundials
> to tell the time with, but I have noticed
> how my irregular footprint horrifies them
>   evenings and Sunday afternoons:
> they spray for hours to erase its shadow.[16]

"Whatever else poetry is freedom," says Layton, yet "mercifully [it] . . . is about poetry itself."[17] Self-realization like self-consciousness is reflexive. It mirrors its own self or, as in the Freudian paradox about the artist, it finds real in fantasy what cannot be found in reality. "Though art transcends pain and tragedy," says Layton, "it does not negate them, does not make them disappear. . . . Poetry does not exorcise historical dynamism, macabre cruelty, guilt, perversity, and the pain of consciousness."[18] The distinction appears to me to be a vital one for this discussion. For what could be the nature of a transcendence that does not negate the reality it transcends? In the context of ethnicity or ethnic literature the answer is the fictional or reflexive character of the subject itself.

If we now turn to a writer outside the Jewish tradition, we find the paradoxes of ethnicity repeating themselves the moment the subject is raised. In the strictest terms F.P. Grove's *A Search for America* is an American pastoral rather than an ethnic novel, but it properly belongs here since it takes its form first of all from an immigrant's experience and from the consequent question of identity, in this case, how to become an American. The dialectic of *A Search for America* is a double one: Europe as opposed to America and, secondly, the true America as opposed to the false one, both versions of what Warren Tallman calls the crude-fine paradox.[19] Grove brilliantly plays off these oppositions, resolving the Europe-America polarity by the further polarity of a true and false America which in turn he seeks to resolve in a final astonishing reversal that turns the true America into Canada. Of course the search for America involves Grove in a search for himself, since it centres on his resolve to "cut himself loose from Europe" and to remake himself as a man in a new land. What is genuinely startling, absolutely explicit and crucial to the argument of this paper is not only Grove's identification of a true self with a fictional (or created) one, but the fact that for some forty-five years historians and critics have taken the fictional autobiography to be an actual one. Who was Frederick Philip Grove? Because of Douglas Spettigue's brilliant scholarship we now know that what Grove told us in his Note to the fourth edition is to be taken seriously. His autobiography is fictional.[20] Grove is a fictional creation, twice removed from the actual in *A Search for America.*

Commenting on his own answer to the question of whether the story presented in the book is fact or fiction, an answer which he says was "pervericating" (sic), Grove adds:

> Imaginative literature is not primarily concerned with facts; it is concerned with truth. . . . The reason for this is that, in imaginative literature, no fact enters as mere fact; a fact as such can be perceived; but, to form subject-matter for art, it must contain its own interpretation; and a fact interpreted, and therefore made capable of being understood, becomes fiction.[21]

How traditional Grove's position here is may be discerned by considering the poetics of Browning or James's theory of the art of the novel. But for our purposes it is not tradition but the created self that matters. Grove tells us that the true self is fictional. He literally wrote himself into existence, created himself, wrote his own mythology—personal and social. The question as to why he did so may never be answered, though Spettigue seems now to have discovered evidence to suggest that disguise was necessary to Grove. Again, for our purpose, what is important is that the reason for the fiction, the motivation behind it, appears to be as much a literary as a biographical one. Grove hints at the power of duplicity as a source of creativity:

> The book which follows is essentially retrospective; which means that it is teleological; what was the present when it was written had already become its *telos.* Events that had followed were already casting their shadows backward. By writing the book, in that long ago past, I was freeing myself of the mental and emotional burden implied in the fact that I had once lived it and left it behind. But the present pervaded the past in every fibre.[22]

"He dramatized a personality", Frye says of Grove.[23] Precisely. But he left us with the endless uncertainties and ambiguities implied by the need to dramatize and so create a self.

III

Two final questions remain. One concerns the generality of this notion of ethnic writing as a self-reflexive form. The other concerns language itself. By now it should be obvious that I have taken a deliberately narrow and partial view of what constitutes ethnic writing. I have viewed it in terms of a literature existing at an interface of two cultures, a form concerned with defining itself, its voice, the dialectic of self and other and the duplicities of self-creation, transformation and identities. By definition that would seem to exclude from ethnic literature those works concerned with the life of a community or culture on its own terms. Whether this immediately excludes much of A.M. Klein's poetry, for example, "Portraits of a Minyan" or "Baal Shem Tov", I'm not entirely certain, but I expect so. I might want to argue that Adele Wiseman's *The Sacrifice* and Klein's *The Second Scroll* could be shown to operate within the structures described here, especially since both are books about books in which questions of identity are uppermost, or that Jack Ludwig's *Confusions* belongs here for obvious reasons. But I would feel less certain about a whole range of other works, for example, Grove's prairie novels or Martha Ostenso's gothic romances. Obviously there is a sense in which the rendering of Jewish experience in Klein, or Mennonite experience in Rudy Wiebe's *Peace Shall Destroy Many* or Scandinavian experience in Laura Salverson's novels, forms part of what normally we would describe as ethnic writing. But to repeat an argument I used in writing about John Marlyn's *Under the Ribs of Death* (a novel, like Kreisel's *The Rich Man,* very much in the pattern I am drawing here), it seems not only tasteless, but futile to confuse questions of cultural identity with local colour. This is not a critical comment on any of the writers I mention, but on the uses of criticism itself.

It seems to me that an integrated community will not see itself in terms of an ethnic group, but as an authentic culture. Ethnicity presents itself as a problem of self-definition. If, for example, we accept the version of the Royal Commission on Bilingualism and Biculturalism, we see at once how this is: "What counts most in our concept of an 'ethnic group' is not one's ethnic origin or even one's mother tongue, but one's sense of belonging to a group, and the group's collective will to exist".[24] This is perilously close to the definition put upon Griffin by Shalinsky, a definition that starts the whirligig going. Says Shalinsky, "A Jew is an idea. Today, you're my idea of a Jew."[25] A linguistic and cultural heritage is different from a definition. And it is on the ground of definition that I argue for the self-reflexive novel or poem of identities as ethnic literature.

It begins to appear as if ethnicity might present itself as a problem only, or perhaps most acutely in linguistic terms. We might say it is a problem of translation. My difficulty with this notion lies in my own lack of competence in languages, but it hardly seems necessary to insist on the cultural confusions involved in the translation process. Translating the poems of Akhmatova, Stanley Kunitz repeats the endless complaint: "The poems exist in the integrity of their form and do not depend on imitable effects."[26] Accepting that perennial limitation, I was moved to think about ethnicity and language when I came across *Volvox,* an anthology of "Poetry from the Unofficial Languages of Canada . . . in English Translation". Twenty-eight poets are represented and more than a dozen languages. As I read, it seemed to me that I was hearing and seeing something very different from the English writing discussed previously. The poets' concerns, I thought, were not so much cultural as universal. For example, in "Literary Criticism" Robert Zend writes:

> Liebnitz thought
> this is the best
> of all possible worlds
>
> Voltaire thought
> Liebnitz was wrong when he thought
> this is the best
> of all possible worlds
>
> Pirandello thought
> Voltaire was wrong when he thought
> Liebnitz was wrong when he thought
> this is the best
> of all possible worlds
>
> I think . . . but I'm wrong anyway[27]

One is led to wonder if the problems of ethnicity disappear in a writer's own language. Not always. Perhaps not with the Yiddish poets. Perhaps not with the writer obsessed with a lost home or the one for whom history is a record of dispossession. But at least once in *Volvox* the problem does appear, and the writer tells us why. It is in the poem, "The Laundress", by Einar Pall Jonsson:

> She worked as a housemaid, then as a laundress in small town
> Winnipeg, full of emigres speaking every language except her own:
> she was Icelandic and as she worked she sang the old Icelandic
> hymns and songs: the songs had all her joy, they brought all her
> peace. She kept reaching for the language that got lost in her life.

She could never speak it again, though it always measured her breath.
Late one summer, as she lay dying, she sang again the Icelandic
hymns, sang in her mother tongue, an other tongue for us; and
as we lay her in a foreign grave, we, who know no Icelandic, who
know then almost nothing of what she loved and lived by, say our
prayers over her in English.[28]

In his recent collection of critical essays George Steiner, who has been
much occupied with questions of linguistics and culture, argues that there
is a sense in which language and its structures of syntax and grammar impose cultural patterns and mythicize the sense of self.[29] Could it be that
speaking another's tongue we cannot be ourselves; that the search for the
lost self begins when we have been translated into another and will not end
until there has been translation, transformation once again? The ending of
John Marlyn's *Under the Ribs of Death* raises the cry for a lost humanity,
for a language free of deception, for a self that has disappeared in a whirligig that begins with our "inescapable doubleness".

And yet another novelist, one who has reasons to know, insists on not
the escape, but the struggle. James Baldwin says:

From this void—ourselves—it is the function of society to
protect us; but it is only this void, our unknown selves,
demanding forever, a new act of creation, which can
save us—"from the evil that is in the world." With the
same motion at the same time, it is this toward which we
endlessly struggle and from which, endlessly, we struggle
to escape.[30]

*Eli Mandel is a professor of English at York University and the author of
numerous books of poetry and criticism.*

NOTES

1 Elizabeth Janeway, *The New York Times Book Review,* 21 October 1973.

2 Margaret Atwood, "Afterword", *The Journals of Susanna Moodie* (Toronto:
Oxford University Press, 1970).

3 M.L. Lautt, "Sociology and the Canadian Plains" in Richard Allen (ed.), *A Region
of the Mind* (Regina: Canadian Plains Studies Centre, University of Saskatchewan,
1973), p. 138.

4 R.D. Laing, *The Self and Others* (London: Tavistock Publications, 1961), pp. 120-
21. Reprinted by permission of Tavistock Publications.

5·Gloria Onley, "In Bluebeard's Castle and Power Politics" in George Woodcock (ed.),
Poets and Critics (Toronto: Oxford University Press, 1974), pp. 202-203.

6 Robert Kroetsch, "A Conversation with Margaret Lawrence" in Robert Kroetsch
(ed.), *Creation* (Toronto: New Press, 1970), p. 63.

7 George Woodcock, *Mordecai Richler* (Toronto: McClelland and Stewart, 1970),
pp. 23-24

8 *Ibid.*, p. 36.

9 Mordecai Richler, *The Apprenticeship of Duddy Kravitz* (New York: Paperback Library, 1964), pp. 249-250.

10 Woodcock, *Mordecai Richler*, p. 52.

11 Rilke, "Archaic Torso of Apollo"; cf George Steiner, *In Bluebeard's Castle* (London: Faber and Faber, 1971), p. 41: "We hate most those who hold out to us a goal . . . which, even though we have stretched our muscles to the utmost, we cannot reach. . . .

12 Edmund R. Leach, "Genesis as Myth" in Vernon W. Gras (ed.), *European Literary Theory and Practice* (New York: Dell Publishing Company, 1973), p. 320.

13 *Ibid.*

14 *Ibid.*, p. 318.

15 Irving Layton, *The Collected Poems of Irving Layton* (Toronto: McClelland and Stewart, 1971), pp. 582-583. Reprinted from *The Unwavering Eye, Selected Poems 1969-1975* by permission of The Canadian Publishers, McClelland and Stewart Limited, Toronto.

16 Irving Layton, "The Fertile Muck" from *The Collected Poems of Irving Layton*, p. 28. Reprinted by permission of The Canadian Publishers, McClelland and Stewart Limited, Toronto.

17 Irving Layton, *Engagements* (Toronto: McClelland & Stewart, 1972), p. 84.

18 *Ibid.*, p. 85.

19 Warren Tallman, "Wolf in the Snow" in George Woodcock (ed.), *A Choice of Critics* (Toronto: Oxford University Press, 1966), p. 75.

20 Douglas O. Spettigue, *FPG The European Years* (Ottawa: Oberon Press, 1973).

21 Frederick Philip Grove, "Author's Note to the Fourth Edition", *A Search for America* (Toronto: McClelland and Stewart, 1971).

22 *Ibid.*

23 Cited in Douglas O. Spettigue, *Frederick Philip Grove* (Toronto: Copp Clark, 1969), p. 1.

24 *Report of the Royal Commission on Bilingualism and Biculturalism,* Vol. IV (Ottawa: Queen's Printer, 1969), p. 7.

25 Mordecai Richler, *Cocksure* (Toronto: McClelland and Stewart, 1968), p. 245.

26 *Poems of Akhmatova,* Stanley Kunitz and Max Hayward (eds. and trans.) (Boston: Little Brown and Company, 1973).

27 *From Zero to One,* J.R. Columbo (co-trans.) (Port Clements: Sono Nis, 1973). Reprinted in J. Michael Yates (ed.), *Volvox* (Port Clements: Sono Nis, 1971) p. 134.

28 *Volvox*, p. 191.

29 Steiner, *In Bluebeard's Castle.*

30 James Baldwin, "Everybody's Protest Novel" in *Notes of a Native Son* (New York: Beacon Press, 1955), pp. 20-21.

3 Quebec: Politics and Change

Réjean Landry 71 The Political Development of Quebec:
A Strategic Interpretation

Michael B. Stein 85 The Dynamics of Contemporary
Party Movements in Quebec: Some
Comparative Aspects of Créditisme
and Indépendantisme

The Political Development of Quebec:
A Strategic Interpretation
Réjean Landry

The future of the past is in the future, the future of the present
is in the past, the future of the future is in the present.

J. McHale

In Canada culture and religion combined with geography and history have
produced at least two easily distinguishable identities: the English-Canadian
and the French-Canadian. Marked boundaries of culture, language and
geography indicate the degree of interconnectedness that prevails between
these two ethnic groups. These are the boundaries which have acted as the
springboard for inter-ethnic bargaining negotiations.

Inter-ethnic bargaining negotiations took, and still take place because the
two groups have always been aware of both their separateness and their interdependence. Political institutions are the result of such inter-ethnic bargaining negotiations as well as the framework within which these bargaining
negotiations take place. But these political institutions, in turn, have consequences for the direction of the ongoing bargaining negotiations.

These inter-ethnic bargaining negotiations describe a situation in which
the best course of action for each ethnic group depends on what the other
does. In a situation of decision a rational ethnic group would then have to:
identify the whole set of alternatives which affect the decision; attach a set
of consequences to each alternative; rank all sets of consequences from the
most preferred to the least preferred; and select the alternative leading to the
most preferred set of consequences. The evolution of these inter-ethnic
bargaining negotiations would then be directed by the formation and the
transformation of these four processes.

However the selection of the best alternative is complicated by two problems. It is difficult to identify the whole set of alternatives and the certainty
of any consequence resulting from an alternative because in politics, where
power dictates the course of action, the unexpected often occurs. Secondly,
it is equally difficult to rank every set of consequences on a preference
scale because different ethnic groups may assign different values to the same
outcome. As a result, the choices that ethnic groups make may be characterized by a disagreement over values which define preference scales of uncertain
outcome.

Analysis of the inter-ethnic bargaining negotiations that have taken place in the past and still take place in Canada today can be divided into many plays. Let us examine seven of these plays.

1760: The Military Conquest

Before 1763 Canada was a French province. Politically, like any other colony it was under the jurisdiction of a mother country. But France was far away and its power would come to an end if French colonization succeeded. History, however, changed Canada's relationship with France. The French regime ended in 1759 when Quebec capitulated to British troops. In 1763, following four years of military rule, the British king made a political reorganization of the new colony. The Royal Proclamation of 1763 and the instructions given to Governor Murray suggest both the tactics and the strategy of the British government.

The set of alternatives from which the British government could choose included at least five tactics: exterminate the Canadiens; deport them; deny them all rights; make some concessions to the Canadiens in exchange for their collaboration; or assimilate them as quickly as possible. The set of alternatives from which the Canadiens could choose included immediate acceptance, passive acceptance, calculated acceptance, or unqualified rejection of British institutions. Matrix I illustrates the twenty outcomes theoretically possible.

Matrix I

Canadiens

	immediate acceptance	passive acceptance	calculated acceptance	rejection
exterminate				
deport				
British Government — deny all rights				
make some concessions				
assimilate				

Some of these outcomes were influenced by others. Let us proceed by eliminating the dominant pairs of tactics. The British government could gain no advantage by using the tactics of extermination or deportation as their first move because the Canadiens would then have been forced to use the tactic of rejection. The Canadiens were in the majority, and the British government could gain more by using the Canadiens to develop Canada's resources than it could by exterminating or deporting them. The main resources of the British government were military and political, whereas the main resource of the Canadiens was their numbers. The British government could win no advantage by denying the Canadiens all rights because, again, the Canadiens would have been forced to reject the British institutions. This tactic also would have involved economic expenditure: it would have necessitated the establishment of a police force to insure that all rights were effectively denied. In reality the British government selected the tactic that would gain the greatest possible acceptance of the British institutions, and the Canadiens used a tactic that involved calculated acceptance of British institutions. The British government chose to make some concessions to the Canadiens in exchange for their collaboration. Their major concession was to allow the Canadiens freedom of religion. This concession was sufficient to make the Canadiens respond with the tactic of calculated acceptance. The British government assumed that this tactic was the most prudent, even if the most preferred tactic would have been to assimilate the Canadiens as quickly as possible. The British government assumed that the Canadiens would soon be assimilated by the English-speaking Protestant settlers, whose arrival they foresaw. This analysis seems to suggest that both the British government and the Canadiens used the most prudent tactics possible.

However the British had miscalculated this first play. The Canadiens' acceptance of British institutions did not break down their strong sense of group identity. They had lived alone in Canada for more than a century and a half and had fought the Iroquois and the British to maintain their separate colony. Thus even military conquest could not destroy their group consciousness: the French-speaking inhabitants of Canada remained Canadiens. Their sense of identity as a group had been formed and expressed by France and the Roman Catholic Church. Although France was no longer the caretaker of this consciousness, the Roman Catholic Church continued to express the French-Canadian identity. And the Church's influence was far more significant than that of the British political institutions.

The British government could not carry out their strategy of assimilation because only a few British settlers arrived in the decade after 1763. This light immigration combined with agitation in the British American colonies increased the bargaining power of the Canadiens.

1774: The Quebec Act

This new situation in the bargaining power of the players produced the Quebec Act of 1774. The Act re-established, with few exceptions, the former limits of New France. It specified that Roman Catholics were to be allowed freedom of worship and that they no longer need take an oath of allegiance in order to hold public office. While it also restored French civil law, the Act did not significantly change the political organization of the colony.

The set of alternatives from which the British could choose included at last two tactics: they could either deny all rights to the Canadiens or make some concessions in exchange for their collaboration. The Canadiens could choose to either support the American Revolution, stay neutral or support the British. Matrix II illustrates the six outcomes theoretically possible.

Matrix II

		Canadiens		
		support the U.S. revolution	stay neutral	support the British
British Government	deny any right			
	make some concessions			

If the British government had denied all rights to the Canadiens, the Canadiens would have reacted by supporting the American Revolution. In other words the only tactic the British government could use to any advantage was that of making some concessions in exchange for the Canadiens' collaboration. For their move, the Canadiens could threaten to use the tactic of supporting the American Revolution if the concessions were not acceptable. Another (but less effective) threat which the Canadiens could use was that of staying neutral. However, if concessions *were* sufficient, the Canadiens could promise to support the British.

The Canadiens obtained few concessions: the Quebec Act still forced them to pay taxes to the seigneurs and maintained the English criminal laws. But the clergy and the seigneurs approved of the Quebec Act and saw in it a great charter of liberties for the Canadiens. The Canadiens' support was necessary since some of the British colonists (Guy Carleton, second Governor of Quebec, for one) wanted to use Canada as a base of operations against the Americans if American agitation culminated in war.

1791: The Constitutional Act

The American Revolution resulted in a massive exodus of Loyalists. Those Loyalists who came to Quebec demanded representative government, British civil law and the formation of a new province within Canada. The Constitutional Act of 1791 was the British government's response to these demands. Quebec was divided into two parts, Upper and Lower Canada. The political structures of each province included a governor, a nominated council and an elected assembly. This new constitutional regime was unable to work efficiently because it generated conflict between the governor and the elected assembly. The governor, who was responsible to the British government, could not accept being controlled by the elected assembly. On the other hand, the elected assembly was not willing to pass laws unless it had control over their management. In Lower Canada this problem was made worse by an ethnic conflict: the Chateau Clique, representing the English ruling class, could not accept being controlled by an elected assembly which was dominated by the French.

Although the Constitutional Act did attempt to limit the control which the assembly exerted over the executive power, it cannot be considered an entirely prudent strategy. It was less than prudent to divide Quebec into two parts since it gave the Canadiens control of the elected assembly of Lower Canada where they were in the majority. The British government then gave the Canadiens a means of promoting and realizing their common goals. One can only wonder if the British government had renounced its goal of assimilating the Canadiens.

The alternatives which dictated the British government's choice were to either create one elected assembly serving both Upper and Lower Canada or to create two elected assemblies. The set of alternatives from which the Canadiens could choose their action included demanding two separate assemblies or agreeing to participate in one central assembly. Matrix III illustrates the four outcomes theoretically possible.

Matrix III

		Canadiens	
		two elected assemblies	one elected assembly
British Government	one elected assembly		
	two elected assemblies		

It is entirely possible that the Canadiens would have participated in one central assembly, but the British government offered two, and in so doing gave the Canadiens power. Supposedly the two governments were structured in such a way that the executive power (the governor and the nominated council) could always govern even if it was opposed by the elected assembly. But it soon became apparent that the government of Lower Canada would be dominated by the Canadiens and that the elected assembly would have more power than the executive.

1840: The Union Act

The Rebellion of 1837-1838 alarmed the British government. The Constitutional Act of 1791 was repealed and Lord Durham was sent to act both as Governor General of the two Canadas and as the Royal Commissioner charged with investigating the political situation of the colonies. "I expected to find a contest between a government and a people," wrote Lord Durham in his report, but "I found two nations warring in the bosom of a single state: I found a struggle, not of principle, but of races; and I perceived that it would be idle to attempt any amelioration of laws or institutions until we could first succeed in terminating the deadly animosity that now separates the inhabitants of Lower Canada into the hostile divisions of French and English." According to Lord Durham, the character of Lower Canada's population should be "the one of the British Empire, the one of the majority of the population of the British Empire, the one of the superior race. . . . The first and firm goal of the British government must consist, in the future, to establish within the province a population having English laws and English language and to give the government to an Assembly resolutely English".

Following the Durham Report, the Union Act of 1840 once again fused Upper and Lower Canada into a single province, United Canada. This act provided for equal representation from both sections, specified that the only official language was English and consolidated the debts of the two provinces.

The set of alternatives from which the Canadiens could choose included asking for the repeal of the Union Act or using the Act to obtain responsible government. The British could choose from two alternatives: they could agree or they could refuse to modify the Union Act. Matrix IV illustrates the four outcomes theoretically possible.

The Canadiens were divided on the question of which tactic was most advantageous. Many of them wanted the Union Act repealed and threatened to withhold their participation in the new political institution unless it was.

Matrix IV

Canadiens

		demand repeal of the Act	use the Act
British Government	refuse to modify the Act		
	modify the Act		

It is difficult to imagine what tactic would have then been the most prudent for the British government. Lafontaine was a proponent of the second tactic. In his manifesto to the voters of Terrebonne he called the Union Act an unjust and despotic measure, but he asked the Canadiens not to demand its repeal. Instead he suggested that they use the Act. According to him, Quebec could be rescued by responsible government, and responsible government could be gained through a coalition with United Canada reformers. This manifesto rallied the majority of the Canadiens. Lafontaine went to the elected assembly and spoke in French in protest against the use of English as the official language. The Draper-Viger government, in the hope of gaining the Canadiens' vote, asked London to give equal rights to both English and French. London granted this in 1848. But representation in the elected assembly still favoured Upper Canada even though it had the smaller population. When, around 1850, Lower Canada gained greater representation, Upper Canada protested against the unfairness of the arrangement and demanded representation by population. The strategic likelihood of equal representation for both sections of United Canada was doubtful: in 1840 the total English-speaking population of United Canada outnumbered the Canadien population.

The Union Act which promised to bring about the assimilation of the Canadiens through British-modelled elected assemblies failed because political parties, divided by language and cultural differences, could not work together in the fight for responsible government.

1867: The British North America Act

The Union Act of 1840, like the 1791 Act, could not avoid producing conflict between the governor and the elected assembly. From 1841 to 1867 there were eighteen different cabinets in office. It was a situation of political crisis. The Union Act of 1840 was a failure: its policies did not satisfy both English and French, but rather drove them further apart. This unstable political situation combined with the threat of American expansion and the need to link the St. Lawrence Valley to the Atlantic provinces and to the western part of British North America convinced political and business leaders that the time had come to separate once more United Canada into two provinces. Their plan included setting up a federation of all British North American colonies.

A new constitutional act, the British North America Act, which became effective in 1867, created the Dominion of Canada. This new constitution gave the provinces powers of a local and private nature and the Dominion government all powers which were not explicitly given to the provinces. The Dominion government had the power to appoint and remove the lieutenant-governor of each province and the power to disallow any provincial law within a year of its passage. An important characteristic of this new federation was that it did not assume that the provinces and the Dominion governments were equal. Instead the Dominion government's role was made comparable to the British government's role as the administrator of the individual colonies. This strategy was carried through by a group of politicians who came to be called the Fathers of the Confederation.

The set of alternatives from which both the English and the French could choose included maintaining the status quo, establishing a federation, or allowing Canada to be annexed by the United States. Matrix V illustrates the nine outcomes theoretically possible.

Matrix V

French Canadians

	status quo	federation	annexation
English Canadians status quo			
federation			
annexation			

Both the French ethnic group and the English ethnic group believed that the status quo was no longer acceptable. Many French Canadians felt that annexation to the United States was a viable alternative and perhaps unavoidable in the long run. But George-Etienne Cartier and the Roman Catholic clergy opposed this alternative and pointed out the dangers which annexation could entail for French Canadians. English Canadians did not consider annexation to the United States a solution to the problems which United Canada faced. Both sides had only one alternative left—the establishment of a federation.

This does not mean that Confederation did not have its opponents. Some English-speaking deputies were against the idea because they foresaw the development of French-Canadian nationalism. But the main opposition came from the Rouges, French-speaking Liberals from Lower Canada, led by Antoine-Aimé Dorion. They thought that the sharing of powers was unacceptable because it gave too much power to the federal government, and they repeatedly asked for a vote on the proposal.

It is not improbable to suggest that French Canadians passively accepted the constitution of 1867 because they were quite unaware of its practical implications. How could it be otherwise? Government intervention was so limited that it did not affect the ordinary citizen in his day-to-day life. Thus most French Canadians were not concerned about having a federal government dominated by English-speaking people.

However history outwitted the Fathers of the Confederation. Sections of the new constitution, such as "the management and sale of the public lands belonging to the province and of the timber and wood thereon" (article 92, paragraph 5) and "property and civil rights in the province" (article 92, paragraph 3), gave the provinces more power than either the English or the French had anticipated.

While the new federal union helped to minimize ethnic conflicts by permitting each ethnic group to satisfy its goals without requiring the consent of the other, in long run it had the potential to increase conflict since provincial boundaries coincided with religious and linguistic cleavages. Looking back, one can see how Quebec was to become more sensitive to policies emphasizing autonomy rather than those emphasizing participation in the federal union.

Honoré Mercier, Premier of the Liberal government in 1887, was probably the first French-Canadian premier to support an autonomist position in federal-provincial relations. As early as 1920 Premier Alexandre Tachereau accused the federal government of reducing the province's sources of income and denounced the federal government's intervention in the fields of education, agriculture and highways. Premier Maurice Duplessis, too, denounced federal intervention. To increase the province's autonomy, in 1954 he instituted a Quebec personal income tax: Quebec taxpayers were then obliged to pay both a federal and a Quebec income tax. Further negotiations allowed Quebec taxpayers to deduct the provincial tax from the federal tax.

1960: The Quiet Revolution

Since 1867 the group consciousness of the French Canadians has been expressed by two elements—the Roman Catholic Church and the Quebec provincial government. The church had sufficient influence to insure the survival of the French ethnic group. But the provincial government was to produce a new frame of reference. The French-Canadian leaders came to consider themselves, not as the representatives of a minority group, but rather as the legitimate representatives of the French-Canadian nationality. They assumed that this legitimacy entitled them to renegotiate the terms of their relationship with the federal (and largely English-Canadian) government. And they learned that a strong English-Canadian government in Ottawa was not a substitute for a strong French-Canadian government in Quebec.

The "quiet revolution" marked the beginning of a strong French-speaking government in Quebec. Major reforms in the fields of education and social welfare combined with the establishment of publicly-owned enterprises created a new sense of self-confidence in the province. This self-confidence, in turn, engendered new and more pressing demands for special status within Confederation. Popular demand and the policies which arose in response to the new self-confidence gave birth to the State of Quebec. French-speaking inhabitants have come to define themselves first as Québécois and secondly, Canadians.

Québecois were faced with two alternatives: they could maintain the status quo or demand special status. The federal government could, like the Québecois, choose to maintain the status quo or it could grant them special status. Matrix VI illustrates the four outcomes theoretically possible.

Matrix VI

		Québecois	
		maintain status quo	demand special status
Federal Government	maintain status quo		
	give special status		

The Québecois probably would have been willing to maintain the status quo if the federal government had been able to guarantee linguistic duality and linguistic equality throughout Canada. However it seems clear that, at the federal level, the practical implications of the two languages have made linguistic equality an impossible dream. French was never a working language but, at best, a language of translation. In short, the status quo was no longer acceptable because official recognition of the French language was not sufficient to assure equality.

The Québecois had no other choice but to demand special status in view of the distinctive character of the province. The acts of 1763, 1774, 1791 and 1867 all recognized Quebec's special status. In 1763 the Canadiens were allowed a separate religion; in 1867, a special language; in 1954, a special income tax; and in 1965, a special Quebec pension plan. The bargaining power of the French-speaking inhabitants of Quebec was such that English-speaking Canadians were unable to deny their special character.

The bargaining power of the Québecois leaders was strengthened not only by the existence of a stronger state in Quebec, but also by their new threat, "equality or independence". The federal government faced a difficult dilemma. If it denied the special character of Quebec and refused to grant special status to the province, the threat of independence might be realized. But did the federal government have any alternative? Could any other arrangement satisfy the Québécois and at the same time preserve the whole federal system?

1970: The Quiet Independence

The present-day Québecois, unlike past generations, are not interested in trying to spread bilingualism across Canada. More than ever they believe that their survival and development are inextricably linked to the development of their province. Their sense of themselves as a group is defined not only in terms of cultural life, but also in terms of political life. Professor Léon Dion has analysed some of the features of this new group consciousness:

> The first basic feature is that the people who acquire the new consciousness reject the old paternalism, which, while offering them security and a certain amount of happiness, denied them justice.
> The second basic feature of the new collective consciousness is that it is caught in a vicious circle of rising expectations and mounting frustrations from which it is difficult to imagine how it can possibly be freed.
> A third feature of the new collective consciousness is the original way in which it defines rationality. In contrast to the abstract concept espoused by scholars and technocrats, it conceives of rationality as vibrant and human. . . . In the first case, it is accepted that to lead a decent life, it is sufficient to have a certain level of education, a certain standard of living, etc., while the extent to which individuals are involved in other activities which concern them is not of primarily importance; in the second place it

is the extent of participation which is the most important factor in determining the quality of an individual life.

The outstanding characteristic of this new consciousness is that it is motivated by a powerful, albeit not yet clearly perceived, desire for self-determination. . . . . Fed up with making submissions to a government that ignores their requests or whose responses are unacceptable or come too late, they decide to take the initiative themselves under new leaders, to formulate their own plans, calling on specialists and on the government to translate these plans into specific programmes.

In short, says Professor Dion, they place their reliance on man as opposed to bureaucracy. They opt for life. This is the philosophy behind the citizens committees. It is still too early to forecast what institutional changes will take place as a result of this new collective consciousness.

In any event, the set of alternatives from which the Québecois can choose has recently been modified to include at least two tactics: they can vote to stay in the Canadian federal system or they can vote for independence. The set of alternatives from which the federal government—and the English Canadians— can choose has also been modified: the government can acknowledge the Québecois' right to vote and accept the outcome, whether it be a vote to stay in the Canadian federal system or a vote for independence, or it can consider a vote for independence as illegitimate. Matrix VII illustrates the four outcomes theoretically possible.

Matrix VII

Québécois

		federalism	independence
Federal Government	legitimacy		
	illegitimacy		

The political chessboard has changed. Since 1970 the proponents of the federal option have been on the defensive. They now have to prove that the federal option is viable. For the past two electoral campaigns Premier Robert Bourassa has been on defensive in his attempts to prove that federalism is a paying proposition. The Union Nationale and the Parti Créditiste ask for renewed federalism and a new constitution, while implicitly suggesting that such an option might well lead, in final analysis, to the independence of Quebec. The Parti Québecois, on the other hand, supports independence: its members believe that independence would be economically viable and that it would allow to the Québecois to be themselves. The federal option is no longer secure. In 1970, with seventy-two seats out of 108 in the National Assembly, the Liberal Party was supported by only 45 percent of the electorate, including only 20 percent of the English-speaking voters of Quebec. Supported by 24 percent of the electorate, the Parti Québecois won six seats in the National Assembly. It is not unrealistic to assume that the Liberal Party will not be in power for ever. The Québecois voters may vote for the Parti Québecois if they believe that the Liberal Party is no longer able to solve the economic, social and political problems that Quebec faces. The "quiet independence" may become a reality. The question is, would the federal government consider a vote for independence an illegitimate vote?

Let us suppose that it would. The federal government would then be forced to say that the democratic system is legitimate only as long as the Québecois vote to remain a part of the federal system. It would also be forced to stipulate that any party advocating independence would be both an illegitimate and an illegal representative of the Québecois and to suggest that legitimacy and legality should be restored.

How should legitimacy and legality be restored? The federal government could set up another election in which the independence party could not participate because illegal, or it could send the army into Quebec. These two tactics could be used simultaneously or separately. Let us assume for the sake of simplicity that they would be used separately.

The possibility of declaring any political party illegal would be abhorrent to those Québecois and those English Canadians who believe in the principle of democracy. At best, many Québecois would refuse to participate in the new political institution. The question then would be, how long can a political system work without minimal participation on the part of the citizens? At worst, some or many Québecois would decide to sabotage or boycott the political institutions and economic goods produced by English Canadians. This new situation would result in significant economic costs. The nature of the Québecois' actions and the magnitude of the economic costs might prompt the federal government to use the army. Psychological and economic costs would then increase very rapidly both for the Québecois and for English Canadians. It is almost impossible to forecast how such an escalation could be stopped. For the Québecois it would prove that independence was the paying but, at the same time, costly option.

One look at the alternative is enough to show why the federal government may be forced to consider a Québecois vote for independence a legitimate vote. One can only hope that, when and if it comes, Quebec's independence will be a "quiet revolution".

Rejean Landry teaches Political Science at the Université Laval.

NOTES

1 Léon Dion, "Towards a Self-Determined Consciousness" in D.C. Thompson (ed.), *Quebec Society and Politics: Views From Inside* (Toronto: McClelland and Stewart, 1973), pp. 29-31.

The Dynamics of Contemporary Party-Movements in Quebec: Some Comparative Aspects of Créditisme and Indépendantisme
Michael B. Stein

The Current Realignment of Political Forces in Quebec

The Quebec election of 1973 has been described by several commentators and politicians as crucial in determining the future of Quebec and Canada. The results may at least help to clarify public preferences, given the unusually large and confusing array of candidates and parties. However in my view the election's most important contribution was that it continued and consolidated a trend which began in 1970. It was what Vincent Lemieux and his collaborators have appropriately labelled "an election of realignment".[1] The term refers to what the authors judged to be a fundamental and long-term change in the alignment of political forces in the province as opposed to the more usual short-term deviations which tend to occur from one election to the next. In the 1970 election the old two-party system, which had operated in Quebec with few important interruptions since Confederation, suddenly collapsed.[2] The Union Nationale, inheritor of the "bleu" tradition, although still officially the major opposition party, began its rapid fall into what appears to be ultimate oblivion.[3] And two new parties, the Parti Québécois and the Ralliement Créditiste, competing for the first time in a provincial election, established important footholds for themselves in future competitions for power with the victorious Liberals.

Realignment involves more than a mere supplanting of old parties by new ones with new names. Since parties are reflections of underlying social forces in a society, the partisan realignment of 1970 signalled an important change in the balance of such forces in the province in recent years. The collapse of the Union Nationale Party and the emergence of the Parti Québécois and Ralliement Créditiste are indicators of the convulsive effect which socio-economic and political modernization have had on the old coalitions of social groupings and classes which held together the party system until the 1960s. The Parti Québécois and the Créditistes seem to articulate two new and distinct protest responses to this process of modernization, respectively a secular, statist, moderate left-wing and nationalistic orientation most attractive to the new expanding sectors of the population whose status is rising, and an anti-secular, anti-statist, right-wing, and less nationalistic outlook identified with sectors of the population facing rapid decline in both

numbers and status. The elements which tend to support the indépendantiste movement include the so-called new middle classes of urbanized, industrialized society: the government bureaucrats, teachers, artists, writers,
media elites, salaried employees in private enterprise, university students
and so on. Also included are expanding sectors within the old elites: the
professionals, skilled labour and owners and managers of small but growing
private enterprises. Clearly these forces are on the rise and provide a fertile
soil for a new and well-organized political formation. The elements which
feel some affinity for the créditiste movement are the lower middle classes
and unskilled workers in the non-urbanized centers of the province: insurance salesmen, shopkeepers, artisans, farmers, journeymen, day labourers and
other workers. These elements are declining in numbers as rural and small-
urban residents are drawn to the large urban centers. They are also experi-
encing a relative decline in status and income.

The largest and still-dominant social force in the province which represents support for the political and economic status quo and slow adaptation
to modernization is now primarily drawn to the Liberal Party. The economic and social programmes of this party have shifted gradually from a fairly
heavy concentration on agricultural and small industrial reforms in the late
1950s to an overwhelming concern for industrial and urban growth in the
1960s and 70s. Intense efforts have been made to attract large-scale foreign
investment. The Liberals have also promoted moderate reforms in the area
of social policy (including family allowances, health insurance and old age
pensions) and have paid lip-service to cultural and linguistic nationalism. It
is not surprising, therefore, that they have come to draw considerable support from major segments of all classes—upper middle class, lower middle
class and working class—including both francophones and anglophones, particularly those who reside in urban areas. They are the conventional bour-
geois and status quo party par excellence, spanning the broad center of the
political spectrum. In the past they have shared this place with the Union
Nationale Party, which propagated a curious blend of populist economic
protest, cultural and political nationalism and conservative economic and
social measures. They attracted an amorphous following including business
and professional elites in the small-urban and rural centers, farmers, some
conservative business and professional elements in the larger urban centers
and many unskilled workers in the metropolitan areas of Montreal and Quebec. Since the late 1950s, their proportion of the popular vote has steadily
dwindled, and they no longer appear to represent a significant proportion
of any social class or occupational grouping.

In this paper I shall be concentrating on the social formations underlying the two new parties which first competed electorally in 1970 and which reflect the emergence of the new social forces—the Parti Québécois and the Parti Crédit Social du Québec. There are very substantial differences between these parties in ideology, programmes, social composition, leadership and electoral styles, and they are bitterly opposed to each other politically. But they share one important characteristic: they are both partisan outgrowths of smaller but older and more deeply-rooted socio-political movements— the indépendantiste and créditiste movements. Therefore they can be treated comparatively under a single conceptual rubric, the socio-political protest movement, and their social composition, evolution and patterns of conflict and schism can be fruitfully compared. Indeed, the indépendantiste and créditiste movements appear to me to be in some respects mirror-images of each other, the former clearly in ascendancy, the latter in obvious decline. A comparative analysis of these two political formations could provide some insight into the evolution and future direction of contemporary political forces in Quebec.

Nature of the Creditiste and Indépendantiste Phenomena

In an earlier study of the créditiste movement in Quebec, I defined the phenomenon as a type of right-wing protest movement. Similarly I would hypothesize that the indépendantiste movement is a type of left-wing protest movement. The Parti Québécois, like the Parti Créditiste du Québec, is merely the most recent partisan outgrowth and structural manifestation of this left-wing protest movement.

The concepts *right-wing protest movement* and *left-wing protest movement* are a composite of three main elements which must be defined: socio-political movement, protest (as opposed to revolutionary) objectives, and right-wing or left-wing orientations. A social movement is defined as any form of collective action which involves the mobilization of individuals and which has as its goal the bringing about of fundamental changes in the social order.[4] The common elements in all definitions of the social movement are a feeling of discontent shared by its members and a general desire to change the society. A socio-political movement is a sub-type of social movement, one which is directed towards change in the political order. It shares a number of traits with other political structures, such as conventional political parties and pressure groups, which are also in competition for influence in the political arena. For example, all involve the organization of individuals around common ideas and interests which are then promoted by political means. But there are important distinguishing features between these structures. Political movements have larger objectives than most other structures of political competition. Their objectives include political education, mobilization of the masses in demonstrations and marches and other modes of action directed towards a general political change. Secondly, political movements are generally organized around a series of beliefs or utopian goals concretized in a political ideology which acts as a unifying force for its members.[5] Finally, these movements exhibit a structuring of political roles and a distribution of power, influence and authority among the members unlike that of other political structures. The organizational structures of such movements tend to be tighter at the leadership level and looser at the level of the followers. The leadership shows a tendency to concentrate power and authority in its hands in order to maintain control over decisions which determine the basic strategy and tactics of the movement.[6]

Socio-political movements may be either protest or revolutionary in their ends. A revolutionary movement is dedicated to the destruction of the existing socio-economic and political systems and to the acquisition of power in order to completely transform the social order. The objectives of protest movements are more limited; they aim to change the manner in which decisions are made or to transform the norms which delimit the decision-making process without destroying the system itself.[7]

On the ideological level there are two main types of protest movements—right-wing and left-wing. In general terms right-wing movements appeal to those sectors of the population which are in long-term decline, either in size or in social status or both (for example, peasants in industrial society and "blue collar" workers in a post-industrial society). Their appeals are characterized by a desire to preserve the existing social and economic conditions which are seen as being eroded or to recreate the more beneficial features of a society of the past. Thus they propound such measures as support for non-secular education, aid to colonization and subsidies to small businesses. In contrast movements of the left appeal to sectors of the population which are increasing in size or in social status or both (for example, blue collar workers in an industrially developing society and "white collar" employees and technocrats in an advanced or post-industrial society). They wish to establish the condition of a future society through measures such as a guaranteed minimum income, strong legislation against pollution, full medical coverage and decentralized health services.[8]

Elsewhere I have demonstrated that the créditiste phenomenon may be considered a type of right-wing protest movement, since it fits each of the criteria for such a movement listed above. The créditiste phenomenon should be considered a movement rather than a party or pressure group because, throughout most of its history, its adherents have sought wider objectives than the mere winning of governmental power. Founded in 1936, the movement did not transform itself into a political party until the establishment of Réal Caouette's Ralliement des Créditistes in 1957. Its members sought to spread their doctrine through newspapers, radio and television broadcasts and correspondence courses. They also engaged in a wide variety of pressure tactics including meetings with members of parliament at both the federal and provincial levels, demonstrations on Parliament Hill and testimony in parliamentary committees. Their efforts were motivated by a strong attachment to the combination of monetary reform ideas and conservative, social, catholic dogma which was propagated as the French-Canadian version of Major Douglas' social credit doctrine by the movement's founder, Louis Even. The early leaders of the movement, Even and Gilbert Côté-Mercier, exercised strong dictatorial control over the rank-and-file through a support cadre known as the Institute of Political Action.

The créditistes were a protest rather than a revolutionary movement because their opposition to the existing financial and political systems was limited in scope. They sought merely to transform the method of distributing credit on the assumption that other changes in the economic, social and political spheres would follow naturally. They did not advocate the abolition or transformation of the capitalist economic system, the method of social organization or the democratic political and constitutional structure. Their appeal was right-wing in orientation: they sought to resuscitate traditional values such as obedience, duty and morality, to root out the corrupt influences of monopoly capitalism, to revitalize the farmer and small-town merchant by offering him credit payments and subsidies, to resurrect church institutions and preserve the confessional school system, to eliminate pornography and drugs, to censor the media for destroying the values of the young and to widen the scope of private freedom against encroachments by the ever-expanding state.[9]

In contrast the indépendantiste phenomenon can be characterized as a left-wing protest movement. The indépendantistes, like the créditistes, manifest the two essential elements of any social movement: the members share a feeling of discontent towards the existing society and they want to change that society. Like the créditistes too, their major focus of activity is in the political sphere. But unlike conventional political parties and pressure groups, the indépendantistes have, since their founding in 1957, fostered political goals other than the mere winning of power through elections. The earliest aims of the movement gave priority to educating the population about the benefits of political independence. Soon after the movement extended its activities and promoted marches and demonstrations in protest against perceived abuses of francophone economic and cultural rights or in support of independence. It was as late as 1966 when the main organization of the movement, the Rassemblement pour l'Indépendance Nationale (R.I.N.), committed itself to electoral and party competition.

Like similar movements, the indépendantiste movement has been organized around a set of utopian beliefs concretized in an ideology. In the early years of the movement this ideology lacked socio-economic content, but it has gradually assumed a social democratic form. The first detailed programme of the indépendantiste movement was published by the R.I.N. in 1965; since that time revisions and modifications have been made on a regular basis, most recently in the manifesto *Quand Nous Serons Vraiment Chez Nous* published in the spring of 1973 by the Parti Québécois (P.Q.). These programmes, which borrow heavily from economic and social reforms in countries such as Sweden, have become, by the admission of the members themselves, more and more social democratic in nature. Thus Claude Ryan wrote in February 1973, after the publication of the P.Q. manifesto, "The P.Q. is orienting itself more and more towards social democracy. One can even state, after attending the birth of the new programme, that it constitutes henceforth a very original Quebec version of this great contemporary current."[10]

The organizational structure of the indépendantiste movement has deviated to some degree from the typical model for political movements. Like most political movements, its organization has been extremely loose at the level of the rank-and-file. But unlike these other movements and in contrast to the créditistes, the indépendantistes lack the tight control at the top which is normally expected during the period of the movement's expansion. Despite the personal prestige of its founders and early leaders—men such as André d'Allemagne, Marcel Chaput and Pierre Bourgault—they were unwilling or unable to impose their will on the rank-and-file member at congresses and party strategy meetings. The conflicts and splits which ensued may have slowed the growth of the movement in its early stages.[11]

The indépendantiste movement has often been characterized as a revolutionary movement, since its explicit aim is to destroy the existing constitutional framework of parliamentary democracy in Canada and to replace it with a presidential system operating exclusively in Quebec. But in most respects its objectives are moderate rather than revolutionary in nature. In political terms it merely wishes to replace one form of democracy (parliamentary) by another (presidential). In economic terms it seeks only to reform the system of mixed enterprise capitalism rather than to replace it by state-controlled socialism. In social terms it seeks to improve the lot of the "have-nots" and remove some of the grosser abuses of the privileged without drastically altering the stratification system or destroying the dominant position of the middle classes. But even its constitutional objective of declaring outright independence from Canada as soon as it gains power has been modified. Since René Lévesque's assumption of leadership in 1968, the desire for political independence has been coupled with the idea of economic interdependence—the maintenance, if possible, of a monetary and customs union with the rest of Canada. More recently Lévesque has suggested that an electoral victory will give him only a mandate to conduct a referendum on the question of independence and the right to bargain on that basis with the federal government over the terms of peaceful secession.[12] Thus the indépendantiste movement may be characterized as a protest rather than a revolutionary movement. Even its members tend to view the movement in these non-revolutionary terms.[13]

Phases in the Evolution of the Créditiste and Indépendantiste Movements and their Catalysts

Analysts of social movements have rarely attempted to describe the patterns of evolution of these movements or to reveal the factors responsible for their transformation. But it has been observed that political movements tend to evolve in three principal phases that correspond to the outstanding traits of their leaders. These phases can be roughly distinguished as mobilization, consolidation and institutionalization. The process of evolution can be considered a gradual secularisation of the movement and a loss of its ideological élan, leading to its eventual transformation into another institutional form or its disappearance.

The phase of mobilization is the period in which militants are recruited, the mass of the population is subjected to propaganda and proselytization, and the basic structures and modes of action of the movement are established. The typical pattern in this phase of evolution is the initial conversion of a small core group of dissidents to the ideology. These persons may come from any social stratum and may be attracted to the movement's ideology for a variety of reasons—economic, social or political grievances, personal needs or interests, and so on. They are more devoted to the cause and more ready to devote time and effort to its promotion than are other members. They are responsible for tapping the feelings and arousing the emotions of the alienated masses.[14] During this phase the leaders take on the aura of prophets. They owe their leadership to their capacity to concretize the main ideas of the movement and to convert new members to the cause. They derive their authority from their superior knowledge of the faith and their superior ability to articulate it to the masses.[15]

In the consolidation phase the movement expands its resources and membership, consolidates its structures, defines its organizational framework and programme with greater precision and modifies its strategy and tactics to deal with new situations. It is generally directed by men whose talents are those of the organizer, administrator or propagandist.[16]

In the institutionalization phase the movement tries to maintain and increase its support by negotiations and alliances with other groups. Its strategy and tactics become more pragmatic and less tied to the original ideology and goals, and it accepts compromises. During this phase it is generally headed by pragmatic and opportunistic men who are not so well versed in the original doctrine as the earlier leaders, nor so devoted to the movement. These leaders are ready to sacrifice to more immediate ends what remains of the original movement.[17]

Students of social movements have also observed that one of the dominant characteristics of such movements is their factionalism and internal division. They have attributed this tendency to a number of factors: the inevitable conflicts which occur between doctrinaire and less doctrinaire members when the militants try to apply their ideology to strategies of action; conflicts between political generations (that is, members of about the same age and similar political experiences) which manifest themselves in different types of leaders and leadership styles;[18] the tendency for new bases of power to develop outside the original leadership group as the movement expands and becomes more heterogeneous;[19] the weakness of the control apparatus and the absence of effective rewards and punishments in such movements, particularly those of a non-revolutionary type.[20]

But what these analysts have failed to do is to link this factionalism to the processes of evolution and change in the movement. Moreover, they tend to consider factionalism a weakness, an enervating force and an aberration from the normal course of development of such movements. In my view, however, whether factionalism produces internal conflict or outright schism, it serves as the prime force generating new phases in the movement's evolution, bringing about the displacement of its leaders, the reorientation of its strategy and tactics and the reorganization of its structures. These new orientations are crucial in determining the relative success or failure of the movement. In other words conflict, not consensus, becomes the norm in political movements and the essential ingredient in determining their pattern of development and their ultimate consequences for the society in which they operate.

In my study of the créditiste movement I have described how the movement has evolved through two of the phases mentioned above—mobilization and consolidation—and has just entered its third phase, institutionalization.

The mobilization phase, led by the first generation of créditistes, extended from 1936, when La Ligue du Crédit Social was founded, until 1957, when a split occurred within the Union des Electeurs, and Réal Caouette founded the Ralliement des Créditistes. This phase was marked by periods of slow growth in the membership followed by periods of stabilization. At its peak in 1948 under the leadership of Louis Even and Gilberte Côté Mercier, the Union des Electeurs estimated its subscription membership at about 65,000, although its active membership was probably much smaller. These miltants were avid readers of the bi-monthly newspaper, *Vers Demain,* and active participants in study groups, policy congresses and (until 1949) electoral campaigns. Louis Even played the role of prophet and ideologue of the movement, translating the abstract theories of Major Douglas into terms which were understandable to the lower middle classes, farmers and unorganized workers of rural and small-town Quebec. Gilberte Côté-Mercier was the major propagandist of the movement. She determined its political strategy and selected its symbols, such as the white berets that the members wore, their flags, songs and emblems. These two leaders maintained a strict control over the movement at all times. Their principal objective was to convert the Québécois to the doctrine of social credit. Electoral objectives were of secondary concern and, after 1949, were discarded altogether.[21] The Union des Electeurs did not achieve their principal objective, but they did manage to plant the seeds of their ideology in the province. In their electoral efforts they failed even more miserably. They competed in six federal and provincial general election campaigns between 1939 and 1957 and during that period were unable to elect a single créditiste. (The sole victory during this period was a seat won by Caouette in a federal by-election in Pontiac in 1946.) However they did manage to win over 150,000 votes in the 1948 provincial election. After 1949 the movement took on a religious cast, and its membership began to decline in numbers.

The consolidation phase, under the leadership of Réal Caouette, extended from 1957 until 1973. Caouette was the outstanding propagandist and electoral campaigner, and he was aided in his efforts by excellent organizers and administrators such as Laurent Legault and Gilles Grégoire. These were men of the second generation of créditistes who had been nurtured in social credit doctrine during the first phase of the movement's development and had finally come to political maturity. Their conflict with the leaders of the first generation was over the emphasis which should be given to educational and religious concerns as opposed to electoral participation. When the directors of the Union des Electeurs refused to accept their plan for a parallel electoral organization these second-generation créditistes split with them and established their own organization, Le Ralliement des Créditistes. Conceived initially as both a party and a movement, the Ralliement oriented itself more and more towards electoral concerns. It organized a series of fifteen-minute television programmes in the northern (Rouyn-Noranda) region and later in several other areas outside metropolitan Montreal. Caouette's popularity as a television performer helped attract many new members to the movement, including several prestige candidates from the liberal professions. But the original "berets blancs" group continued to be the nucleus of the party. The party retained the electoral structures and the methods of finance which were used by the Union des Electeurs in the first phase. Its ideology, although stripped of its religious content, was essentially unchanged. At the polls the Ralliement did considerably better than its predecessor. Whereas the Union des Electeurs had never earned more than 10 percent of the popular vote, the Ralliement des Créditistes expanded its support to between 15 and 30 percent of the electorate. However this base was concentrated in rural and semi-urban areas and was drawn principally from the lower classes. The support for the Ralliement, which reached its peak in the federal election of 1963, declined steadily thereafter.[22]

The institutionalization phase was signalled by Caouette himself in March 1970, when he attempted unsuccessfully to have Yvon Dupuis elected leader of the newly-established provincial party. However the real beginning of institutionalization came when a group of third-generation créditistes seeking to modernize the movement and extend its popular base into the expanding urban areas, decided to displace Camil Samson as provincial leader and to support Yvon Dupuis, an old-time créditiste foe, as their new chief. Dupuis is in many respects the personification of the pragmatic leader of the institutionalization phase. He is better educated, better dressed, more elegant in speech and more sophisticated and urbanized than most créditiste leaders. Although he shares the conservative orientation of the créditistes, he seems to be less concerned with the old shibboleths of social credit doctrine. In fact his knowledge of Major Douglas' ideas is minimal. His major concern is to win power for himself and his party, and he is likely to make any pragmatic adjustment or forge any alliance which would assist him in this objective. However his attempts at striking a balance in his appeals to rural and

small-urban supporters in créditiste strongholds and his enticements to new
urban voters in the metropolitan areas seem to have failed thus far. His
bitter attacks on some typical manifestations of modern urban life–decline
in the birth rate, secularization of the schools, liberalism in dress, freedom
of the media, the youth culture, separatism and socialism–seem to have
alienated much potential support. The steady decline of support for both
Dupuis and his party in public opinion polls seems to foreshadow a severe
electoral defeat. His own future and that of the movement as a whole are in
some doubt.

If the future of the créditistes seems bleak, that of the indépendantistes
appears very bright indeed. The evolution of the indépendantiste movement,
like that of the créditiste, can be conceived of in terms of three phases–
mobilization, consolidation and institutionalization. The mobilization phase
occurred in the period between 1957 and 1970 largely under the banner of
the Rassemblement pour l'Indépendance Nationale. The original founders
of this movement, André d'Allemagne and Marcel Chaput, were middle-class
nationalists who first expressed their profound sense of alienation concerning the Québécois condition in book-length treatises published in the late
1950s. In 1960 they organized their small band of supporters into a loosely-
knit and diffuse structure known as the Rassemblement pour l'Indépendance
Nationale. Shortly after they were joined by the fiery journalist and propagandist Pierre Bourgault. These three men were, and continue to be the
prophets of the movement. Like the créditistes, the indépendantistes depended on voluntary contributions from their members to finance their
activities. At first the movement's activities were confined to non-electoral
concerns. But after Marcel Chaput split with the movement in 1962 in an
effort to orient it more toward electoral concerns, the leaders began to revise
their thinking, and, by 1965, they were ready to compete wholeheartedly in
provincial elections. Following their limited success in the 1966 election
(7 percent of the popular vote), they organized a recruiting campaign which
more than doubled their pre-election membership. In this period (1966-68)
the original group of intellectuals and middle-class leaders who expounded
a moderate social democratic ideology and a peaceful electoral transition to
political independence were joined by a more radical minority faction under
the leadership of Andrée Ferretti. This faction called for a greater orientation
toward working class concerns and more direct involvement in non-electoral
nationalist causes. When Ferretti's group split away from the R.I.N. in early
1968, and René Lévesque's breakaway liberal faction, known as the Mouvement Souveraineté Association, began to draw members away from the R.I.N.,
the influence of the main wing of the movement began to wane. In October,

1968, it voted to dissolve itself. Most of its members then joined the Parti Québécois, a union of dissident Liberals, créditistes and rinistes, formed by René Lévesque in 1968. A vast recruiting drive followed, and the membership of the indépendantiste movement, which had never exceeded 8,000 members during the R.I.N.'s strongest period, reached an estimated 25,000 by the 1970 election.

The consolidation phase began after the election of April, 1970. The outstanding success of Lévesque's P.Q., which won 23 percent of the popular vote, strengthened the hand of the moderates who proposed to confine the movement almost exclusively to electoral activity. This majority faction, called "électoralistes", argued forcefully that the movement could only make headway in its quest for power if it projected an image of respectability and moderation and eschewed extremism in every form. Lévesque's own preference, first stated clearly in his book *Option Québec,* was for continued economic association with the rest of Canada even after political independence. His strategy helped to attract many prestigious French Canadians who had formerly belonged to or served other political parties, including economist Jacques Parizeau, technocrat Claude Morin and several erstwhile Liberal and Union Nationale Members of the National Assembly. He also consolidated the organizational and financial structures of the party, maintaining the pattern of voluntary self-finance and increasing the donations from affluent middle-class groups. The platform of the party was carefully defined and adopted in party convention and then consolidated in an election brochure. The party also hired public relations specialists to aid them in future campaigns. The "électoralistes" were opposed for a time by a minority faction known as the "participationistes", who, like the Ferretti faction in the R.I.N., advocated greater involvement in social causes and more support for popular demonstrations and marches. This faction was consistently defeated in its efforts to win executive positions and now occupies a marginal position in the power circles of the movement.

The process of institutionalization of the indépendantiste movement has already begun and overlaps with that of consolidation. This process is likely to accelerate if the movement finds that its commitment to complete independence prevents it from increasing its popular vote much beyond 25 percent of the Quebec voting population. At that stage the leadership may attempt to further de-emphasize the independence and social democratic programmes and transform the movement into a moderate, nationalist left-of-center party. A final split between the électoralistes and participationistes may occur. Thus we see that both the créditiste and indépendantiste movements have passed through the typical phases of evolution common to political protest movements. But it is still necessary to examine the catalysts that caused these changes. A comparative study of the two movements sheds some light on these catalysts.

In the créditiste movement each new phase in evolution was triggered by the coming to power of a new generation of créditiste leaders. But in the indépendantiste movement the phase of consolidation began when the founding leaders voluntarily subordinated themselves to a new group of converts headed by Lévesque. In the former case, the "outsider" Dupuis continued to be the instrument of the third-generation créditistes after winning the leadership, and this may have handicapped him in his efforts to define a new strategy for the movement in the institutionalization phase. In the case of the indépendantistes, the rapid rise of Lévesque and his group seems to have given him a freer hand in reorienting the strategy of the movement and refashioning the organization to suit his own preferences.

Secondly, each new evolutionary phase in both movements and each fundamental reorientation in strategy was preceded by a period of intense internal factionalism and conflict leading to outright schism. For example, in the indépendantiste movement evolution from the mobilization phase to that of consolidation, and the reorientation of the movement towards a more moderate ideology and greater emphasis on electoral action was preceded by internal factionalism between the Bourgault and Ferretti factions and the eventual splitting off of the latter. The subsequent weakening of the R.I.N. encouraged the riniste leaders to take the unusual step of subordinating themselves to the souverainiste newcomers.

Thirdly, in the case of the créditistes, factionalism was most intense during the consolidation phase because conflict between those most attached to the original movement concept and those who put the emphasis on party and electoral action was greatest at this stage. The internal control mechanisms were weaker under Caouette's leadership than they had been under the Union des Electeurs. External political forces generated by the "quiet revolution, such as nationalism, economic modernization, educational reform and cultural transformation, were most intense during this period and had a direct influence on internal policy decisions. And the movement had reached its limit of expansion electorally. In the indépendantiste movement, on the other hand, factionalism and internal conflict were greatest during the mobilization phase. The conflict between ideologists and the more moderate and pragmatic supporters of independence was most intense at this stage,[23] and the internal control mechanisms were weak. There were few sanctions available to the leaders other than expulsion from the party, and the prevailing norm of internal democracy counterbalanced those of solidarity and secrecy,

permitting dissidents to air their grievances with comparative impunity.[24]
As in the case of the créditistes, external political forces exerted a great influence on the indépendantistes during the 1960s and caused much internal
perturbation. The riniste movement reached its limit of expansion in 1968
with about 8,000 members and then began to decline in numbers. Financial
resources within the R.I.N. were limited and unlikely to increase. The original "little circle" of indépendantiste militants was broken after 1966 when
the movement expanded, bringing in new and heterogeneous elements with
different perspectives, so that group solidarity could no longer be maintained.[25]

The fourth and perhaps most important catalyst in both movement's
evolution, was the fundamental conflict which existed between sub-groups
of leaders because of their different social backgrounds, political attitudes
and patterns of participation. It is this fundamental conflict which, in my
view, is the major catalyst of change in all political protest movements. In
order to understand this conflict more clearly, it is necessary to describe the
social, attitudinal and behavioural characteristics of the two movements.

Social Background Characteristics, Political Attitudes and Patterns of Participation of the Activists and their Relation to Schism

In my study of the créditiste movement I was able to isolate two major sub-
groups of leaders: the moderates, who formed the dominant majority group
and the highly disaffected, who were an important minority. They could be
distinguished not only by their political attitudes, but also by their socio-
economic characteristics and their modes of political participation.

The moderate créditiste leaders were born and brought up in small towns
and villages in Quebec and most still live outside the metropolitan areas of
Montreal and Quebec City. Most joined the movement as young men when
they were suffering economic hardships. Today they exhibit many of the
characteristics of the traditional small-town Quebec elite: they are better
educated than the average French Canadian and have higher-than-average
incomes. They are active in social and church groups and on municipal and
school boards. They were generally the first members of their family to join
the movement, and they did so largely for economic and ideological reasons.
They have achieved some upward status mobility over their fathers, but still
probably feel some sense of status deprivation. They articulate moderate
dissenting attitudes against the existing political and economic system and
a moderate desire for their reform. However they are not revolutionary in
any sense and show neither conspiratorial attitudes nor authoritarianism in

background or personality. They are active participants in the local associations of the movement and occupy most of the official positions.[26]

The highly disaffected leaders, who comprised about 20 percent of our sample, tend to be of lower socio-economic status than the moderate leaders. They also tend to be less involved in voluntary associations and to hold fewer official positions within the community. They are most attracted to the movement by the negative aspects of its appeal. They show great dissatisfaction with all of the fundamental aspects of the existing economic and political systems, particularly the pattern of federal politics, and advocate a radical transformation of the federal structure. They display many of the personality and attitudinal traits associated with the ethnocentric or anomic personality: they are more conspiratorial in their outlook, more authoritarian in personality and attitude and more anti-intellectual than the moderates. These characteristics seem to be primarily a function of status deprivation, arising from relatively inferior education.[27]

Because of these differences, the two sub-groups are in constant conflict over the objectives, strategies and tactics. Their conflicts are muted during the mobilization phase, since the movement is in the process of expansion and élan is high. But in the consolidation phase, the absence of structural, social and personal controls, the importance accorded to the over-riding goals of the movement, and the inevitable setbacks which the movement suffers cause the latent conflicts between the sub-groups to surface. When these conflicts are reinforced by differences in origin and social status, disagreements erupt over status and the distribution of roles. The conflict and resulting alliances lead to schism and ultimately to a reorientation of the movement. This hypothesis has been summarized graphically in Figure 1.[28]

An analysis of the social composition of the indépendantiste movement may lead to somewhat comparable findings. Gingras who studied R.I.N. militants by means of a mailed questionnaire and in-depth interviews, found two distinct sub-groups: the "moderates", who formed a large majority of the militants, and the more "engagés", about 6 percent of whom were "genuine extremists".[29]

The average riniste militant, according to both Gingras and Pelletier, was male, married, younger than thirty-five years of age, highly educated (college- or university-trained), had a high income ($10,000 plus annually), occupationally part of the new middle class and linked to new social sectors recently developed and still in transformation. About the same proportion perceived themselves to be of upper and of lower middle class (40 percent), while very few were of working-class background or identified with that class. Their motivations for joining the movement were not economic, but rather

Figure 1   **A model of schismatic behaviour**

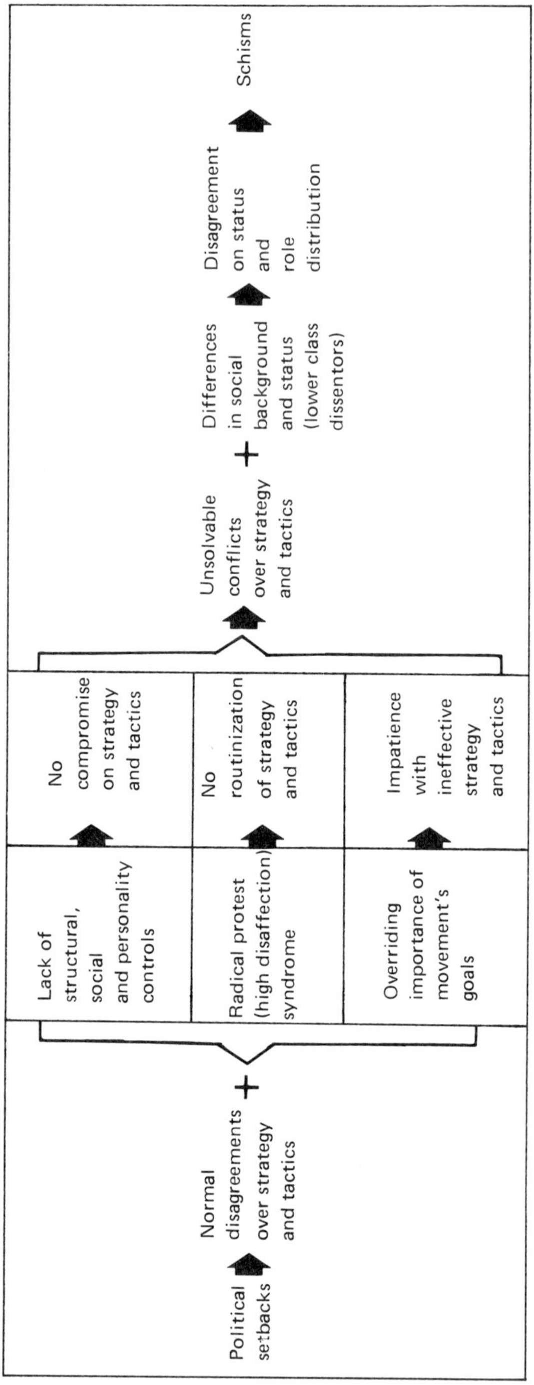

Political
setbacks → Normal
disagreements
over strategy
and tactics

+

Lack of
structural,
social
and personality
controls → No
compromise
on strategy
and tactics

Radical protest
(high disaffection)
syndrome → No
routinization
of strategy
and tactics

Overriding
importance of
movement's
goals → Impatience
with
ineffective
strategy
and tactics

→ Unsolvable
conflicts
over strategy
and tactics

+

Differences
in social
background
and status
(lower class
dissentors)

→ Disagreement
on status
and
role
distribution

→ Schisms

"a complex of socio-psychological factors directing them to a cause".[31] They felt a moderate sense of status deprivation.

The genuine extremist, on the other hand, was among the most frequent demonstrators in the R.I.N. He sometimes held an official position in the movement and was ready to go to any extreme for the cause. His attitude towards the existing political and economic system was most negative: he considered the existing system to be a "parody of democracy", he demanded that "power flow into the streets", and he supported the violent overthrow of the system as a last resort in the effort to achieve independence. In personal terms, unlike the moderate riniste, he was dissatisfied with his income. Conversely, and paradoxically, he felt too much prestige was accorded to those who held his job. He had little trust in others and a pessimistic vision of the human condition; he showed himself thereby to be more anomic than his copartisans. He was among the most active in assemblies and at demonstrations, but he contributed little to the movement's "caisse" (fund) or to the daily functioning of the party.[32]

Given the differences between moderates and extremists, it is relatively simple to explain the schism within the R.I.N. In the R.I.N. as in the créditiste movement, there was a general sharing of the goal of independence but a clear disagreement over the means for achieving it. The lack of structure and the absence of sanctions permitted these disagreements to manifest themselves internally between the two major sub-groups. The genuine extremists were able to join the movement and even rise to positions of some leadership. Although they remained a distinct minority, they had some success in attempting to orient the movement towards their ideological concerns. While the movement was expanding, the internal conflicts remained submerged, and the major energies of both sub-groups were concentrated on their external enemies. However when decline set in, the genuine extremists turned inward and attacked the moderate leaders. When these extremists lost their struggle for power and influence within the movement, they either split with the moderates and established their own dissident wing or became inactive. The movement was thereafter able to adopt a more moderate course.

This pattern, which emerged in the conflict between the Bourgault and Ferretti factions between 1966 and 1968, may have repeated itself with less intensity in the Parti Québécois during the consolidation phase. In his 1967 study of the R.I.N. militant Pelletier shows that the "activistes", who take part in demonstrations, would resort to arms to oppose a military intervention against an independent Quebec, and would be willing to take up arms in order to hasten the advent of independence, outnumbered the "electoralistes", who advocated converting others peacefully to the cause of independence, by almost four to one.[33] But by February, 1973, the latter group, under Lévesque's leadership, was clearly in ascendancy. Most of the former leaders of the R.I.N. party, including Bourgault, Chaput and d'Allemagne, had lost their influence over the new wing of the movement. This may well explain the success which Lévesque has had in altering the movement's electoral strategy and popular image.

Conclusion: The Consequences of these Party-Movements for Quebec Politic

Each of the party movements analyzed here reflects larger socio-economic and political forces present in Quebec society. The créditiste movement is an authentically Quebec movement which first appeared in the province during the Depression years and responded to the feelings of anxiety and insecurity of certain segments of the Quebec population. People were unable to comprehend and consequently they feared the new trends towards urbanization, industrialization, bureaucratization, secularization and the explosion of the communications media. This trend, which first manifested itself in Quebec in the early years of the century, intensified after World War I and particularly after World War II. Changes in the economic structure were followed by changes in the social, cultural and political spheres: the relations between church and state changed, education was expanded and secularized, the communications media grew rapidly, social security and health benefits were extended, and cultural and political nationalism were strengthened. The "quiet revolution" of the 1960s symbolized the maturation and ultimate acceptance of these changes.

Créditisme, with its right-wing protest ideology and its rural and urban base, is a movement that responds to the fears and aspirations of the segment of the Quebec population which still sees itself threatened by these changes. But the rural and semi-urban traditions are eroding, and the regions in which créditisme is strong are in a state of long-term economic decline. The out-migration in these areas is increasing, and the old values are being rejected by the young. Thus créditisme is bound to decline as a political force unless it transforms itself into a fundamentally different phenomenon. While the factionalism and schisms have produced gradual reorientations in the movement's strategy, they have failed thus far to enable the movement to break out of its narrow right-wing rural and semi-urban mold. If the créditiste movement is to survive, it must transform itself into a moderate right-of-center party with both urban and rural support. Undoubtedly a move in this direction will involve considerable internal struggle, because the forces of factionalism in the movement have not yet run their course.

The indépendantiste movement, on the other hand, has adapted itself re-
markably well to this process of modernization, and its future appears much
brighter. The movement itself was a by-product of modernization, and it
continues to attune itself to the new and rapidly changing currents in Quebec politics. Its original ideology reflected the conservative and clerical
nationalism of Raymond Barbeau. It has gradually embraced the successive
waves of cultural nationalism, political nationalism, socio-economic nationalism and finally social democracy and nationalism.[34] It has also transformed
itself from a movement of middle-class intellectuals inclined to impose their
image of the utopian state on the population to a pragmatic left-of-center
party with an evolving programme closely attuned to, and derived from the
cultural, social and economic aspirations of modern Québécois of all classes.[35]
The ultimate test of the movement will be its readiness to subordinate its
political objectives to its socio-economic concerns should the former prove
to be a barrier to future electoral success. It is entirely possible that there
will be a renewal of the process of factionalism and schism between the de-
votees of the movement's original independence ideals and the pragmatists
seeking electoral success. If the pragmatists prevail, the ideal of independence
will die, and the Parti Québécois will transform itself into a conventional,
left-of-center nationalist party with strongly autonomist tendencies which
will alternate in power with the Liberals. At this stage, the two-party system
based on conventional parties may be re-established in Quebec, and social
democrats and liberals will vie for power in what one political scientist has
labelled a "mature party system" in the "center-left" or "liberal-social democratic" mold.[36]

*Michael B. Stein is an associate professor of Political Science at McGill Uni-
versity.*

NOTES

1 Vincent Lemieux, Marcel Gilbert and André Blais, *Une Election de Réalignement,
l'élection générale du 29 avril 1970 au Québec* (Montréal: Editions du Jour, 1970),
chapter 1.

2 The exceptions to this pattern of bipartism were due to temporary incursions by
Mercier's Parti Nationaliste in 1888 and l'Action Libérale Nationale under the joint
leadership of Paul Gouin and Maurice Duplessis in 1935.

3 The Union Nationale had begun to lose popular support as early as the mid-1950s.
From a high of over 50 percent at the height of Duplessis' power, its proportion of
the popular vote had fallen gradually in the late 1950s and 1960s. In the election
of 1966, despite winning power under Daniel Johnson, the party amassed just over
40 percent of the popular vote. In 1970 its proportion of the popular vote plum-
metted to just over 20 percent. Since that time, in seven successive CROP polls, its

support has continuously dropped to its most recent low of only 4 percent in a survey conducted between October, 18 and October, 22, 1973. See *Le Devoir,* le 26 octobre 1973, p. 1.

4 Rudolf Heberle, *Social Movements: An Introduction to Political Sociology* (New York: Appleton Century-Croft, 1951), p. 6.

5 *Ibid.,* pp. 12, 434.

6 K. Lang and G.E. Lang, *Collective Dynamics* (New York: Thomas Y. Crowell, 1961), p. 495.

7 R.J. Jackson and M.B. Stein, *Issues in Comparative Politics: A Text with Readings* (New York and Toronto: St. Martin's Press and Macmillan, 1971), p. 266.

8 This must be understood as the description of a mere tendency. Obviously in some instances measures identified with the left will attract individuals belonging to declining sectors of the population, and programmes of the right will appeal to people belonging to expanding sectors. Moreover some programmes are presented in terms which are sufficiently ambiguous and emotive to attract people from both sectors.

9 For a more detailed discussion of créditiste ideology, see Michael B. Stein, *The Dynamics of Right-Wing Protest: A Political Analysis of Social Credit in Quebec* (Toronto: University of Toronto Press, 1973), chapter 2.

10 *Le Devoir,* le 26 février 1973, quoted in Réjean Pelletier, "Une voie québécoise vers la social-démocratie", *Le Devoir,* le 19 octobre 1973, p. 5.

11 Francois-Pierre Gingras, "Militants, Leaders et Dynamique d'un Mouvement d'Indépendance" (Paper delivered to the Ninth World Congress of the International Political Science Association, Montreal, August 1973), p. 25.

12 This view has since been adopted as party dogma.

13 Réjean Pelletier, "Le Militant du R.I.N. et Son Parti",*Recherches Sociographiques,* XIII, no. 1 (janvier-avril, 1972), p. 68.

14 Lang and Lang, *Collective Dynamics,* p. 495.

15 The ideas in this paragraph are drawn primarily from Eric Hoffer, *The True Believer* (New York: Harper, 1951), chapters I-III, XV; Hadley Cantril, *The Psychology of Social Movements* (New York: Wiley, 1944), chapters 2 and 3; C.W. King, *Social Movements in the United States* (New York: Random House, 1956), p. 72; Neil Smelser, *The Theory of Collective Behavior* (New York: Free Press, 1963), p. 361; and Lewis N. Killian, "Social Movements" in Robert E.L. Faris (ed.), *Handbook of Modern Sociology* (Chicago: Rand McNally, 1964), pp. 441-3.

16 The ideas in this paragraph are drawn from Hoffer, *The True Believer,* chapter XVII; King, *Social Movements,* pp. 72-4; Lang and Lang, *Collective Dynamics,* p. 520; Faris (ed.), *Modern Sociology,* pp. 441-2; and Smelser, *Collective Behaviour,* p. 361.

17 The ideas in this paragraph are adapted from Lang and Lang, *Collective Dynamics,* pp. 359, 518-520.

18 Heberle, *Social Movements,* pp. 118-19.

19 Lang and Lang, *Collective Dynamics,* p. 533; Smelser, *Collective Behaviour,* p. 361; and M. Zald and R. Ash, "Social Movement Organizations: Growth, Decay and Change" in Barry McLaughlin (ed.), *Studies in Social Movements: A Social Psychological Perspective* (New York: Free Press, 1969), p. 478.

20.Lang and Lang, *Collective Dynamics,* p. 533. See also Joseph Nyomarky, *Charisma and Factionalism in the Nazi Party* (Minneapolis: University of Minnesota Press, 1961).

21 The Union des Electeurs did make one further foray into electoral politics after 1949 in the provincial election of 1956. They formed an alliance with the opposition Liberals under Georges Lapalme and ran four of their members under the Liberal banner. All four were soundly defeated by the Union Nationale.

22 In 1962 the Ralliement des Créditistes received 26 percent of the popular vote, and obtained 26 seats; in 1963 they amassed 29 percent of the popular vote but won only 20 seats; in 1965 they captured 19 percent of the popular vote but retained only 9 seats; in 1968 they received 16 percent of the popular vote but increased

the number of their seats to 14. The exception to this downward spiral in popular vote support after 1963 was in the federal election of 1972, in which the Ralliement Créditiste won 24 percent of the popular vote in Quebec and retained 14 seats. Provincially, the Ralliement Créditiste du Quebec first contested an election in 1970, winning about 12 percent of the popular vote and 12 seats.

23 These more ideological militants were probably also among those who showed greater "revolutionary potential" and a greater spirit of involvement (engagement) in the questionnaire conducted by Gingras. See François-Pierre Gingras, "Les Sources du Comportement Indépendantiste: quelques traits du militant" (Paper delivered to the Canadian Political Science Association, Montreal June, 1972), p. 4. They comprised a distinct minority of riniste militants. Only about 6 percent of them were "genuine extremists", in the sense of considering violent means as the most desirable method of "liberating" Quebec. *Ibid.,* p. 2.

24 Gingras, "Militants, Leaders et Dynamique", pp. 26-28.

25 *Ibid.,* p. 15.

26 For a more detailed description of the social background characteristics, attitudes and patterns of participation of the moderate Créditiste leaders, see Stein, *The Dynamics of Right-Wing Protest,* chapters 4-6.

27 For a more detailed discussion of the highly disaffected créditiste leader, see Stein, *The Dynamics of Right-Wing Protest,* chapter 7.

28 This figure has been directly extracted from Stein, *The Dynamics of Right-Wing Protest,* p. 182.

29 Gingras, "Les Sources du Comportement Indépendantiste", pp. 1-6.

30 Pelletier, "Le Militant du R.I.N. et Son Parti", pp. 46-50.

31 Gingras, "Les Sources du Comportement Indépendantiste", p. 11. See also Francois-Pierre Gingras, "De l'Aliénation Politique au Militantisme, un essai de réformulation à parti du cas des indépendantistes" (Paper delivered to the Societé canadienne de science politique, Université d'Ottawa, octobre 1972).

32 See Gingras, "Les Sources du Comportement Indépendantiste", pp. 1-6 and "De l'Aliénation Politique au Militantisme".

33 Pelletier, "Le Militant du R.I.N. et son Parti", pp. 59-60. In his recent article in *Le Devoir* entitled "Une voie québécoise vers la social-démocratie" (le 19 octobre 1973, p. 5), Pelletier showed that, according to a sample of their leaders, an overwhelming proportion (72 percent) of the main effort of the P.Q. is now directed towards elections and the desire to win power. Only about 16 percent of the sample thought that the main effort of the party is directed to the political education of the Québécois. This reflects the change in orientation of the movement in the evolution from the R.I.N. to the P.Q.

34 For a description and definition of these different currents see Pelletier, "Le Militant du R.I.N. et son Parti", pp. 41-42.

35 See Francois-Pierre Gingras, "L'Evolution de l'Idéologie Indépendantiste, 1957-1972" (Paper delivered to the Joint Congress of the Canadian Political Science Association and the Societé canadienne de science politique, Sir George Williams University, Montreal, August 1973). On the deliberate appeal of the P.Q. to all classes see Pelletier, "Une Voie Québécois vers la social-democratie".

36 This concept of a "mature party system" is defined in John M. Wilson, "The Canadian Political Cultures: Reflections on the Problem of National Integration", (Paper delivered to the Joint Congress of the Canadian Political Science Association and la Societé canadienne de science politique, Sir George Williams University, August 1973).

4 Ethnicity: Power, Commitment or Segregation?

Donald G. Baker 109   Ethnicity, Development and Power: Canada in Comparative Perspective

John Goldlust and 132   Factors Associated with Commitment
Anthony Richmond   to and Identification with Canada

Sally M. Weaver 154   Segregation and the Indian Act: The Dialogue of "Equality" vs. "Special Status"

Alexander Matejko 162   Commentary on Section 4

Ethnicity, Development and Power:
Canada in Comparative Perspective

Donald G. Baker

In his preface to the edited collection, *Canadian Society,* Professor Ossenberg suggests that Canadian society "cannot be properly understood unless its similarities to and differences from other societies are compared".[1] He proposes that studies be macroanalytical, historical and comparative, an approach with which Schermerhorn, in *Comparative Ethnic Relations,* concurs. Schermerhorn, however, suggests that initial studies focus on societies with somewhat comparable cultural traditions because, by heightening cultural similarities, differences are accented.[2] It is this approach which Hartz employs in his analysis of fragment cultures.[3]

Canada and the United States are often characterized by the contrasting metaphors of "ethnic mosaic" and "melting pot". But these are deceptive terms; they distort or obscure many of the more fundamental similarities and differences that exist.[4] Comparisons are possible. Although there were earlier comparative studies such as the Carnegie-sponsored series, Lipset's studies of the 1960s prompted more recent analyses.[5] Since then, studies which compare Canada to other countries have also appeared.[6] In this paper ethnicity and culture in Canada are compared with that of two other countries: the United States and South Africa. What can be said comparatively is that all three fall within Hartz's "Anglo fragment tradition",[7] all are within the same category in Schermerhorn's classification scheme,[8] and all three can be analyzed in terms of the plural society theory or model.

The plural society model, used initially to describe developing countries in Africa, Asia and the Caribbean, can be modified and applied to more developed nations such as Canada, the United States and South Africa.[9] Plural society theory focuses on power relationships and the cleavages within a society caused by the presence of diverse cultural, ethnic and racial groups. These cleavages appear most sharply in the forms or types of cultural integration which characterize the society, and in the types and differential rates of incorporation of specific groups within the major structures—political, economic, social—of the society. Plural societies are analyzed "as fields of social, economic, and political power",[10] because group power differentials largely determine the characteristics of cultural integration and structural incorporation which occur.

Plural society theory, like conflict theory, emphasizes the dominant group's power in making these determinations, and both theories provide a basis for comparative analysis.[11] But the emphasis on the dominant group's power does not discount subordinate group power or other factors. Rather, relations are evaluated in terms of the relative power capabilities (whether equal or unequal) of the given actors or groups. Plural society and conflict theory provide a framework within which such variables as development and power can be traced as determinants of the forms which cultural integration and structural incorporation take in Canada, the United States and South Africa. From these comparisons the major characteristics of culture and ethnicity within the three societies emerge.

The emphasis here is on economic development. Political and social development are also significant, but they will be so labelled when they are considered. Power, and particularly the equal or unequal power capabilities of groups, has significantly influenced in the past and continues to influence the types of cultural integration and structural incorporation found within these countries.[12]

Historically, Canada, the U.S. and South Africa were Anglo fragment societies. Either initially or subsequently they were settled and controlled by English settlers who, in conjunction with the British government, held and exercised power. That control provided them with the basis for determining both the types of cultural integration and how other groups would be structurally incorporated. For an extended period of time the English manipulated political and economic institutions to retain power. Their decisions, based on their cultural values, were tempered by two factors: first, the economic imperatives or needs of the society and secondly, the power capabilities of other groups. Circumstances and conditions often changed over time and those changes necessitated reappraisals or modifications of existing group relations, especially when the power capabilities of groups changed. Moreover such changes often necessitated modifications in the patterns of cultural integration and structural incorporation.

The impact—and ramifications—of economic development appear most clearly in the dominant group's relations with three specific groups: non-whites, including indigenous and non-indigenous groups, immigrant white groups, and what emerged as three white siege cultures, namely, French Canadians, white southerners and Afrikaners. Because of their encounters with the dominant groups, these siege groups feared the extinction of their culture or way of life. There are numerous parallels in their defence strategies. Differences in strategies or outcomes are partly attributable to variations in the siege groups' resources and the political structures of the three countries.

Besides power, developmental factors shaped the dominant cultural group's response to the three major groups—the non-whites, immigrant whites, and siege culture. Where changes occurred in the patterns of intergroup relations, they can be traced to developmental factors and alterations in power capabilities. These patterns and changes can be explored in two ways: first, by sketching in the major characteristics of intergroup encounters and relations, and secondly, by comparing ethnicity and culture in Canada, the United States and South Africa.

Within these three plural societies, settler-indigenous encounters very early resulted in settler domination. The French and Dutch originally settled what later became Canada and South Africa, but Britain annexed these countries and English settlers became the dominant cultural group in all three nations. By exercising control, the English largely determined acceptable forms of cultural integration (be that assimilation, pluralism, segmentation or some combination of these) and the types of structural incorporation (including the degree of inclusion/exclusion of various groups within economic, political and social structures). These decisions were based in part on the country's developmental necessities and the power capabilities of the other groups.

Power should be distinguished in two ways: first, as the resources available to a group (including, for example, natural resources, finances, skills, organization, numbers, culture, etc., whether in economic, political, social or military sectors), and secondly, as the given group's ability to mobilize its resources for given ends including contests or confrontations with other groups.[13] Group encounters and relations, whether past or present, constitute power confrontations in which groups mobilize their resources to contest (a) for control of resources and (b) for control of the institutions through which are allocated or reallocated the resources, power and privilege of that society.[14]

Two brief examples illustrate the links between these factors. In pre-Civil War United States rapid northern economic development and the influx of immigrants threatened the existing north-south political/economic power balance. Southerners recognized that northern political supremacy would result in the abolition of the south's slave culture. Fearing cultural extinction, the south defended itself through states' rights appeals, while demanding political structural revisions (for instance, Calhoun's "concurrent majority" proposals) which would preserve north-south political parity. When that strategy failed, the south opted for secession, believing it possessed the requisite resources (military and otherwise) to preserve its way of life should the north prohibit secession.

In the other example the recent rapid economic developments in Canada have exacerbated French-English relations. Development brought external (mostly English-Canadian and U.S.) control of Quebec industry. Likewise the federal government's increasing involvement in welfare, education and other fields has propelled it into areas formerly considered provincial responsibilities. These factors, Quebec maintains, threaten French culture. Fearing for its cultural survival, Quebec defends itself by appeals to provincial rights while proposing political structural revisions (for example, special provincial status) which will re-establish a power parity and protect its way of life.

These examples are simply suggestive, but they illustrate the link between development and power factors as they affect ethnic and cultural groups. The links emerge more clearly when the dominant group's relations with the three groups noted (non-whites, immigrant whites, and the siege cultures) are traced more fully.

Non-white groups

Non-white groups, indigenous and non-indigenous, are present in all three countries. Indigenous group subordination usually resulted from conquest, disruption of their economy and culture or dispossession from their land.[15] Non-indigenous subordination was the consequence of enslavement, indentured status, or the group's entry into the country in a relatively powerless position.

Rarely needed in the nation's economic development, indigenous groups in Canada and the U.S. were shunted aside. Placed on reserves or reservations, they became wards of the state. When seeking employment, those who left the reserves were usually discriminated against on the basis of their color and culture. Settlers, their descendents and white immigrants filled the major labor needs. Where labor shortages occurred, non-whites were imported, usually as slaves, indentured laborers or migrant workers.[16] For example, the south's plantation economy relied upon slavery. When slavery was abolished, techniques such as share-cropping, debt peonage and migrant status were utilized to retain blacks as cheap and powerless labor.[17] In what later became South Africa the Dutch and English utilized indigenous non-whites as well as imported slaves to fill their labor needs. After slavery was abolished in 1834, a head tax was imposed on indigenous non-whites, and they were compelled to work for low wages to pay the tax. Where labor shortages occurred, as on the Natal sugar plantations, indentured East Indians were imported. Later indentured Chinese were brought in, but white opposition forced their repatriation. However the Indians, who had settled much earlier, remained.[18]

Slavery existed in all three countries. There were few slaves in Canada, so the British government's abolition of slavery in 1834 had little impact. But the British action angered the Boers in South Africa. The abolition of slavery combined with the British government's liberal policies toward blacks, threatened the Boer belief in white supremacy and prompted their exodus from the Cape Colony into the hinterlands on what is called the Great Trek. For decades thereafter the Voortrekkers fought with the Bantu-speaking groups with whom they contested for possession of frontier lands. Until British troops defeated the Zulus in 1879, the Boers felt themselves constantly threatened.[19]

In the U.S. slavery proved uneconomical in the northern states and territories, and it had disappeared in those areas by 1800. Even so, blacks in the north were discriminated against; their rights were circumscribed and in some states and territories laws prohibited their entry.[20] But slavery was fundamental to the economy of the south, and whites justified it by referring to the Bible and to the black man's supposed inferiority.[21] When granted their freedom by the Civil War and enfranchised during Reconstruction, blacks participated widely in the political system. But southern white antipathies persisted. Following the withdrawal of northern troops in 1877, white fears of increasing black political and economic power prompted new efforts, legal and otherwise, to disfranchise them and curtail black power.[22] By early 1900 racist sentiments in both the south *and* the north effectively blocked black efforts at improving their position in society. Northern whites who had previously supported the blacks now felt threatened as blacks migrated north and competed for jobs.[23]

In South Africa non-indigenous non-whites (initially, slaves from West and East Africa, later, East Indians and Chinese, and, more recently, migrant black labor from other African nations) were utilized to alleviate labor shortages.[24] A similar policy was followed in Canada and the United States. Where the supply of white European immigrants proved inadequate, as it did in the west for railroad building, mining and other industries, Asians, including Chinese and later Japanese, were imported. Paid lower wages than whites, the Asians threatened white labor, and strife resulted. Consequently both countries enacted legislation excluding further Chinese entry. The Japanese were not excluded by that legislation, and their later entry prompted similar strife. At that time both Canadian and U.S. governments established "gentlemen's agreements" with Japan, whereby Japan agreed to restrict the emigration of its citizens to North America.[25] But latent antipathies persisted toward Asians, particularly the Japanese. With the outbreak of World War II and under the guise of national security, both foreign and American-born Japanese were removed from the west coast, incarcerated in concentration camps or settled in the interior of Canada and the U.S.[26] Although changes have occurred since World War II, discriminatory treatment of non-whites persists in the two countries. Institutional racism is clearly indicated in the low rates of structural incorporation of non-whites, a rate (especially in economic and political institutions) much lower than that for immigrant whites or the dominant cultural groups.[27]

In South Africa the 1948 Afrikaner electoral victory marked a sharp change in the relations between whites and non-whites. The gradual incorporation of non-whites into the political structure was terminated as Afrikaners warned that continuation would lead to a black political majority and ultimate black rule. Apartheid, the policy of separate development, was imposed. Blacks were classified as migrants who possessed no political rights within the white state. Rather, their homeland was the bantustan, the reserves or internal colonies, which, while granted a limited degree of political autonomy, nevertheless remained under white control.[28] Within the white economic structure blacks hold low level positions: the higher positions, whether in mining or industry, are reserved for whites. After the Afrikaner victory, political, economic and social restrictions were also imposed on other non-white groups, including Indians and coloureds. Thus to maintain political power and preserve a culture based on white supremacy, the Afrikaners established a segmented society. They have removed the non-white from the political structure, locked him into the lower levels of the economic structure, excluded him from the white social structure and thereby developed a modernized system of racial domination.[29]

Historically, whites have regarded themselves as superior to non-whites in each of the three countries. Their greater command over resources and technology combined with organizational skills and cultural attitudes that condoned domination of non-whites has contributed to the perpetuation of white dominance systems.[30] Power and dominance came to be seen as a confirmation of white superiority. Although cultural differences and other factors originally contributed to this belief, the color factor subsequently has emerged as the basis for distinguishing superior from inferior.[31] When needed for economic development, non-whites have been utilized. Non-whites who have acquired white skills and behavioral patterns have been incorporated more readily into lower levels within the economic structures, but the acquisition of white culture and behavior has not provided entry into white social structures. Rather, non-whites remain segmented. They are considered "outsiders", a separate and inferior segment of the society.[32]

Immigrant whites

The types of cultural integration and structural incorporation of white immigrants in Canada, the United States and South Africa have been determined usually by three factors: (a) the historical period in which the immigrants settled, (b) the extent to which society needed them for economic development, and (c) their power (actual or potential), based on available resources and their mobilization of those resources.

Cultural integration usually assumes one of three forms, and it is the dominant cultural group which determines the form (or forms) allowed in the society. In the process of cultural assimilation the dominant group assumes the superiority of its own culture, and other groups are expected to discard their cultures for that of the dominant group. Where there is cultural pluralism, the dominant group accepts that the cultures of the other groups are of equal worth, and these groups are allowed to retain their cultures. Thus a society can be culturally heterogenous even though its thrust is toward assimilation. In a segmented society the dominant group considers other groups inferior on the basis of color or other attributes. Even though these groups discard their cultures for that of the dominant group, they are still regarded as inferior because of other (usually physical) factors. Anglo societies, for example, are segmented societies in which non-whites are considered inferior "outsiders".[33] The dominant group utilizes its power to determine how and to what extent the other groups will be incorporated within the economic, political and social structures.[34]

Assimilation was not the only type of cultural integration in the early years of United States: there was cultural heterogeneity. But the post-Civil War industrializing society needed assimilated workers who could be readily incorporated into the lower levels of economic structures. Before this time, particularly in rural areas, cultural pluralism prevailed: Germans and other European groups retained their cultures and languages.[35] But assimilationist pressures existed and gathered momentum with industrialization and the influx of southern European immigrants. Nativists, fearing the "contamination" of their culture, demanded the Americanization of immigrants. Americanization programmes were established; English was the exclusive language of the schools; and pressures intensified for conformity to Anglo cultural and behavioral norms. Industry supported this effort: it needed workers who spoke English and accepted the Anglo work ethic. There was also a political motive. Fearing the loss of political power to newer immigrant groups, Anglos saw their culture endangered unless immigrant groups were rapidly assimilated. It was assumed that anglicized immigrants, when given the vote, would uphold the dominant Anglo culture.[36] The myth of the United States as a "new nation" also contributed to assimilationist pressures. Viewing itself as born in revolution and free from European corruptions, American society feared possible "contamination", whether by culturally different European groups or by radical European political ideas such as Marxism.[37] Thus, even though the society welcomed (indeed, encouraged) the immigrants needed for industrial development, it feared their corrupting influence unless they were hurriedly purified—that is, Americanized.

The degree of assimilation of an immigrant group determined its rate of structural incorporation. Whether willingly or under duress, those who more readily assimilated were more rapidly incorporated and granted opportunities within economic, political and social structures. Rates of incorporation varied; the door to economic incorporation was usually opened before those leading to political and social institutions. The melting pot was clearly an anglicized vat, and the immigrant who immersed and melted most rapidly emerged a new man, an American. Assimilation was clearly the prerequisite for access to the American Dream of economic success.[38]

South Africa and Canada had difficulties in recruiting immigrants. More immigrants headed to Canada than South Africa, but many of them considered Canada simply a stepping stone before moving to the United States. Although British annexation terminated any future Dutch immigration from Europe, the Dutch (later known as Boers, then Afrikaners) remained the majority white population, their birth rate easily offsetting the limited English immigrants. But Britain retained political control over the colony: the dominant culture was Anglo and the English controlled economic, political and social structures. Later immigrants, mostly English, were assimilated into the Anglo culture and structures.[39] However, after the 1948 Afrikaner electoral victory, and especially following South Africa's break from the Commonwealth, non-Anglo white immigrants increasingly assimilated into Afrikaner and Anglo cultures, depending partly on where they settled in South Africa. Those settling in urban areas were more readily assimilated and incorporated into the Anglo economic system, but increasing pressures are being exerted to Afrikanerize more recent immigrants.[40]

South Africa's cultural pluralism, like that of Canada, results from the presence of two distinct white cultural or ethnic groups. Historically, non-whites were segmented, and major tensions in both countries arose from clashes between the two white groups over cultural, political and economic differences.[41] In contrast, in what later became the United States, colonial society witnessed the gradual assimilation and incorporation into Anglo society of Dutch, French and other groups. There was some cultural heterogeneity, and other language and culture groups did persist for a while, but, as Crevecoer noted, assimilationist forces were pervasive. Canada's ethnic mosaic metaphor is partly myth. As recent studies indicate, numerous forces (particularly within the economic structure) pressure for cultural assimilation.[42] The presence of English and French groups has contributed to the mosaic myth. Their recent confrontations refurbish the myth and, simultaneously, encourage the development of cultural pluralism. Nevertheless, when viewed historically, it becomes clear that Anglo society wanted assimilation. It denigrated French culture and envisioned the ultimate anglicization of the French. But the latter's stubborn resistance to assimilationist thrusts prevented that, and within the fortress of Quebec the French were able to avoid contact with the Anglo melting pot.[43]

Other factors have contributed to Canada's cultural heterogeneity. As previously noted, the country desperately needed immigrants. To prevent its settlers from moving to the U.S., Canada embraced cultural pluralism, warning immigrants they would be forced to assimilate and shed their identities in the United States. Canada encouraged groups to retain their cultural identities, and many did, including the Ukrainians, Slavs, Doukhobors and the Hutterites. Most of these groups settled in rural areas in the western provinces. There was little need for their assimilation, but on occasion even they were pressured to change their values and culture.[44] In contrast, most of the immigrants settling in the U.S. in this period (the late nineteenth and early twentieth centuries) remained in the cities. They joined the industrial work force and found advancement easier if they assimilated. The experience of the immigrants who settled in Canada after World War II presents a closer parallel with the United States. Most settled in, or subsequently moved to urban areas and, despite the persistence of ethnic enclaves and the government's support of ethnic pluralism, immigrant groups which assimilated found readier access to Anglo-dominated economic structures. Recent immigrant groups usually retain their own social structures, but they believe that at least a degree of language and cultural assimilation leads to greater economic opportunities.[45]

As plural societies, Canada and South Africa have more sharply-differentiated cultural and ethnic groups than does the United States. This is also reflected in economic, political and social structures. In all three societies industrialization, with its demands for uniformity, has been, and remains a compelling force behind cultural conformity, and it is most readily evident in pressures exerted upon white immigrant groups.[46]

Siege cultures

In each of the countries a siege culture—respectively, French Canadian, white southerner, Afrikaner—has emerged. The dominant culture, wanting assimilation and economic development, used its power to accomplish those ends. In the process it threatened the cultural survival of the siege group. Fearing cultural extinction and deprived its full share of the society's benefits, the siege group mobilized its resources and pursued strategies which took into consideration its own and its opponent's power capabilities. Usually the defensive response of the siege culture was prompted by conflict, conquest or economic development which threatened its survival. In Canada and South Africa, for example, the attitudes of English settlers and the British government prompted the French and Dutch to feel threatened, and in the U.S., northern behavior similarly solidified the south.

The English were viewed as interlopers, while the French and Dutch, having originally settled Canada and South Africa, viewed themselves as legitimate possessors of the land. To preserve their way of life, they isolated themselves, turning to the land for sustenance and security, the French in Quebec and the Boers in the hinterlands.[47] But the British retained control, and circumstances determined the degree to which that control was exercised. White southerners, too, viewed theirs as the legitimate culture and felt threatened by increasing northern economic domination, abolitionist efforts to terminate slavery and shifts in north-south political power.[48] Survival was the fundamental concern of all three groups. To them, the dominant culture, with its emphasis on business, industry and democracy, was an anathema. For the siege cultures, agrarianism as a way of life was their salvation; agrarian society provided security from the contaminating beliefs and culture of the dominant group.[49] But agrarianism had another and not fully recognized consequence: it isolated the siege culture from the economic sector, and, with the advent of industrialism, the dominant culture preempted control of economic structures and development. Consequently siege cultures, similar to indigenous non-white groups on reserves, became more and more dependent on the dominant culture.[50]

The components of a group culture include a common language, values, history, social system and symbols which serve as a binding force. Originally southerners did not consider theirs a separate culture. It was forged from those factors and events previously noted, including an economy based on slavery, northern opposition to slavery, increasing northern domination of the south's economy, and the rapid northern population increase which clearly indicated eventual northern political hegemony. Because of these threats to its way of life, the south became defensive. And when its view of states' rights was rejected, the south demanded a political restructuring (Calhoun's concurrent majority) whereby political parity with the north could be re-established.[51] When those efforts failed, the south, fearing cultural extinction, opted for secession, even risking war. Defeat brought the termination of slavery, but it also solidified the southerners' white supremacy ideology. Thus the war and its aftermath (as, later, with the Boers) forged an ideology based on agrarianism and white supremacy.[52]

Even though blacks were accorded political rights, those rights were tenuous and depended on the presence of northern troops during Reconstruction. The withdrawal of those troops did not result in immediate disfranchisement. But, as blacks mobilized their resources for economic and political gains, the white south, its power threatened, counterattacked, and both legal (Jim Crow laws) and illegal (terrorism) measures were implemented to re-establish white supremacy.[53] The north's role in this was significant. Totally immersed in industrial development, it ignored the black man's plight. Moreover, northern attitudes were changing. As blacks moved north seeking work, they competed with white labor causing white prejudices and racial conflicts to surface. Southern efforts to convince northerners of the black man's inferiority found increasing support. By World War I, notions of Anglo-Saxon and white superiority were widely held in both north and south,[54] and even the federal government, reflecting this new attitude, moved to curtail the black man's rights and opportunities.

In the meantime the south discovered yet another means for assuring white supremacy. By maintaining a one-part system, the south assured the re-election of a senior congressman. Through his seniority, the south controlled the chairmanships of major congressional committees and prevented consideration of federal legislation which threatened white control. Although defeated in war, the south shifted strategies and, by manipulating the political structures, succeeded in keeping black people subordinate. Only in the 1960s, prodded by the civil rights movement and black mobilization efforts, were major efforts undertaken to protect the black man's rights. However, with its partial control of political structures, the white south has preserved the major vestiges of white supremacy.

Agrarianism and white supremacy were also fundamental tenets of the Boer/Afrikaner siege culture. The British, who had temporarily annexed the Cape Colony during the Napoleonic wars, annexed it permanently in 1806. Like the French settlers in Canada, the Dutch settlers were separated from their mother country. The Boers, most of whom were farmers, were considered culturally inferior by the British. British missionary and liberal thought held that native groups should be considered equal to whites before the law. These notions shocked the Boers and prompted an easily-suppressed Boer rebellion in 1815. The British government's abolition of slavery in 1834 further alienated the Boers, promoting the trek inland in 1836 to escape British rule. British policy toward the Boers vacillated. Often they were ignored. But when their frontier movements prompted African-Boer clashes, British troops intervened and Britain reasserted its control.[55]

Britain's efforts to control the Boers prompted the two Boer wars of 1880-1881 and 1899-1902. Successful in the first, the Boers in the Transvaal temporarily were accorded independence. But gold discoveries changed that. Prospectors and adventurers from the United States and the British empire converged on the Transvaal. They demanded political rights and, when the Boers rejected their demands, these *uitlanders* asked the British government to intervene. Angered at British pressures and fearing for their cultural survival, the Boers declared war. There was certainly some basis for Boer fears. Earlier Sir Alfred Milner, the British High Commissioner to South Africa, had suggested that, to resolve the British-Boer clashes, Britain should "break the dominion of Afrikanerdom" and anglicize the Boers, a view reminiscent of Lord Durham's solution to French-English tensions in Canada.[56]

The British-Boer War, like the American Civil War, left deep scars, but it did unify the Afrikaners. Although defeated, they readily agreed to later British proposals to establish a unitary state made up of the former Boer and British colonies. Under such a union the Boers, who were the majority white population, ultimately would hold power even though in the interim they would be under an English-Boer coalition government. Concerned primarily with South Africa's economic development, Britain acceded to Boer wishes, including limitations on indigenous rights. Britain believed that Boers would be anglicized and that English immigration would result in an Anglo majority. But after the union of 1909, Britain did little to encourage immigration, and the Boers remained the majority white group.[57]

The British retained limited control over "native affairs", and the British parliament could reject that legislation which it considered unconstitutional. Anglo-Afrikaner political coalitions ruled for most of the period until 1948, when the Afrikaners, capitalizing on mounting racial fears, captured control of the government without English support. Two factors had intensified Afrikaner antipathies toward the English. The first was the racial issue. The Afrikaners feared the English plan to incorporate blacks (to a limited degree) in the political structure because it threatened eventual black control. The second issue concerned South Africa's support of Britain in two world wars, a step opposed by many Afrikaners but supported by English South Africans and the British government. These factors influenced the 1948 election and, later, the British government's criticisms of Afrikaner racial policies prompted South Africa's withdrawal from the Commonwealth in 1961.[58]

Since 1948 the Afrikaner government has utilized its political power to restructure the political system so that white racial domination is secure.[59] Agrarianism remains a basic component of Afrikaner culture, but increasingly Afrikaners are moving into the economic structures controlled by the English. Although in South Africa the siege culture lost the war, because of its majority in the white political structure it eventually achieved absolute political power. In the United States white southerners also lost the war. While they eventually gained control of the political structure in the south, at the federal level they were a minority and had to modify the political system to fit their own ends. Both siege cultures survived by using tactics which modified the political structure of their country and reflected their power capabilities.

French Canada evolved into a siege culture after 1763. Canada's history is marked by English-French rivalry. The "quiet revolution" of the 1960s is the most recent manifestation, as French Canada's attempts to defend its cultural/ethnic identity from Anglo and American domination and assimilation.

While most upper-class French Canadians fled to France with the British takeover, some 70,000 settlers stayed. In the 1774 Quebec Act and in subsequent measures, the British government allowed the French to retain their language, laws and religion. But other measures of that government and the actions of Anglo settlers clearly indicated to French settlers that they were expected to assimilate the English language and culture. Although prior to Confederation the French exercized a degree of autonomy in Lower Canada, English-French tensions prompted the 1837 Rebellion. Evaluating the conflict, Lord Durham recognized that cultural/ethnic differences were the basic cause, and he proposed elimination of French culture and language. Assimilation, he concluded, was the only means for resolving the ethnic tensions. In defense the French turned to the land and to agrarianism as a means of preserving their way of life.[60]

Confederation brought the two groups into closer contact, and political parties thereafter usually had French and English branches. Nevertheless subsequent events prompted French fears. Most significant in creating tensions were the execution of Louis Riel, the abolition of the French language in Ontario and Manitoba schools, French opposition to Canada's support of Britain during the Boer War and the conscription crises of the two world wars.[61] While it was nineteenth-century industrialization and immigration that caused assimilationist demands in the U.S., in Canada it was intensifying Anglo-Saxonism that created a demand for a "Canadian nationality which . . . would be English."[62] This prompted French nationalism, for "its survival openly threatened, French Canada resorted to every defensive mechanism at its disposal".[63] That defensiveness led to continued agrarianism and increasing isolation of French Canadians in Quebec and to a nationalism which, by the 1920s, espoused a Laurentian Republic and became the precursor for more recent separatist movements.

Even though it proclaimed itself an ethnic mosaic, Canada remained Anglo controlled in terms of economic, political and social structures. Immigrants seeking access to economic opportunities quickly recognized the necessity for acquiring the English language and culture. Those who refused to be assimilated found their economic opportunities blocked. This pattern continued as English- and U.S.-controlled industries moved into Quebec. French Canadians who spoke English and acquired accepted Anglo values and behavior were more readily incorporated into those industrial and business enterprises.[64] French recognition of this subtle assimilation and the concern over external control of Quebec industry intensified French apprehensions for their cultural survival. Increasingly, French control over industry and education is seen as the only means of preserving that culture. But Quebec's desire to shape its own destiny brings it into conflict with the federal government over the control of welfare measures, taxation policies and other programmes. The issue of federal vs. provincial rights represents one level of the conflict, but the clashes have prompted even more fundamental proposals for political restructuring, proposals ranging from granting Quebec special status to the establishment of a separate Quebec nation.[65]

Thus in Canada, the United States and South Africa the siege cultures have adopted diverse strategies to preserve their culture, their strategies shaped by different political structures and power differentials. In the U.S. and South Africa the siege groups were led into war when their cultural survival was threatened. Although both were defeated, both emerged more unified. They regrouped their resources, modified strategies to fit new circumstances and rallied to preserve their cultural identity. Somewhat comparable ethnic/cultural tensions have beset Canada throughout its history, and its present problems represent but another stage in which two disparate ethnic groups attempt to resolve their differences. What emerges in all three cases is the significance of economic development and group power differentials as determinants of ethnic and cultural nationalism. Ethnicity and culture are shaped by the dominant cultural group's assimilative efforts and the manner and degree to which it incorporates other ethnic/cultural/racial groups in the society's economic, political and social structures. Based on the preceding brief appraisal of the dominant group's relations with the three groups noted (non-whites, immigrant whites and siege cultures), it is possible to assess the relationship of ethnicity, development and power within these three countries.

Ethnicity and culture in Canada, the United States and South Africa have been shaped essentially by two factors—power and economic development. Power can be evaluated relationally, in terms of group power capabilities, whether equal or unequal and structurally, in terms of the control which a given group exerts over the major structures (economic, political, social) of the society. In the former instance a group's power is determined by its resources and its ability to mobilize those resources for given ends. In the latter case a group's power capabilities are measured by the extent of its control over society's structures.

This control is demonstrated in the group's ability (or inability) to influence and determine decisions, particularly at two levels: (a) in the allocation (or reallocation) of the society's resources, privileges and power and (b) in the determination of the character and types of cultural integration and structural incorporation within society. It is therefore possible to appraise group power capabilities and to observe the transformations in group power capabilities and relationships. It is these power capabilities, whether shifting or constant, which account for system maintenance or system change.

Economic development is also a crucial variable; economic transformations can radically alter or strengthen the resources and mobilization abilities of groups. When development alters group power capabilities, system change may occur. However, if dominant group power is pervasive, that group may be able to structure changes to solidify or support its domination. Although the dominant group may even grant concessions to a subordinate group, such concessions may do little to enhance either the resources or mobilization capabilities of that latter group. South Africa illustrates this. While granting minor concessions, the Afrikaners have managed to modernize racial domination by utilizing industrialization to strengthen their control over other groups.[66] But developmental forces can, despite the continuation of dominant group power, activate a new awareness or consciousness within a subordinate group, which may, in turn, generate new subordinate group mobilization efforts. This happened with the siege cultures, and it is presently occurring among other groups, including Africans in South Africa, Amerindians in Canada and the U.S., and blacks, Mexican-Americans and Puerto Ricans in the United States. Activation prompts these groups to seek and develop new resources for confronting dominant group power. For example, recent confrontations in Canada and the U.S. have strengthened the resources of non-white groups, and despite government efforts to curtail their mobilization activities, Africans in South Africa are also achieving some success in recent confrontations. In South Africa leaders of some bantustans have challenged the Afrikaner government, and recent black labour strikes in industry and the mines have prompted salary increases. Although this is a minor concession, it is a step toward intensified African mobilization efforts.

Some generalizations can be made with regard to cultural integration and structural incorporation within these three countries. These generalizations focus primarily on power and development as determinants of culture and ethnicity. Evident in all three countries is a white ethnocentricity that is exclusive in character. Non-whites are considered to be "outsiders" and inferiors. Whenever possible non-white groups are isolated or segmented from the white society. They may acquire white culture, but their color precludes cultural assimilation. In terms of their society's structure they are usually excluded from white social institutions, including white social classes. The lines of division are sharpest in South Africa, but in Canada and the United States segregated schools and living areas, group pressures (and legislation) against interracial marriage, and other discriminatory practices excluding non-whites from white social life clearly indicate white society's desire to maintain control.

Fearing black power, Afrikaners have barred non-whites from the political structure. Similarily, in the U.S. and Canada non-whites, although accorded political rights, have not been encouraged to participate. Indeed, when non-white political mobilization activities have threatened white power, as in the post-Civil War south or more recently at the national level in the United States, whites have mobilized to "keep the black man in his place". In both North American countries other devices and tactics have been employed to exclude or limit the Amerindian's participation in the political system.

When needed, all three countries have utilized non-white labor, but all have taken care to limit the integration of this sector of the labour force. White society has established reserves, bantustans and ghettos, all of which serve as massive pools of unskilled labor. But with industrialization and automation the need for a supply of unskilled labor has decreased. As a consequence non-whites are classified as "redundant"—they are no longer needed by the society. Even when they are incorporated into the economic structure, non-whites usually encounter job restrictions (whether sanctioned by law or custom) which protect whites from competition with non-whites. This practice is most evident in South Africa, but low incorporation rates of non-whites within the economic structures in the two North American countries clearly indicate that discriminatory practices are pervasive. Thus, neither fully assimilated nor incorporated, the fate of non-whites is largely in the hands of white society. Historically, they have lacked the necessary resources or power to demand equal treatment or opportunity. Recent mobilization efforts have strengthened the position of non-whites in Canada and the U.S., and in South Africa the Africans are discovering the bantustan as a vehicle for resource mobilization.[67]

The nature of this exclusive ethnocentricity is also reflected in the dominant cultural groups' response to immigrant whites. The history of each of the countries studied shows that the dominant group wanted assimilation, for it considered immigrant group cultures inferior to its own. Unlike non-whites, immigrant whites could gain structural incorporation if they renounced their own for the dominant culture. The various immigrant groups were not incorporated at the same rate, and social incorporation generally came later than economic or political incorporation. Assimilationist pressures varied in the three countries, and it was these pressures, not the dominant groups' attitudes toward cultural integration, which accounted for the somewhat divergent forms of cultural integration evident in the three societies.

Dominant group and siege culture relations reaffirm the preceding conclusions. Their cultural survival threatened by the dominant groups' assimilationist thrust, the siege groups mobilized resources, accepted agrarianism and geographical isolation as a means of defense and ignored economic developments. This assured the dominant groups' control of economic structures, and, as a consequence, the siege groups found themselves in a position of economic dependency. Geographically isolated and economically dependent, the siege groups came to assume a position somewhat comparable to that of the non-whites on reservations, bantustans or in ghettos. They became internal colonies within the larger society.[68] In contrast to non-whites and immigrants, the siege cultures possessed numerous resources generally unavailable to non-white groups. They were able to mobilize these resources, thereby strengthening their power position vis-à-vis the dominant cultural group. For example, in South Africa the Afrikaners' mobilization efforts were translated into eventual political control; the white southerner tempered northern power and preserved the major manifestations of white supremacy through political maneuvering; and French Canadians, presently mobilizing their resources, contest, confront and struggle to assure cultural survival.

Given their political control, the Afrikaners have manipulated economic development to support racial domination. But industrialization is prompting somewhat different, and often quite opposite responses in the southern states and in Quebec. In the former industrialization slowly erodes the siege culture and incorporates (though at distinctly different rates) both white and black into the economic structure. This has been advantageous to blacks; increased opportunities have enhanced their resources and assisted in their mobilization efforts. As a result, the white southerner is forced to recognize the reality of emergent black power, a factor which tempers and diminishes white power in some areas of the south. However in Quebec development and external control have intensified nationalist feelings. Increasingly French-English confrontations over economic and political issues parallel (except for the slave issue) the pre-Civil War north-south dialogue.

In all three countries group power capabilities and development needs have determined the character of ethnicity and culture. South Africa remains a segmented society, and intensifying Afrikanerization suggests that the English culture will begin to assume the characteristics of a siege culture. Both Canada and the United States remain segmented societies, too, but gradual changes leading to non-white incorporation suggest that those societies will become increasingly plural. The three countries represent variants of the plural society model, and in all three the major determinants of culture and ethnicity have been power and developmental factors.

Donald G. Baker is a professor of Political Science at Southampton College, Long Island University.

NOTES

1 Richard Ossenberg (ed.), *Canadian Society: Pluralism, Change and Conflict* (Scarborough: Prentice-Hall, 1971), iv.

2 R.A. Schermerhorn, *Comparative Ethnic Relations* (New York: Random House, 1970), chapters v-vi.

3 Louis Hartz, et al., *The Founding of New Societies* (New York: Harcourt, Brace and World, 1964). There are reservations to Hartz's approach. See, for example, Gad Horowitz, "Conservatism, Liberalism and Socialism in Canada", *Canadian Journal of Economics and Political Science,* XXXII (May, 1966).

4 Allan Smith, "Metaphor and Nationality in North America", *Canadian Historical Review,* LI (September, 1970), pp 247-49.

5 The earlier studies of the 1930s and 1940s, sponsored by the Carnegie Foundation, are appraised in Carl Berger, "Comments on the Carnegie Series" in Richard Preston (ed.), *The Influence of the United States on Canadian Development* (Durham: Duke University Press, 1972). See Seymour Lipset, "Canada and the United States:

A Comparative View", *Canadian Review of Sociology and Anthropology,* I (November, 1964) and *The First New Nation* (New York: Basic Books, 1963). Illustrative of the later studies are: Marian McKenna, "The Melting Pot: Comparative Observations in the United States and Canada", *Sociology and Social Research,* LIII (July, 1969); and Erwin Hargrove, "On Canadian and American Culture", *Canadian Journal of Economics and Political Science,* XXXIII (February, 1967).

6 See, for example, Henry Albinski, *Canadian and Australian Politics in Comparative Perspective* (New York: Oxford University Press, 1973); and J.O.N. Perkins (ed.), *Macro-Economic Policy: A Comparative Study of Australia, Canada, New Zealand, South Africa* (Toronto: University of Toronto Press, 1973).

7 Hartz, *New Societies,* chapters i, vi-vii.

8 Schermerhorn, *Ethnic Relations,* chapter v.

9 Ira Katznelson, "Comparative Studies of Race and Ethnicity", *Comparative Politics,* V (October, 1972); John Rex, "The Plural Society: The South African Case", *Race,* XI (April, 1971). See also, Pierre van den Berghe, *Race and Ethnicity: Essays in Comparative Sociology* (New York: Basic Books, 1970) and Oliver Cox, "The Question of Pluralism", *Race,* XII (April, 1971). Originally proposed by J.S. Furnivall, the plural society model was subsequently developed by M.G. Smith in *The Plural Society of the British West Indies* (Berkeley: University of California Press, 1965). Its most recent application and modification can be found in the articles by him and by Leo Kuper in Kuper and Smith (eds.), *Pluralism in Africa* (Berkeley: University of California Press, 1969).

10 Katznelson, *Comparative Politics,* V, p. 143.

11 See *ibid.*; Schermerhorn, *Ethnic Relations,* chapter i; and Gerhard Lenski, *Power and Privilege* (New York: McGraw-Hill, 1966), chapters i-iv.

12 On developmental aspects, see Cynthia Enloe, *Ethnic Conflict and Political Development* (Boston: Little, Brown, 1973); on power and development, Schermerhorn, *Ethnic Relations,* chapters iv-v, and Lenski, *Power and Priviledge,* chapters ii-iv. Milton Gordon, in *Assimilation in American Life* (New York: Oxford University Press, 1964), chapter iii, distinguishes between cultural (behavioral) and structural assimilation. The terms are confusing, for assimilation is but one form of cultural integration. For example, the dominant group may demand that other groups discard their culture and accept the dominant group culture (assimilation), may accept the presence of other cultures as equals (pluralism), or may reject other cultural groups as being of less worth (segmentation) and dominate them as superiors. In terms of plural society analysis the term structural incorporation, rather than structural assimilation, more clearly distinguishes how and to what extent various groups are incorporated into the dominant group's economic, political and social structures, or whether they retain their own structures willingly (pluralist) or as a consequence of being outsiders (segmented). One can analyze the differential rates of incorporation of specific groups within dominant group structures.

13 Katznelson, *Comparative Politics,* V, pp. 145-46; Hubert Blalock, Jr., *Towards a Theory of Minority-Group Relations* (New York: Capricorn, 1967), chapter iv; James S. Coleman, *Resources for Social Change: Race in the United States* (New York: Wiley, 1971); Schermerhorn, *Ethnic Relations,* chapter vii; and Enloe, *Ethnic Conflict.*

14 Lenski, *Power and Priviledge,* chapters iii-iv; Schermerhorn, *Ethnic Relations,* pp. 39-48; Philip Mason, *Patterns of Dominance* (New York: Oxford University Press, 1970). Amos Hawley in "Community Power and Urban Renewal Success", *American Journal of Sociology,* LXVIII (January, 1963), p. 422, clearly describes the ramifications of power: "Every social act is an exercize of power, every social relationship is a power equation, and every social group or system is an organization of power."

15 A. Grenfell Price, *White Settlers and Native Peoples* (Westport: Greenwood Press, 1972); Melbourne: Georgian House, 1950); E. Franklin Frazier, *Race and Culture Contacts in the Modern World* (Boston: Beacon Press, 1957); E. Palmer Patterson II, *The Canadian Indian* (Don Mills: Collier-Macmillan, 1972); Peter Cumming and Neil Mickenberg (eds.), *Native Rights in Canada,* 2d ed. (Toronto: Indian-Eskimo Association, 1972), part IV; Harold Fey and D'Arcy McNickle, *Indians and Other*

Americans (New York: Harper and Row, 1970); George Ellis, *The Red Man and the White Man in North America* (Boston: Little, Brown, 1882); William MacLeod, *The American Indian Frontier* (New York: Knopf, 1928); C.T. Loram and T.F. McIlwraith (eds.), *The North American Indian Today* (Toronto: University of Toronto Press, 1943); G.H.L. LeMay, *Black and White in South Africa* (New York: American Heritage Press, 1971); Pierre van den Berghe, *South Africa: A Study in Conflict* (Berkeley: University of California Press, 1970); and Monica Wilson and Leonard Thompson (eds.), *The Oxford History of South Africa* (Oxford: Clarendon Press, 1969-1971).

16 Price, *White Settlers and Native People,* chapters i, iv; Frazier, *Race and Culture Contacts,* chapters v-viii; David B. Davis, *The Problem of Slavery in Western Culture* (Ithaca: Cornell University Press, 1966), part II; Kenneth Stampp, *The Peculiar Institution* (New York: Vintage, 1956); Eugene Genovese, *The Political Economy of Slavery* (New York: Vintage, 1965) and *The World the Slaveholders Made* (New York: Vintage, 1969); Robin Winks, *The Blacks in Canada* (New Haven: Yale University Press, 1971); van den Berghe, *Race and Ethnicity*; Charles Young and Helen Reid, *The Japanese Canadians* (Toronto: University of Toronto Press, 1939); Forrest LaViolette, *Americans of Japanese Ancestry* (Toronto: Canadian Institute of International Affairs, 1945); Roger Daniels, *The Politics of Prejudice* (New York: Atheneum, 1970); S.W. Kung, *Chinese in American Life* (Seattle: University of Washington Press, 1962); and Gunther Barth, *Bitter Strength: A History of the Chinese in the United States, 1850-1870* (Cambridge: Harvard University Press, 1964).

17 W.E.B. DuBois, *Black Reconstruction in America, 1860-1880* (Cleveland: World Publishing, 1964); Rayford Logan, *The Betrayal of the Negro* (New York: Collier-Macmillan, 1965), part I; C.Vann Woodward, *Origins of the New South, 1877-1925* (Baton Rouge: Lousiana State University Press, 1951).

18 van den Berghe, *South Africa*; H.J. and R.E. Simons, *Class and Colour in South Africa, 1850-1950* (London: Penguin, 1969).

19 Wilson and Thompson (eds.), *South Africa*; Eric Walker, *The Frontier Tradition in South Africa* (London: Oxford University Press, 1930).

20 Eugene Berwanger, *The Frontier Against Slavery: Western Anti-Negro Prejudice and the Slavery Extension Controversy* (Urbana: University of Illinois Press, 1967); V. Jacque Voegeli, *Free But Not Equal: The Midwest and the Negro During the Civil War* (Chicago: University of Chicago Press, 1967), chapters i-iii; and Leon Litwack, *North of Slavery: The Negro in the Free States, 1790-1860* (Chicago: University of Chicago Press, 1961).

21 Genovese, *The World the Slaveholders Made*; Thomas Gossett, *Race: The History of an Idea in America* (New York: Schocken, 1965), chapters i-iv; Stampp, *The Peculiar Institution*; Winthrop Jordan, *White Over Black: American Attitudes Toward the Negro, 1550-1812* (Baltimore: Penguin, 1969), parts iv-v.

22 C. Vann Woodward, *The Strange Career of Jim Crow* (New York: Oxford University Press, 1966).

23 Logan, *The Betrayal of the Negro,* parts ii-iii; Allen Trelease, *White Terror: The Ku Klux Klan Conspiracy and Southern Reconstruction* (New York: Harper and Row, 1971); Forrest Wood, *Black Scare: The Racist Response to Emancipation and Reconstruction* (Berkeley: University of California Press, 1968); John Haller, Jr., *Outcasts from Evolution* (Urbana: University of Illinois Press, 1971); George Fredrickson, *The Black Image in the White Mind: The Debate on Afro-American Character and Destiny, 1817-1914* (New York: Harper and Row, 1971); and I.A. Newby, *Jim Crow's Defense: Anti-Negro Thought in America, 1900-1930* (Baton Rouge: Louisiana State University Press, 1965).

24 van den Berghe, *South Africa*; Heribert Adam, *Modernizing Racial Domination* (Berkeley: University of California Press, 1971), chapter ii; and Francis Wilson, *Migrant Labour in South Africa* (Johannesburg: SPRO-CAS, 1972).

25 Charles Price, " 'White' Restrictions on 'Coloured' Immigration", *Race,* VII (January, 1966); see also LaViolette, *Americans of Japanese Ancestry*; Daniels, *The Politics of Prejudice*; Kung, *Chinese in American Life*; and Young and Reid, *The Japanese Canadians.*

26 Forrest LaViolette, *The Canadian Japanese and World War II* (Toronto: University of Toronto Press, 1968) and "Canada and Its Japanese" in Edgar Thompson and Everett Hughes (eds.), *Race* (Glencoe: Free Press, 1958); and Jacobus tenBroek et al., *Prejudice, War and the Constitution* (Berkeley: University of California Press, 1968).

27 Richard Burkey, *Racial Discrimination and Public Policy in the United States* (Lexington: Heath, 1971); Louis Knowles and Kenneth Prewitt (eds.), *Institutional Racism in America* (Englewood Cliffs: Prentice-Hall, 1969); *Report of the National Advisory Commission on Civil Disorders* (New York: Dutton, 1968); John Porter, *The Vertical Mosaic: An Analysis of Social Class and Power in Canada* (Toronto: University of Toronto Press, 1965); Bernard Blishen, et al. (eds.), *Canadian Society: Sociological Perspectives,* 3rd ed. (Toronto: Macmillan, 1968); John Harp and John Hofley (eds.), *Poverty in Canada* (Scarborough: Prentice-Hall, 1971); Jean Elliott (ed.), *Minority Canadians* (Scarborough: Prentice-Hall, 1971); and Morris Davis and Joseph Krauter, *The Other Canadians* (Toronto: Methuen, 1971).

28 Wilson and Thompson (eds.), *South Africa*; van den Berghe, *South Africa*; Gwendolyn Carter, *The Politics of Inequality: South Africa since 1948,* rev. ed. (New York: Praeger, 1962); L.E. Neame, *The History of Apartheid* (London: Pall Mall, 1962); and N.J. Rhoodie, *Apartheid and Racial Partnership in Southern Africa* (Pretoria: Academica, 1969).

29 Heribert Adam (ed.), *South Africa: Sociological Perspectives* (New York: Oxford University Press, 1970); and Adam, *Modernizing Racial Domination.*

30 Mason, *Patterns of Dominance*; Michael Banton, *Race Relations* (New York: Basic Books, 1967); Pierre van den Berghe, *Race and Racism* (New York: Wiley, 1967); Frazier, *Race and Culture Contacts,* parts III-IV; Jordan, *White over Black,* parts I-II, IV; and Joel Kovel, *White Racism: A Psychohistory* (New York: Vintage, 1970).

31 H. Hoetink, *Caribbean Race Relations: A Study of Two Variants* (New York: Oxford University Press, 1971).

32 Donald G. Baker, "Identity, Power and Psychocultural Needs: White Responses to Nonwhites", *Journal of Ethnic Studies,* I (Winter, 1974).

33 *Ibid.*

34 Schermerhorn, *Ethnic Relations,* chapters ii-iii, vi; Tamotsu Shibutani and Kian Kwan, *Ethnic Stratification: A Comparative Approach* (New York: Macmillan, 1965); van den Berghe, *Race and Racism,* chapters vi-vii; and John Rex, *Race Relations in Sociological Theory* (New York: Schocken, 1970), chapters i, iv-v.

35 J.A. Fishman, *Language Loyalty in the United States* (The Hague: Mouton, 1966).

36 John Higham, *Strangers in the Land: Patterns of American Nativism, 1860-1925* (New York: Atheneum, 1971).

37 Charles Sanford, *The Quest for Paradise: Europe and the American Moral Imagination* (Urbana: University of Illinois Press, 1961); see also, R.W.B. Lewis, *The American Adam* (Chicago: University of Chicago Press, 1955); David Noble, *The Eternal Adam and the New World Garden* (New York: Braziller, 1968); Felix Gilbert, *To the Farewell Address: Ideas of Early American Foreign Policy* (Princeton: Princeton University Press, 1961); and Clinton Rossiter, *Marxism: The View from America* (New York: Harcourt, Brace, 1960).

38 Gordon, *Assimilation in American Life,* chapters iv-v.

39 van den Berghe, *South Africa,* chapter ii; Isobel Edwards, *The 1820 Settlers in South Africa* (New York: Longmans, 1934); Leonard Thompson, *The Unification of South Africa, 1902-1910* (Oxford: Clarendon, 1960), chapter i; and W.M. Macmillan, *Bantu, Boer and Briton: The Making of the South African Native Problem* (Oxford: Clarendon, 1963).

40 John Stone, *Colonist or Uitlander: A Study of the British Immigrant in South Africa* (New York: Oxford University Press, 1973).

41 Hartz, *New Societies,* chapters vi-vii.

42 Allan Smith, "Metaphor and Nationality in North America", *Canadian Historical*

Review, LI (September, 1970); J.M.S. Careless, "Limited Identities in Canada", *Canadian Historical Review,* L (March, 1969); Anthony Richmond, *Post-War Immigrants in Canada* (Toronto: University of Toronto Press, 1967) and "Immigration and Pluralism in Canada" in W.E. Mann (ed.), *Social and Cultural Change in Canada* (Toronto: Copp Clark, 1970), Vol. I.

43 Edward Corbett, *Quebec Confronts Canada* (Baltimore: Johns Hopkins Press, 1967); Ramsay Cook, *Canada and the French-Canadian Question* (Toronto: Macmillan, 1967); J.M.S. Careless and R. Craig Brown (eds.), *The Canadians, 1867-1967* (New York: St. Martin's Press, 1968); and J.R. Mallory, "The Canadian Dilemma: French and English", *Political Quarterly,* XXXXI (July/September, 1970).

44 Davis, *The Other Canadians;* Elliot (ed.), *Minority Canadians;* and McKenna, *Sociology and Social Research,* LIII.

45 Richmond, *Post-War Immigrants in Canada;* Porter, *The Vertical Mosaic;* Wsevolod Isajiw, "The Process of Social Integration: The Canadian Example", *Dalhousie Review,* XXXXVIII (1968-69).

46 Enloe, *Ethnic Conflict;* W.W. Rostow, *Politics and the Stages of Growth* (London: Cambridge University Press, 1971).

47 Hartz, *New Societies,* chapter vii; Cook, *Canada and the French-Canadian Question,* chapter iv; Corbett, *Quebec Confronts Canada,* chapters i-iii; Careless and Brown (eds.), *The Canadians,* chapters i-v; Janet Morchain, *Search for a Nation: French-English Relations in Canada Since 1759* (Toronto: Dent and Sons, 1967), chapters i-v; Arthur M. Lower, *Colony to Nation: A History of Canada* (Toronto: Longmans, Green, 1946), chapters vi, xv; Richard Ossenberg, "The Conquest Revisited: Another Look at Canadian Dualism", *Canadian Journal of Sociology and Anthropology,* IV (November, 1967) and "Social Pluralism in Quebec," in Ossenberg (ed.), *Canadian Society;* Richard Jones, *Community in Crisis: French-Canadian Nationalism in Perspective* (Toronto: McClelland and Steward, 1972), chapters i-ii; Macmillan, *Bantu, Boer and Briton;* Walker, *The Frontier Tradition;* Ian MacCrone, *Race Attitudes in South Africa* (Johannesburg: Witwatersrand University Press, 1937); William Vatcher, Jr., *White Laager: The Rise of Afrikaner Nationalism* (New York: Praeger, 1965), chapters i-ii; Wilson and Thompson (eds.), *South Africa;* Thompson, *The Unification of South Africa,* chapter i.

48 Gossett, *Race,* chapters iii-iv; Stanley Elkins, *Slavery: A Problem in American Institutional and Intellectual Life* (New York: Grosset and Dunlap, 1963); Fredrickson, *The Black Image,* chapters ii-v; David B. Davis, *The Slave Power Conspiracy and the Paranoid Style* (Baton Rouge: Louisiana State Univorsity Press, 1969).

49 Stampp, *The Peculiar Institution;* Genovese, *The World the Slaveholders Made,* part II; see also note 47.

50 Adam (ed.), *South Africa,* chapters v, vii; LeMay, *Black and White,* chapters i-ii; Hartz, *New Societies,* chapters iv, vi-vii; Mallory, *Political Quarterly,* XXXXI; Ossenberg, *Canadian Journal of Sociology and Anthropology,* IV.

51 Davis, *The Slave Power Conspiracy and the Paranoid Style.*

52 Trelease, *White Terror;* Wood, *Black Scare;* and Fredrickson, *The Black Image.*

53 Woodward, *The Strange Career of Jim Crow;* and Claude Nolen, *The Negro's Image in the South* (Lexington: University of Kentucky Press, 1968).

54 Logan, *The Betrayal of the Negro,* parts II-III; Fredrickson, *The Black Image;* Haller, *Outcasts from Evolution;* and Newby, *Jim Crow's Defense.*

55 LeMay, *Black and White,* chapters ii-iii; Vatcher, *White Laager,* chapters ii-iii; and Thompson, *The Unification of South Africa,* chapters i-ii.

56 G.H.L. LeMay, *British Supremacy in South Africa, 1899-1907* (Oxford: Clarendon, 1965); and Ronald Robinson and John Gallagher, *Africa and the Victorians* (New York: St. Martin's Press, 1967), chapters iii, vii, xiv.

57 Nicholas Mansergh, *South Africa, 1906-1961: The Price of Magnanimity* (New York: Praeger, 1962); Thompson, *The Unification of South Africa;* and B.G. Pyrah, *Imperial Policy and South Africa, 1902-1910* (Oxford: Clarendon, 1955).

58 Carter, *The Politics of Inequality;* Leonard Thompson, *Politics in the Republic of South Africa* (Boston: Little, Brown, 1966).

59 *Ibid.*, chapters iii, v; Rhoodie, *Apartheid and Racial Partnership*; van den Berghe, *South Africa*; and Adam, *Modernizing Racial Domination.*

60 See note 47; Michael Brunet, "The French Canadians' Search for a Fatherland" in Peter Russell (ed.), *Nationalism in Canada* (Toronto: McGraw-Hill, 1966).

61 Cook, *Canada and the French-Canadian Question,* chapter iv; Morchain, *Search for a Nation*; and Careless and Brown (eds.), *The Canadians.*

62 *Ibid.*, p. 121.

63 *Ibid.*

64 S.D. Clark, "The Position of the French-Speaking Population in the Northern Industrial Community" in Ossenberg, (ed.), *Canadian Society.*

65 Jones, *Community in Crisis*; Cook, *Canada and the French-Canadian Question*; Corbett, *Quebec Confronts Canada*; A.R.M. Lower et al., *Evolving Canadian Federalism* (Durham: Duke University Press, 1958); Stanley Lieberson, *Language and Ethnic Relations in Canada* (New York: Wiley, 1970); Donald Smiley, *The Canadian Political Nationality* (Toronto: Methuen, 1968) and *Canada in Question: Federalism in the Seventies* (Toronto: McGraw-Hill Ryerson, 1972).

66 Harold Wolpe, "Industrialism and Race in South Africa" in Sami Zubaida (ed.), *Race and Racialism* (London: Tavistock, 1970); Heribert Adam, "The South African Power Elite" in Adam (ed.), *South Africa*; and Adam, *Modernizing Racial Domination,* chapters iv, vi.

67 Patterson, *The Canadian Indian,* part II, chapter iv; Forrest LaViolette, *The Struggle for Survival: Indian Cultures and the Protestant Ethic in British Columbia* (Toronto: University of Toronto Press, 1961), chapter v; Cummings and Mickenberg, *Native Rights,* parts IV-VI; Harold Cardinal, *The Unjust Society* (Edmonton: Hurtig, 1969); Winks, *The Blacks in Canada*; chapters xiv-xv; Hazel Hertzberg, *The Search for an American Indian Identity: Modern Pan-Indian Movements* (Syracuse: Syracuse University Press, 1972); Alvin Josephy Jr., *Red Power: The American Indians' Fight for Freedom* (New York: McGraw-Hill, 1971); Vine Deloria Jr., *Custer Died for Your Sins* (New York: Avon, 1969); and Joseph S. Himes, *Racial Conflict in America* (Columbus: Charles Merrill, 1973).

68 Robert Blauner, *Racial Oppression in America* (New York: Harper and Row, 1972).

Factors Associated with Commitment
to and Identification with Canada*
John Goldlust and Anthony H. Richmond

This study of identification with Canada is part of a larger research project concerned with the development of a multivariate model of immigrant adaptation. It is based on the premise that the experiences of immigrants and their interactions with the receiving society are the complex result of a multitude of different factors, only a few of which can be effectively observed and measured. The outcome cannot be adequately represented in terms of a single dimension of "assimilation" or "integration". The general characteristics of the multivariate model have been described elsewhere.[1] The present paper deals with only one dimension of the total immigrant experience, namely, those factors which induce a strong sense of permanent commitment to the new country. Another aspect of what is generally considered "identification" concerns the individual's definition of his own ethnic identity. An examination of that question with respect to both Canadian- and foreign-born householders in Toronto has been reported elsewhere.[2]

Previous studies have thrown light on some of the factors which contribute to the immigrant's identification with his new country.[3] Although they differ in their specific conclusions and emphases, the authors of these studies appear to agree on certain major points. The experience of identifying with a new country involves a learning process which has cognitive, conative and evaluative aspects. This learning experience cannot take place without effective communication with members of the receiving society. Therefore a knowledge of the receiving country's language, acquired before or after migration, is a necessary condition for identification. Prior knowledge of the receiving society's dominant language facilitates the immigrant's acquisition of the information and practical skills required to perform effectively in that society's economic and social systems. But prior knowledge of the language may also have a negative effect on identification because it reduces the necessity for the immigrant to make subjective changes in his own personality, attitudes and values—changes which normally occur in the process of learning the language.

*The research for this paper was carried out under the auspices of the Ethnic Research Programme, York University and was supported financially by the Canada Council, the Department of Manpower and Immigration and the Federal Department of the Secretary of State, Ottawa. The authors wish to thank Karen Kaplan for her valuable assistance.

132

From a socio-psychological point of view, immigrant adaptation involves a certain degree of desocialization and subsequent resocialization into the cultural norms of the new society.[4] An immigrant who arrives in a new country without a knowledge of its language must literally regress to a child-like state until he has at least an elementary command of the new language. The necessity for this may be delayed when he is able to live, find employment, recreation and religious participation in an ethnic community consisting mainly of others from his own country. This security, although valuable from the point of view of the immigrant's adjustment and mental health, is likely to delay the process of his resocialization into the new society.

In addition to language the other factors which are generally recognized to contribute to the immigrant's commitment to the new country are the speed of his acculturation, his economic success and his social integration at the primary and secondary levels. It has also been suggested that those experiences prior to, or immediately after immigration which sever the individual's ties with his former country may contribute to more rapid identification. These often traumatic experiences include that of being a refugee or displaced person together with the experience of occupational status dislocation after migration.[5] Such experiences appear to have a drastic desocialization effect and consequently make the individual more receptive to the experiences of the new society, particularly when these are, in the long run, relatively rewarding.

The Canadian Identification Index

The data for this analysis were derived from a stratified, strict probability sample survey of householders in metropolitan Toronto. The survey was carried out in the autumn of 1969 and spring of 1970 by a multilingual team of interviewers.[6] The sample was representative of all householders in Toronto, 17 percent of whom were women. However the latter were not representative of the female population generally, as they consisted mainly of single women, those who were separated, divorced or widowed. Therefore they have been excluded from the present analysis which is based on 1,929 foreign-born male householders. A detailed account of the characteristics of householders in metropolitan Toronto, including their ethnic characteristics, economic status and residential distribution, has already been published.[7] It is sufficient to note here that approximately 52 percent of the male householders were immigrants to Canada. Of these, only one in three had English mother tongues.

An index was designed to measure identification with Canada in terms of commitment to permanent residence, feeling a sense of belonging, of being at home and of becoming, or wanting to become a naturalized Canadian citizen. This was based on the answers to seven questions.[8] The items, when combined, comprised an index ranging from 0-6. The mean score for the foreign-born males in the sample was 3.9, with a standard deviation of 1.8.

Ethno-Linguistic Groups[9]

The mean scores on the Canadian identification index by ethno-linguistic group and length of residence are shown in Table I and in graphic form in Figure 1. In all cases identification increased with length of residence: after immigrants had lived in Canada for twenty years or more, there seemed to be little difference between them and immigrants of other nationalities. Slavic and Jewish immigrants identify more rapidly with their new country, and those of Italian origin more slowly than average. Very few Greek or Portuguese immigrants have been in Canada more than twenty years, and most black or Asian immigrants in the sample have been Canadian residents less than ten years. Since the number of non-whites in the sample was small, the mean identification scores for those who had been in Canada for more than ten years were subject to a larger than usual margin of error. The identification of black and Asian immigrants in the first four years appears to be very low but increases quite rapidly in the next five year period.

Immigrants whose mother tongue is English showed a somewhat erratic pattern and high standard deviations from the mean, even after residing in Canada for over twenty years. This suggests that there is considerable variability within the group. Furthermore English-speaking immigrants were more likely to be found in either the short- or long-term residence groups rather than in the middle residence group (ten to nineteen years). Many of those who had resided in Canada for less than five years did not plan to settle permanently.

Length of Residence

Length of residence in Canada was the single most important determinant of the degree of identification and commitment as measured by the identification index. This was entirely predictable. It has been noted that the process of identifying with the new country involves a degree of resocialization. This process takes time. Furthermore there were significant interaction effects between length of residence and other variables. Many immigrants who originally did not plan to settle permanently were still in Canada in the first quinquennial cohort and swelled the ranks of those with low identification with Canada. In fact 17 percent of those who had lived in Canada for less than five years had firm plans to re-migrate or return to their mother country. There was a curvilinear relationship between length of residence and those who had English as mother tongue. As noted above, English-speaking immigrants were found proportionately more often among those resident less than ten years and more than twenty years than in the middle residence category. Therefore English-speaking groups showed both high and low identification when the effect of length of residence was taken into account. Overall the association between identification and length of residence appeared to be linear with a Pearson product moment correlation of .47 for all males in the sample. According to normal conventions, this may be said to explain 22 percent of the variance in the Canadian identification index.[10] Although the multivariate model generated a larger multiple correlation and explained more of the variance, no single variable in the analysis was as strongly associated with identification as length of residence.

In interpreting the effects of any characteristic upon the subsequent identification of immigrants with a new society, care must be taken to distinguish between direct and indirect influences. For example, differences between householders in degree of identification by age of arrival, education, etc., may be due to the indirect association between these characteristics and other important factors such as length of residence. Even when the influence of length of residence is taken into account, there may be other intervening variables, such as speed of acculturation, which directly influence identification and which are found differentially among particular nationalities or categories of immigrants. Therefore it is essential to analyze the findings in terms of a multivariate model which examines the additive and interaction effects of a number of interdependent variables simultaneously.

The Multivariate Analysis

Although length of residence and education proved to be important determinants of almost all aspects of immigrant adaptation, their effects were both direct and indirect.[11] Various scales and indexes were devised to measure such factors as economic achievement, satisfaction, acculturation, primary and secondary social integration, exposure to Canadian and ethnic mass media, ethnic attitudes, social distance and the perception of ethnic discrimination in Canada.[12]

The results of combining these various measures into a multiple correlation and regression analysis of the identification index are shown in Tables II and III. Due to the evident influence of mother tongue, separate analyses were made for the English- and non-English-speaking immigrants. After eliminating those factors which appeared to have little or no effect on identification, the results have been represented graphically in figures 2 and 3. The figures are modified path diagrams. The direct and indirect effects of significant determinants are represented and their relative influence is indicated by single or double lines. The direct paths are based on standardized Beta coefficients which indicate the relative weight of the variable in question when all other variables are held constant. However actual path coefficients have not been entered on the diagrams. It was felt that emphasis should not be attached to the precise figures, particularly since the measures used were of varying reliability. The general configurations represented here are supported by the evidence in the tables and by the separate analyses that have been made of each of the intervening variables. A complete exposition of the latter findings will be reported elsewhere.[13]

The multiple correlation and regression analyses for the English- and non-English-speaking categories differed in that items relating to English fluency and use were omitted from the former, as were a number of "dummy" variables representing ascribed ethnic characteristics and refugee status. In both groups length of residence and age of arrival were examined first, and the ascribed characteristics, such as mother tongue and religion, were grouped last. Other factors were free to enter the equation according to the amount of variance they explained. Regardless of the order of entry, the standardized Beta coefficients indicate the direct effect of the variable in question when all others are held constant. In the tables the second column indicates the correlation with the identification index when the effect of length of residence was partialled out. The third column shows the multiple correlation; R^2 is the amount of variance explained by the model at each step. And the penultimate column indicates the amount of variance added to the explanatory model by the variable in question. It will be noted that the model explained 61 percent of the variance in the identification index for those whose mother tongue was English but only 41 percent in the case of others.

While in both language groups length of residence explained the largest part of the variance, it should be noted that the effect was more direct in the case of those whose mother tongue was not English. Among English-speaking immigrants the standardized Beta coefficient was lower, suggesting that the effects of length of residence were being mediated to a greater extent through other variables, such as cognitive acculturation and formal social participation. Measures of secondary integration, such as the Chapin scale of social participation and the scale of "non-neighbourhood" integration, were quite strongly associated with identification among those whose mother tongue was English but not among others. In the case of English-speaking immigrants cognitive acculturation and general acculturation (including English fluency and use) were positively associated with identification. Reliance on ethnic newspapers and radio was negatively associated with acculturation and identification.

Satisfaction with life in Canada was positively correlated with identification in both cases. Reluctance to move (high neighbourhood integration) contributed to the identification of the English-speaking group, but did not contribute to the identification of other groups. Primary social integration, measured by the frequency of seeing close relatives, was positively associated with identification among those whose mother tongue was not English, although a friendship network that was strictly homogeneous and whose members were like the respondent had a negative effect on identification. The similarity of the respondent's spouse in terms of ethnic background was not important.

Education and Socio-Economic Status

There was no linear association between identification with Canada and education: the effects of education differed according to circumstances. Previous studies of immigrants' plans to become naturalized Canadian citizens have indicated the complexity of the relationship between education and citizenship. This relationship appears to vary according to nationality and the immigrant's residence in a metropolitan or urban area.[14] In addition more stringent selection criteria in recent years suggest that there is a negative association between education and length of residence.

The present study revealed important interaction effects between education and other variables which tended to obscure the direct influence of education itself. This varied according to mother tongue, length of residence and other factors. In general there was a small negative zero order correlation of -0.08. However there were important differences between those whose mother tongue was English and others when length of residence was taken into account. Among English-speaking immigrants, the tendency for those with higher education to identify less than the average was very marked among those who had lived in Canada less than ten years. Among longer-term residents, those with between ten and thirteen years of education tended to identify less than any other groups. The combined effect was to produce a zero order correlation of -0.27 and a first order partial correlation of -0.18

when the effects of length of residence were controlled. The negative association of education and identification was also characteristic of those with other mother tongues in the first ten years of residence. However the reverse was the case among the non-English-speaking immigrants in the middle residence group (ten to nineteen years). Among the longer-term residents, those with average education were the most committed to their new society.

These apparently contradictory findings were the result of intervening variables (such as satisfaction and primary integration) with which education was negatively associated, and acculturation, with which education was positively associated. When the effect of all other variables was held constant, there was a small negative Beta coefficient of −0.08 in the case of those whose mother tongue was not English. Education explained 2 percent of the variance. The negative influence of education on identification was much stronger in the case of English-speaking immigrants, explaining 3 percent of the variance and indicating a Beta coefficient of −0.40.

Other indicators of socio-economic status, such as income and occupation, revealed somewhat inconsistent associations with identification. As a whole there was a slight positive correlation of 0.11 between income and identification. This persisted when length of residence was taken into account. However an examination of the detailed tabulations shows that (as in the case of education to which income was closely related) the association tended to be negative among those who had resided in Canada less than ten years, positive in the middle residence cohort, and of little consequence among those who had been in Canada more than twenty years. There was similar inconsistency with regard to occupational status as measured by the Blishen index.

Although the occupational status of the immigrant at the time of the survey was an important determinant of the degree of his identification with Canada, the experience of status dislocation and social mobility was even more important. Previous studies have shown that the desire to take out Canadian citizenship is greater among those who are upwardly mobile than among those who retain the same occupational status as they had in their former country.[15] Under certain circumstances downward mobility, particularly when followed by recovery or improvement of status after the initial decline, had the effect of changing the individual's self-image. Status dislocation appeared to compel the migrant to make a more radical re-adjustment to his situation and rendered him more open to the socialization and other experiences conducive to identification with the new country. The evidence from the metropolitan Toronto survey appeared to substantiate these findings only partially. An examination of the detailed tabulations reveal that upward mobility is generally associated with higher identification but, in the case of English-speaking immigrants, so also is downward mobility. This is confirmed by the zero order correlations shown in Tables II and III. The tabulations further reveal that among non-English-speaking immigrants, downward mobility is associated with low identification unless it is followed by recovery or improvement of status compared with the individual's occupation in former country. If recovery follows, the effect is similar to immediate upward mobility. With the exception of English-speaking immigrants who have resided in Canada for ten to nineteen years, those who retained the same occupational status in the new country generated levels of identification as low as, and in some cases lower than those who had fallen in status and had not recovered. However the low Beta coefficients for both English- and non-English-speaking immigrants indicate that, when all other things are equal, the effect of occupational status dislocation and social mobility is minimal. It seems likely that these variables have a more direct influence on satisfaction with life in Canada and that satisfaction explains most of the variance that might otherwise be attributed to socio-economic factors.

Ethnicity and Religion

It seems reasonable to hypothesize that commitment to Canada, as measured by the Canadian identification index, would be greater among those immigrants who most closely resemble the dominant charter group in Canada— that is, white English-speaking Protestant immigrants. In fact the reverse proved to be true. Regardless of language, Protestants were less committed than immigrants of other religions. This was particularly true among the English-speaking group, as indicated by a positive Beta coefficient of 0.38 between identification and *not* being Protestant. When other things were equal, Catholics, Jews or members Eastern Orthodox religions (i.e. Greek, Ukrainian, Russian and other Orthodox denominations) showed a higher degree of identification. An examination of the detailed breakdown by length of residence and religion revealed that Jewish immigrants and Eastern Orthodox adherents scored above average on the Canadian identification index. Catholics scored above average in the less-than-ten- and more-than-twenty-years residence groups, and close to average in the middle-residence category. Protestants were about average in the ten-to-nineteen-year residence categories, and below average in the earlier and later categories.

It should be noted that the Slavic-speaking group included a substantial proportion of Catholics and Eastern Orthodox adherents, thus explaining some of the variance. The operational definition of Slavic-speaking immigrants excluded Jewish householders. Undoubtedly if they had been included, they would have further increased the association between high commitment and speaking a Slavic language. A high proportion of refugees were also Jewish and/or Slavic, and being a refugee had a direct and positive effect on identification. Despite the positive influence of being Catholic, there was a slight negative association between being Italian and the identification index.

In a monistic society nationality may be the principal basis for defining one's own ethnic identity, but in a pluralistic society like Canada there may be other legitimate bases of self-identification which are ethnic in character but independent of birthplace or citizenship. As a consequence there need not be any association between commitment to the new country, including becoming a naturalized citizen, and the definition of ethnic identity in nationalistic terms. In the course of the metropolitan Toronto survey householders were asked to state the ethnic group (if any) to which they felt they belonged. (This question was distinct from the "ethnic origin" question used in the census which traces paternal ancestry.) The question was open-ended and respondents were free to say they were Canadian if they wished.

There was a small positive correlation between the Canadian identification index, measuring commitment, and whether the foreign-born respondent described himself as Canadian (or hyphenated Canadian) as opposed to such descriptions as "British", "Jewish", etc. Although those of Jewish ethnic origin were least likely to call themselves Canadian, they had the highest average scores on the identification index. In fact 40 percent of those who described themselves as Jewish had the highest score on the index compared with 22 percent of those who called themselves Canadian, 17 percent of those using a hyphenated Canadian description, 16 percent of the British, 10 percent using any other self-definition, and 8 percent who said they belonged to no ethnic group.[16] However, with the exception of the low commitment of English-speaking Protestants, the direct effects of ethnicity on identification were limited.

Commitment to Canada as measured by the Canadian identification index is only one dimension of the complex process of immigrant adaptation. Given the pluralistic and multicultural character of Canadian society and particularly the situation in metropolitan Toronto in the last two decades, it is possible for immigrants to maintain their own ethnic identity while at the same time developing a strong sense of belonging permanently in Canada. This appears to be primarily a function of long residence reinforced by concomitant acculturation, social integration and increased satisfaction. A low degree of commitment is particularly characteristic of recent immigrants with higher levels of education. This may be related to the phenomenon of transilience—that is, the propensity of those who have marketable professional and technical qualifications to move readily from one country to another.

TABLE I

Mean Scores on Canadian Identification Index by Ethno-linguistic Group and Length of Residence

		Total	0–4	5–9	10–14	15–19	20–24	25 & over
English*	Mean	3.8	2.9	3.6	3.4	4.4	4.3	5.2
mother tongue	s.d.	1.7	1.9	1.6	1.4	1.3	1.3	0.8
Slavic**	Mean	4.7	3.1	4.1	4.6	5.0	5.0	5.3
mother tongue	s.d.	1.1	1.1	1.5	0.9	0.8	0.7	0.7
Jewish	Mean	5.1	2.8	4.5	4.8	5.4	5.4	5.6
origin	s.d.	1.2	1.8	1.2	1.1	0.5	0.6	0.5
Italian	Mean	3.5	2.5	2.8	3.2	4.0	5.1	5.2
mother tongue	s.d	1.6	1.8	1.5	1.5	1.2	0.6	0.9
West	Mean	4.1	2.3	3.9	4.2	4.7	4.7	5.1
European***	s.d.	1.6	1.7	1.8	1.5	1.1	0.7	0.3
Greek &	Mean	3.8	3.5	3.5	4.1	4.3	4.6	–
Portuguese	s.d.	1.4	1.4	1.3	1.4	1.5	0.9	–
Other	Mean	4.1	3.0	3.3	4.6	4.2	4.5	4.8
languages	s.d.	1.5	1.9	1.9	1.1	1.3	1.0	0.6
Black &	Mean	2.7	1.7	3.5	5.1	–	–	–
Asian	s.d.	2.1	1.7	1.9	1.0	–	–	–
All male	Mean	3.9	2.7	3.4	3.9	4.4	4.8	5.2
householders	s.d.	1.7	1.8	1.6	1.5	1.2	1.0	0.7

Years of residence in Canada

*   Excludes those of black, Asian and Jewish origin with English mother tongue

**   Excludes those of Jewish origin with Slavic mother tongue

***   Includes French, German, Netherland and Scandinavian mother tongues

—   = not available due to small number in sample

s.d. = standard deviation

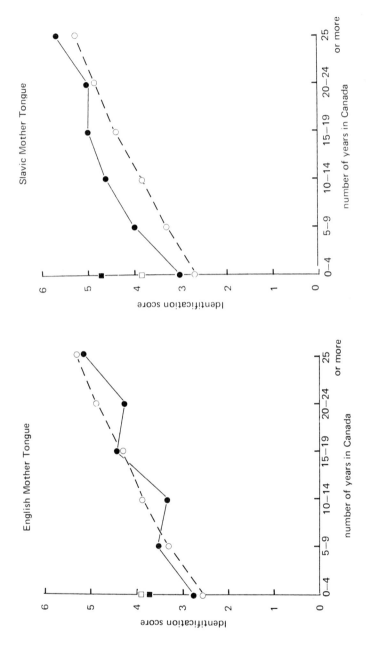

Figure 1

Identification Index by Length of Residence in Canada for each Ethno-Linguistic Group (Foreign-born Males)

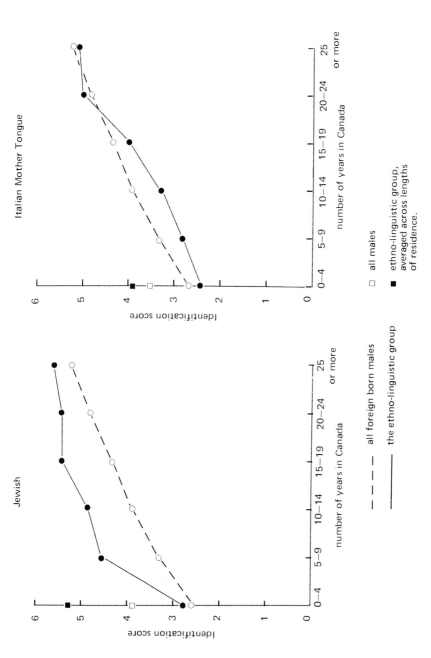

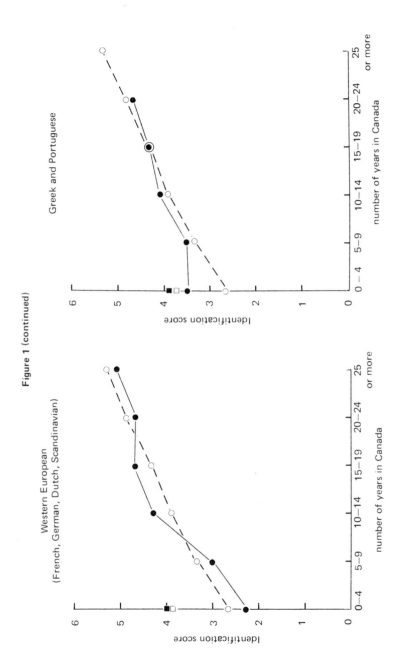

Figure 1 (continued)

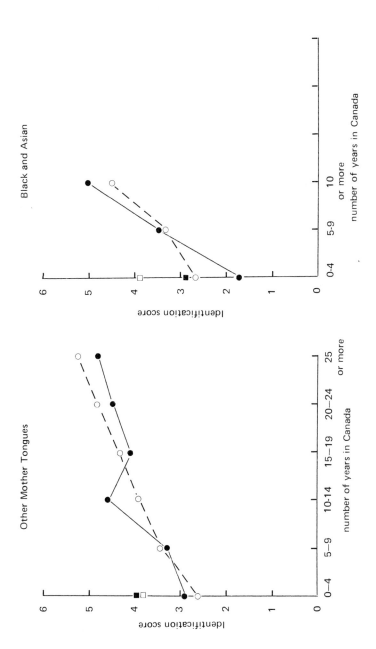

TABLE II

**Multiple Correlation and Regression
with Canadian Identification Index**

English Mother Tongue

	Zero order correlation	1st. order partial*	Multiple correlation	R^2	Addition to variance explained	Standardized Beta coefficient
Length of residence in Canada	.50	–	.50	.25	.25	.16
Aged over 30 yrs. on arrival	–.21	–.16	.52	.27	.02	–.02
Aged 15 yrs. or less on arrival	.25	.02	.52	.27	.00	.14
Non-neighbourhood integration	.42	.35	.59	.35	.07	.19
Formal social participation (Chapin scale with labour unions)	.28	.28	.63	.39	.04	.23
Education	–.27	–.18	.65	.42	.03	–.40
Satisfaction	.20	–.01	.67	.45	.03	.22
Preference for same ethnic neighbourhood	.07	–.17	.69	.47	.02	–.14
Frequency of reading Canadian papers	.05	.17	.70	.49	.02	.22
Cognitive acculturation	.40	.21	.71	.51	.02	.20
Neighbourhood integration	.47	.19	.72	.52	.01	.25
Homogeneity of friends	.07	.07	.73	.53	.00	–.05
Income	.10	.11	.73	.53	.01	.07
Occupational mobility c.f. former country: up	.10	.20	.73	.53	.00	.07
Occupational mobility c.f. former country: down	.02	.01	.73	.53	.00	–.04
Perception of discrimination	–.11	–.05	.73	.53	.00	.06

* Controlling for length of residence

Table II cont'd.

	Zero order correlation	1st. order partial*	Multiple correlation	R^2	Addition to variance explained	Standardized Beta coefficient
Frequency of seeing close relatives	.38	.18	.73	.53	.00	−.02
Similarity to spouse	−.19	−.07	.73	.53	.00	.07
Reads British and/ or American papers	−.04	−.03	.73	.53	.00	−.01
Not Protestant	.08	.31	.78	.61	.08	.38

TABLE III

Multiple Correlation and Regression with Canadian Identification Index

Other Mother Tongues

	Zero order correlation	1st. order partial*	Multiple correlation	R^2	Addition to variance explained	Standardized Beta coefficient
Length of residence in Canada	.46	–	.46	.21	.21	.28
Aged 15 yrs. or less on arrival	.13	−.04	.46	.21	.00	−.07
Aged over 30 yrs. on arrival	−.09	.00	.46	.21	.00	.05
Reliance on ethnic media	−.34	−.29	.53	.28	.07	−.16
Satisfaction	.26	.16	.56	.31	.03	.15
General acculturation	.35	.25	.58	.33	.02	.17
Education	−.01	.06	.58	.34	.01	−.09
Homogeneity of friends	−.23	−.21	.59	.35	.01	−.18
Frequency of seeing close relatives	.11	.03	.60	.36	.01	.08
Occupational mobility c.f. former country: down	−.14	−.13	.60	.36	.00	−.07

*Controlling for length of residence

Table III cont'd.

	Zero order correlation	1st. order partial*	Multiple correlation	R^2	Addition to variance explained	Standardized Beta coefficient
Formal social participation (Chapin with labour unions)	.20	.15	.60	.36	.00	.06
Perceived discrimination	−.05	−.05	.61	.37	.00	−.05
Non-neighbourhood integration	.19	.12	.61	.37	.00	.05
Preference for same ethnic neighbourhood	−.10	−.14	.61	.37	.00	−.05
Occupational mobility c.f. former country: up	−.21	.16	.61	.37	.00	.03
Income	.11	.11	.61	.37	.00	−.00
Similarity to Spouse	−.20	−.15	.61	.37	.00	.00
Neighbourhood integration	−.22	−.00	.61	.37	.00	−.00
Slavic	.21	.15	.62	.39	.01	.07
Refugee	.10	.11	.63	.39	.01	.08
Sponsored by relative	−.05	.01	.63	.40	.00	.08
Jewish	.19	.05	.63	.40	.00	.09
Eastern Orthodox	.06	.09	.64	.41	.01	.10
Roman Catholic	−.06	−.02	.64	.41	.01	.13
Italian	−.20	−.18	.64	.41	.00	−.06

*Controlling for length of residence

Figure 2

Factors Associated with Commitment to and Identification with Canada

English Mother Tongue Only

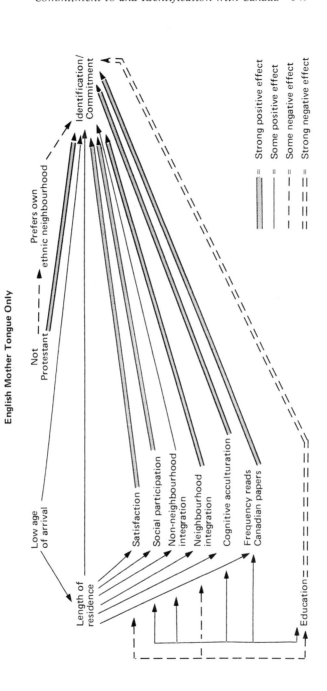

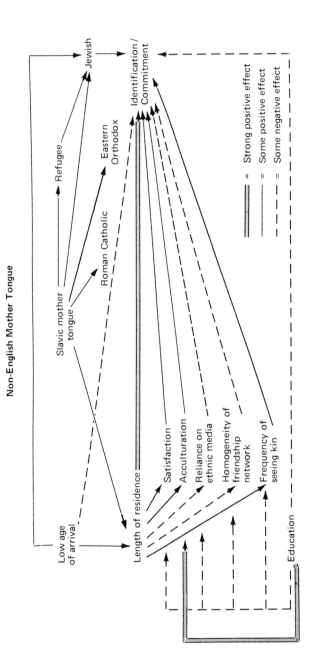

Figure 3

Factors Associated with Commitment to and Identification with Canada

John Goldlust is lecturer in Sociology at La Trobe University, Australia. Anthony Richmond is a professor of Sociology and Co-ordinator of the Ethnic Research Programme, York University, Toronto.

NOTES

1 John Goldlust and Anthony Richmond, "A Multivariate Model of Immigrant Adaptation", *International Migration Review,* 8 (1974), 193-225.

2 Anthony Richmond, "Language, Ethnicity and the Problem of Identity in a Canadian Metropolis", *Ethnicity,* 1 (1974), 175-206.

3 See, for example, Alan Richardson, "A Theory and Method for Psychological Study of Assimilation", *International Migration Review* (Fall, 1967), 3-30; R.W. Bar Yosef, "Desocialization and Resocialization: The Adjustment Process of Immigrants", *International Migration Review* (Summer, 1968), 27-43; Jerold Heiss, "Sources of Satisfaction and Assimilation among Italian Immigrants", *Human Relations,* 19 (1966), 165-77; Heiss, "Residential Segregation and Assimilation of Italians in an Australian City", *International Migration Review,* 4 (1966), 165-71; Heiss, "Factors Related to Immigrant Assimilation: The Early Post-Migration Situation", *Human Organization,* 26 (1967), 265-72; Heiss, "Factors Related to Assimilation: Pre-Immigration Traits", *Social Forces,* 47 (1968), 422-28; S. Alexander Weinstock, *Acculturation and Occupation: A Study of the 1956 Hungarian Refugees in the United States* (The Hague: Martinus Nijhoff, 1956).

4 S.N. Eisenstadt, *The Absorption of Immigrants* (London: Routledge & Kegan Paul, 1955); Bar Yosef, *International Migration Review* (Summer, 1968), 27-43.

5 J.T. Shuval, *Immigrants on the Threshold* (New York: Prentice-Hall, 1963); A.H. Richmond, *Post-War Immigrants in Canada* (Toronto: University of Toronto Press, 1967); Heiss, *Social Forces,* 47 (1968), 422-28.

6 The study was carried out by the Survey Research Centre of York University directed by Dr. Michael Lanphier, using a multilingual team of interviewers. The principal investigator was Anthony H. Richmond, assisted by Brigitte Neumann. Designed by Dr. Ivan Fellegi of Statistics Canada, the sample was a two phase, stratified random sample with a probability of selection determined according to locality of residence and the ethnicity of the household head. This enabled interviewers to talk to a larger number of household heads of Jewish, Italian and Slavic origins than would have been obtained using an equal probability sample. Appropriate weighting procedures ensured that the sample was representative for metropolitan Toronto as a whole. All tables are based on weighted estimates of number of household heads. Weights were calculated as inverse of probability of selection adjusted for overall response rates to the survey by ethnic sub-stratum (response rates of 84 percent to phase 1 and 86 percent to phase 2 interviews were obtained). However response rates to individual questions varied and some questions (such as those relating to the labour force) were irrelevant for some householders. Therefore the unweighted N(on which any table is based) varies, causing variation in estimated populations depending on the size of the "missing data" category. Due to the complexity of the sample (which also involved some clustering of the households selected), tests of significance and of association involving the assumptions underlying the use of simple random samples are not applicable. For a more detailed discussion of "design effects" and other characteristics of the sample, see Appendix I to A.H. Richmond, "Ethnic Residential Segregation in Metropolitan Toronto", mimeographed (Toronto: Institute for Behavioural Research, York University, 1972).

7 A.H. Richmond, "Ethnic Segregation in Metropolitan Toronto", mimeographed (Toronto: Institute for Behavioural Research, York University, 1972).

8 An index designed to measure the degree of identification with Canada was based on six items derived from seven questions in the original interview schedule. These questions are listed below. In calculating the index whether or not a respondent had become a Canadian citizen was given double weight; if the respondent had been in Canada less than five years, double weight was given to the item concerning his intention to become a citizen.

Seven questions from the interview schedule:

1. Taking into account all of the places in which you have lived, which place would you call home?
2. Of what country are you a citizen?
3. If not already naturalized, do you plan to become a Canadian citizen?
4. When you first came to Canada, what were your plans (e.g., to settle, to return home, to move on)?
5. Have your plans changed since then?
6. Do you feel now that you are fully a Canadian, or do you belong more in your old country?
7. If a football match or other game was being played between a Canadian team and one from your former country, which side do you think you would cheer for?

The Canadian identification index had an average inter-item correlation of 0.28 and a coefficient of reliability of 0.67.

9 The ethno-linguistic groups were created on the basis of information concerning birthplace, mother tongue, religion, and, in the case of black immigrants only, interviewers' designation. The particular groupings chosen depended partly on a judgment of relevant criteria for predicting immigrant adaptations and partly on the size of the unweighted numbers in each category. These numbers had to be large enough to minimize the sampling error. The category of Jewish origin included all those, irrespective of mother tongue, who reported their religion as Jewish or, if they said "no religion," reported that one of their parents was Jewish by religion. Therefore the other ethno-linguistic groups exclude those defined as Jewish.

10 I am indebted to Dr. Brent Rutherford, director of the Methods and Analysis Division, Institute for Behavioural Research, York University, for drawing my attention to the effects of measurement reliability on correlations. The convention that the proportion of variance explained is the square of a correlation (or multiple correlation) was derived originally from biometric research and subsequently adopted in psychology and elsewhere. However it is based on the assumption that the dependent variable can be measured exactly or with a high degree of reliability, as in the case of age, height, weight, etc. This is manifestly not the case with many sociological variables. The maximum possible correlation between any two variables is the square root of the product of their respective reliability coefficients (in this study the Canadian identification index had a reliability coefficient of .67). As a consequence, unadjusted product moment correlations probably underestimate substantially the strength of the actual relationships between the variables concerned, if they could have been more precisely measured. It is safe to assume that estimates of variance explained by particular items or scales or by the multivariate model as a whole, using multiple correlation and regression techniques, are conservative ones. For a fuller discussion of these methodological questions, see C. Michael Lanphier, "Attenuation in a Reliability and Multiple Correlation: An Example from Survey Data' (Paper delivered to the seminar of the Survey Unit of the Social Sciences Research Council, London, England, May 16, 1976).

11 John Goldlust and Anthony Richmond, "A Multivariate Model".

12 Full details of how each variable was measured, giving a description of the items on which it was based, how they were coded, inter-item correlations and reliability measures, will be included in an appendix to the final report. When possible, standard scales, such as the Blishen Index of Socio-Economic Status, Bogardus Scale of Ethnic Social Distance, the Chapin Scale of Social Participation, etc. were used. When new scales were created, they were subjected to appropriate tests of reliability and validity.

13 John Goldlust and Anthony H. Richmond, "Multivariate Analysis of Immigrant Adaptation: A Study of Male Householders in Metropolitan Toronto", mimeographed (Toronto: Institute for Behavioural Research, York University, 1974).

14 Richmond, *Post-War Immigrants*; W.E. Kalbach, "The Impact of Immigration on Canada's Population", *1961 Census Monograph* (Ottawa: Dominion Bureau of Statistics, 1970).

15 Richmond, *Post-War Immigrants,* pp. 216-20.

Segregation and the Indian Act:
The Dialogue of Equality vs. Special Status
Sally M. Weaver

In the late 1960s Canada underwent a re-examination of its substance and worth in debates on integration, national identity and cultural complexity. Part of this re-examination involved a growing consciousness of its native population and the civil liberties which this population did or should have. The mass media rapidly focused on the moral, social and legal web surrounding the Indian Act, and the Act became the instrument for examining the relationship between the native people and the government/society at large. (The formalization of this issue around treaties, poverty and marginality also occurred, but these will not be considered in the following discussion.)

The Indian Act has been, and still is Canada's major instrument for dealing with an aboriginal population which is racially different from the other residents of the country. While recently the Act has become an embarrassment to the federal government, it has come to be seen as a source of ethnic salvation by the Indian people. The purpose of this paper is to address the events and ideologies which led to this conflict and to describe briefly the current arenas of power and activity where resolutions are being attempted.

The Indian Act is a product of a historical obligation to protect and, at the same time, "civilize" the aboriginal people. It pre-dates Confederation and has roots in British treatment of aboriginals. The Act has legitimate roots in the B.N.A. Act (Section 91, Head 24): Indians were singled out as a category of persons deserving special attention under a federal mandate. Although one legal interpretation[1] holds that this mandate was discretionary, Canada apparently interpreted it as impelling and exercised its mandate. The evolution of the Indian Act has witnessed increasing federal power within the realm of Indian Affairs which has produced the only clientele department now in existence in the federal structure.

Although some Indians have consistently criticized the Act for its constraints, most have mixed emotions about it. They resent the authority it exerts over their daily lives, yet see it as an important device for protecting their special rights. These "rights", supposedly enshrined in the Act, are variously perceived. Formulations vary according to region, tribe, personal experiences and local folklore. In some areas treaty rights have become confused with Indian Act rights. On the whole they usually involve statements of freedom to maintain their lands, freedom of trespass from whites, freedom from taxation, free medical services, freedom from accountability for debts accrued

154

to whites and freedom to follow their cultural patterns and to retain their languages. These rights carry high emotional content, and, although many *are* derived from the Indian Act, the Act is more often used as a means of defending the legitimacy of all such rights when they are challenged. Rights comprise the core of the "special status" argument.

As a necessary background, it should be noted that the Act specifically addresses itself to the following topics:

1. definition of Indian status as it pertains to individuals and bands
2. definitions and safeguarding of reserves
3. land
4. monies
5. taxation
6. estates and testimentary disposition
7. local government
8. economic exchanges
9. ministerial powers
10. education and farming

These categories of concern have changed little in the course of history, and the Act today is fundamentally the same as it was in the late 1800s.

As an ethnic category Indians have received unique treatment. Despite the Indians' extensive linguistic and cultural diversity, they have been lumped under one rubric which does not reflect or represent a social or cultural unit or collectivity. While this has presented a problem to the public and the government, it is emerging as a major concern for Indian associations. The constraints, which include social, legal and physical segregation, have become embarrassing to the federal government and to many white liberals.

The issue at hand is whether the Indians as a group and as individuals should be treated equally with other Canadians or whether they should be granted special status. Empirically it could be said that they experience a little of both, but this paper is not addressed to strictly empirical issues. Instead, it focuses on two questions: are Indians discriminated against because they are treated differently, and secondly, how does society resolve the seemingly opposite demands of special status and equality? To be sure these are old issues in any democratic society, but they are now crucial issues for Canadian society. In order to understand how these issues are being formulated and treated, it is necessary to look at their roots in history.

In the past legislation, drafted without Indian commentary, built in the dilemma of protection from, yet exposure to civilizing agents. Although the policy was designed to assimilate the Indians (i.e. to replace Indian culture with that of the dominant society), it was considered necessary to build legal and administrative walls around the native population to prevent anomie before "civilization". One means of achieving this "balance" was to physically isolate Indians on reserves and to protect them from white intrusion. (The relocation policy practiced in the U.S.A. whereby Indian communities were moved to areas of sparse white population did not occur in Canada, although it was proposed in the 1830s.) But in order to protect and isolate, it was necessary to define the protected population. Originally, the principle of self-determination was used to establish this definition: an Indian was defined as a person whom the community considered a member. But this rapidly gave way to the principle of patrilineal descent which still holds today.[2] Because this meant that an individual's legal status as an Indian was related to his right to occupy land, it was necessary to establish a cut-off point. As a result, Indian women who married white men in theory forfeited membership in the band, rights of residence and the right to pass legal Indian status on to their off-spring. This marriage-to-secure-land process occurred early in Upper Canada's history and later was transformed into legislation which affected all Canadian Indians.

But Indian land had to be guarded against other dangers. Indians might be persuaded to sign their land over in return for cancellation of their debts, they might barter it for goods, sell it under the influence of alcohol, lose it through taxation or, through testimentary disposition, give it to non-Indians. Ministerial authority was exerted to protect reserve lands from these threats. Boundary-maintaining mechanisms, which other ethnic groups evolved internally, were imposed on the category Indian by external, federal governmental agencies. The protection of the band and individual rested not on the Indian or his community, but on the government. Certainly some boundary-defensive mechanisms existed at the band level through cultural and social factors such as identity, rituals, mythology and ideologies. But it is important to stress that legal fortifications were erected (not always successfully) to insure community isolation.

To understand the native people's reaction to the re-awakening of interest in their problems in the 1960s, it is necessary to examine the general characteristics of their population. Canada's Indians are roughly 500,000 in number, of which only half hold legal status and half of those, treaty status. Generally they are poor, unskilled or semi-skilled, linguistically and culturally diverse, geographically dispersed in small pockets of reserves across the country or in city ghettos, manifest an extensive range of acculturation, have a low level of education and literacy, and have weakly developed leadership at the band or community level. These characteristics of marginality, poverty and lack of political leadership have, in the past, rendered interaction among individual groups difficult, if not impossible. Such interaction or communication between bands across the country is needed in order to create a national identity or nexus of contact and information dispersal. The critical point is that the Indian population is a cateogry of individuals and bands, not an interacting nation-wide ethnic group as some would think.

Clearly influenced by the birth of the participatory democracy ideology of the 1960s, Canada began to re-examine the Indian Act as an instrument of ethnic relations. From July of 1968 to early May of 1969 regional consultation meetings were held between representatives of the bands and Department of Indian Affairs officials to discuss revisions to the Act. The booklet *Choosing a Path* was published by the department to assist Indians in crystallizing their opinions.[3] The recorded results of the consultations indicated a wide diversity of Indian opinion on revisions to the Act and an unmistakable preoccupation with treaties and special rights.[4]

The discussions were aimed at producing a new policy, but when this policy was announced in 1969,[5] a cry of alarm went up from Indian communities across the nation. The policy would remove the federal presence in Indian Affairs, extend provincial involvement and pass land title to Indian bands. Indian indignation at the "consultation" process was intense. They had understood that the Act was to be revised, not abrogated.

This new Indian policy provided the needed impetus for Indian interaction and dialogue. Although in the past Indian associations above the band level had been formed, most were short-lived and no nation-wide movement had occurred. Such a movement began to emerge with the formation of provincial and regional associations which were federally funded and balanced precariously between a desire for independence and an equally strong emotional dependence on the Indian Act and treaties. A few provincial leaders received nation-wide acclaim, if not recognition from the Indian people, and a national organization was created to articulate their interests to the federal government. Indian involvement was characterized by a diversity of Indian organizations which at times had ample funds, but often lacked well-defined goals and objectives, leadership and grass roots support or understanding from their constituents, the bands. Historical allegiances and animosities between tribal groups placed severe stress on these associations, as did the lack of clear goal formulation and bureaucratic skills.

But, however falteringly, the social movement began to put pressure on the federal government's "termination" policy. The Indians were met with sympathetic support from the press and confusion from the white liberals who, convinced that the Indian Act was discriminatory and that the Indians did not want it, though it was proper to remove this oppressive legislation.

The most immediate product of the associations was the formulation of counter-proposals on the new Indian policy. Although the associations differed over specific recommendations, they promoted a common stance.[6] In general they denounced the termination policy, demanded a renegotiation of treaties before they would consider any changes in the Act, asked for more local self-determination, urged support for economic development and educational up-grading, and argued for special status or "citizens plus" treatment.

With the emergence of these position papers the dilemma—special status vs. equality— crystallized. The equality policy put forward by the government in 1969 argued that treating Indians differently than other Canadians denied the Indians equality before the law and certain goods and services that the nation had to offer. The government felt that the Indians would continue to be powerless, marginal and ineffective. This situation, it was said, was intolerable and unjust. The solution lay in abolishing the Indian Act and developing a partnership between Indians and government to deal with the problem.

The special status or citizens plus argument, articulated most eloquently by Cardinal,[7] was founded on the premise that, by their aboriginal occupation of the country, the Indians were "first citizens". It was further argued that they had been treated unjustly in the past, that their rights either had not been recognized or had been inadequately defended if recognized, and that they wanted to participate in the nation and be recognized for their contributions. They demanded the re-negotiation of treaties and recognition of their aboriginal land rights.

As discussion of these issues began to intensify, other civil rights causes emerged providing new rhetoric and suggesting other avenues of exploration. Poverty, ecology and the status of women were directly related to some of the issues concerning special status and equality. An important legal event was the passing of the Bill of Rights by parliament in 1960. The Bill was tested in the courts in the Drybones case where it was found that the provisions on intoxication in the Indian Act were harsher than those in the laws of the Northwest Territories where Drybones lived. On this basis, the Supreme Court of Canada declared the relevant section in the Indian Act to be discriminatory against Indians, contrary to the Bill of Rights and had that section rendered inoperative.[8] This case had far-reaching implications for the Indian Act because future judgements could declare the entire Act discriminatory.

After this judgement, the dialogue on Indian rights began to shift from the political-parliamentary arena to the judiciary. This shift occurred for many reasons: Indians were becoming impatient with unnecessarily restrictive provisions in the Indian Act; Indian organizations were in the process of responding to the White Paper and were even less inclined to trust government with the defense of their special rights; and the government had agreed to take no further action until the responses to the White Paper had been made by Indian organizations.

Some court judgements indicated that the judiciary considered the general question of Indian rights, and the more specific one of aboriginal land title claims, to be a political matter rather than a judicial one, but the government had closed the avenues for political consideration of Indian rights by its "equality" policy in the White Paper. Consequently Indian groups such as the Nishga Tribal Council in British Columbia and the Grand Council of the Cree in Quebec took their land claims to the courts for redress. In the Nishga case the Supreme Court of Canada decided against the Indians' claim to aboriginal title.[9] This decision came from a divided court and was made on the grounds of a technicality rather than on the substance of the issue. The public was unimpressed with the judgement and increased pressure was put on the government to recognize aboriginal land claims. The decision is still pending in the case of the Grand Council of the Cree who are asking for a settlement of their land claims before the James Bay hydroelectric project further damages their lands and livelihood.[10] A more encouraging judgement has recently come from the Superior Court of the Northwest Territories.[11] Faced with possible damage to their lands by the construction of the Mackenzie pipeline, several bands in the area filed a caveat claiming that their aboriginal title to the lands had not been properly extinguished. Although the court recognized the need for a full examination of the matter, it found sufficient evidence to validate the filing of the caveat.

More recently an Indian case tested the Bill of Rights in relation to the status of women. The conjunction of these two causes led to certain dilemmas for white liberals and for the courts, but not for the Indian associations who argued the case on a Bill of Rights vs. Indian Act basis, rather than on the basis of women's rights. The case involved two Indian women who claimed that they were being discriminated against on the basis of sex. Both had been forced to forfeit their Indian status when they married whites, whereas an Indian male in the same situation would not lose his status. In the lower courts of Ontario where the original decisions were made the issue was judged almost solely on the basis of the status of women, and the decisions favoured the Indian women retaining their status.[12] But upon appeal to the Supreme Court of Canada the decision was reversed.[13] To some, this reversal represented a defeat for the cause of women, while to Indians it was a victory for their special rights and a successful defense of the Indian Act against the Bill of Rights.

The present confrontation between the Indian Act and the Bill of Rights in the courts clearly reflects the special status versus equality argument. An earlier legal solution would have been relatively easy. Parliament could have declared the Indian Act exempt from the application of the Bill of Rights, but it took no such action.[14] As a result of these cases, the courts were seen by Indians as possible avenues for the recognition of their special rights, and the Minister of Indian Affairs, in August of 1973, changed his position indicating that the government was willing to negotiate a settlement in the Yukon, the Northwest Territories, northern Quebec and British Columbia where Indians claimed their aboriginal land title had not been extinguished.[1]

In summary it is clear that Indians have come to depend upon the Indian Act and the treaties (real or promised) as boundary-maintaining mechanisms They have socialized succeeding generations to these protections, but these protections require the compliance of the government if they are to be main tained. Historically, Indians have not built and maintained strong, self-maintained controls against external forces to the extent that such groups as the Hutterites and Mennonites have done. Recently Indian reliance on a single external institution (the government) to protect their interests has proved precarious as the 1969 termination policy demonstrated. Since the mid-1960s Indians have begun to play a more active role in defining and defending their own ethnic boundaries and rights. They have sought support from the judicial arena and from other personnel in society and thus have diversified their external supports for the maintenance of their special rights This diversification involved risk, but the future will hold even greater risk and further demands for native initiative because the collective forces of the welfare state, mass communication, urbanization and resource development will not by-pass Indians. At the ideological level, there will remain a strong need for a realistic rationalization of their special rights ideology, because the prevailing liberal ideology which seeks to abolish privilege will continue to prevail.

Sally Weaver is an associate professor of Anthropology at the University of Waterloo.

NOTES

1 H.B. Hawthorn and M.A. Tremblay, *A Survey of the Contemporary Indians of Canada* (Ottawa: Queen's Printers, 1966), part I, chapter xii.

2 S.M. Weaver, "Report on Archival Research Regarding Indian Women's Status, 1868-1869" (1971). Unpublished report.

3 Canada, Department of Indian Affairs and Northern Development (Ottawa, 1968).

4 Canada, Department of Indian Affairs and Northern Development, *Reports of the Indian Act Consultation Meetings, 1968-1969* (Ottawa, 1969).

5 Canada, Department of Indian Affairs and Northern Development, *Indian Policy* (Ottawa, 1969).

6 *Citizens Plus* Prepared by the Indian Chiefs of Alberta and presented to the Prime Minister, June 1970 (mimeo): *A Declaration of Indian Rights: The B.C. Indian Position Paper.* Prepared by the Union of B.C. Indian Chiefs, November 17, 1970. Vancouver (mimeo); *Wahbung: Our Tomorrows.* Prepared by the Manitoba Indian Brotherhood, presented to the Minister of Indian Affairs, October 1971 (Manitoba Indian Brotherhood, Winnipeg, Man. mimeo).

7 H. Cardinal, *The Unjust Society* (Edmonton: Hurtig, 1969).

8 The Queen v. Drybones, Supreme Court of Canada, S.C.R. (1970), pp. 282-298.

9 Calder et al v. Attorney General of British Columbia, Supreme Court of Canada, S.C.R. (1973).

10 For a review of the James Bay issue see B. Richardson, *James Bay: The Plot to Drown the North Woods* (Sierra Club of Canada, Clarke Irwin: Toronto, 1972), and H. Bourassa, *James Bay* (Montreal: Harvest House, 1973).

11 Paulette's Application to file a Caveat, 6 *Western Weekly Reports* (n.s.) 97 (N.W.T. Supreme Court, 1973).

12 Lavell v. The Attorney General of Canada, Federal Court of Appeal (1971), and Bedard v. Richard Isaac et al, Supreme Court of Ontario (1971).

13 Richard Isaac et al v. Yvonne Bedard, Supreme Court of Canada (1973), and The Attorney General of Canada v. Lavell, Supreme Court of Canada (1971).

14 D.E. Sanders, "The Bill of Rights and Indian Status", *U.B.C. Law Review,* vol. 7 (1972), pp. 81-105.

15 Statement by the Hon. Jean Chretien on Claims of Indian and Inuit People. Ottawa, August 8, 1973. Press Release, Department of Indian Affairs and Northern Development, Ottawa.

Commentary on Section 4
Alexander Matejko

Immigrants' commitment to, and identification with Canada has several
dimensions which should be clearly distinguished. These distinctions
are blurred to some extent in the paper presented by Anthony Richmond and John Goldlust. There are several practical reasons why immigrants
are either eager or reluctant to accept the Canadian citizenship, and one
should be very careful when drawing conclusions on this basis. Social identity is to a large extent a cultural phenomenon, and it is necessary to look
much deeper into this issue. Many years ago Thomas and Znaniecki studied
immigrants to the U.S. in terms of their self-identification in *The Polish
Peasant in Europe and America,* and later Znaniecki developed the concept of the "humanistic coefficient". In Canadian ethnic studies much more
attention to a similar coefficient is badly needed.

Commitment to a given society and the identification with it is influenced
by a whole variety of external and internal factors. All of these factors are
in some way experienced by immigrants, evaluated, and then accepted or
rejected. A Canadian passport means something different to the holders of
"good" British passports than it does to refugees from eastern Europe or
Uganda. People who come from a clearly defined socio-cultural environment with long-standing traditions may have more difficulty in identifying
with a new culture than people with a relatively poor or impoverished
social background.

Canadians may be overly concerned with the behavioristic approach and
may underestimate what can be learned from gaining insight into the mentality of people. Investigations of the spiritual life of the ethnic groups are
carried out by writers, priests and journalists, rather than by sociologists.
The ethnic press is not utilized as a source of information. The original
ethnic cultures are almost unknown to people who speak only English.

The Iroquois, French and the Ukrainian experience, like all other ethnic
experiences, must be located in a broader socio-cultural context. People
who must decide about their own identity evaluate the relative attractive-
ness of various alternatives. For the destitute people who arrived long ago
from eastern Europe to work in the lowest jobs there was often no other
choice than to remain in their own ethnic communities. But the young generation is now in an entirely different situation. They speak English fluently
and many alternatives are open to them. Such freedom of choice is still not

available to young Indians. They are restricted to their own reserves by the Indian Act, family affiliations, local traditions, prejudices and, most of all, by the lack of opportunities for them in the outside white world. The whole issue of French identity may be also explained partly by the changes in external opportunities (among others, the limited utility of the French language) and partly by the spiritual comfort of being different from Anglo-Saxons and enjoying it. It is true that several ethnic groups in Canada presently lose their young generation, while others, especially the Indians, do not. But the young Indians who do not leave the reserves become increasingly frustrated with their situation.

It is necessary to pinpoint the factors which contribute to the traditional ethnic identity. The middle-class ethic has only limited attraction for the young generation. And these same young people have begun to question the American mass culture as it is portrayed by the media. Many Canadians are still not clear as to what constitutes the Canadian identity. The double or even triple identity may be one possible solution for Canadian ethnic groups. However the main question is not how many identities people can reconcile, but rather what these identities mean to peoples' lives, how deeply they are rooted in their souls, and what is the social impact of the moral and intellectual turmoil of changing identities? Many more cross-cultural studies are needed to show how Canada's ethnic experience differs from that of other countries.

Although a policy of multiculturalism flourishes in Canada, several ethnic groups survive only because of their older and middle generations. The young people at best pay the lip service to what has been so dear to their parents and grandparents. Studies of ethnic groups in Canada do not as yet pay enough attention to the growing generation gap and internal tensions within ethnic groups. The latter is not so much a question of personal rivalries and political dissonance as of the changing meaning of ethnic identity. As long as the existence of ethnic groups was endangered, they could improve their position in the Anglo-Saxon world only by a group effort. Thus it was valuable and meaningful for them to support ethnic church groups and parishes, to organize mutual aid associations, to operate ethnic halls and other group meeting places. The younger generation does not feel this threat or feels it much less than did the older generation. The present generation of ethnics shares common problems and anxieties with the Anglo-Saxon youth. In ethnic groups such as the Ukrainians and Poles, which are not rejuvenated by large numbers of new immigrants, it remains to be seen to what extent these groups will be willing and able to maintain their socio-cultural identity and for how long. An ethnic culture makes sense only as long as it shows some vitality and a spiritual meaning for individuals involved.

Sociologists should pay more attention to the eufunctional as well as to the disfunctional qualities of various ethnic cultures. The strong conservative bias of certain ethnic groups may be attributable to a social and moral deterioration which makes these groups little more than objects of external manipulation. The use of ethnicity in the U.S. presidential elections may be a good example of such manipulation, rather than of the politicians' genuine concern for the well-being of ethnic groups. The current revival of interest in ethnicity on the North American continent may be traced to two opposing sources: the first is the genuine search for identity shared by uprooted people who have lost themselves in the mass society; the second is the politicians' search for new clichés with which to manipulate the masses

In research on various ethnic groups in Canada one must consider the capacity of ethnic groups to provide a meaningful identity for their members. It is an unacceptable simplification to say that ethnicity is always meaningful and therefore desirable. Ethnic cultures differ widely in their vitality, stages of development, autonomy and spiritual appeal. In Canada little is known about the vitality of various ethnic cultures. Obviously all ethnic groups would like to present themselves as being dynamic, but it is up to social scientists to distinguish between truth and window-dressing. An ethnic group's appeal to its young generation may serve as a valuable measure of its vitality.

In my comments I have tried to discuss various dimensions of ethnic commitment and identity. More studies should be done so that multicultural Canada may better understand the vital issue of Canadian identity.

Alexander Matejko is a professor of Sociology at the University of Alberta.

5 Research on Ethnicity in Canada

Howard Palmer 167 **History and Present State of Ethnic Studies in Canada**

Jerzy Zubrzycki 184 **Research on Ethnicity in Australia and Canada**

History and Present State of Ethnic Studies in Canada
Howard Palmer

There has been a good deal of excellent research done in the area of ethnic studies in Canada. Many of the best Canadian sociologists and several sociologists of international repute have done scholarly studies of ethnic groups. However there are also weaknesses in the research to date, and there are areas where research is urgently needed. In discussing the "state of the art" attention will be directed towards the weaknesses and the gaps.

Ethnic studies as it is used here refers to non-British, non-French and non-native groups. This is not to imply that Canada's two dominant groups— the French and the British (a very broad term which conceals more than it reveals)—and Canada's native peoples are not ethnic groups. Of course they are. However scholars have given more attention to these groups than to immigrant groups, or, as they were called in the terms of reference and the report of the Royal Commission on Bilingualism and Biculturalism, the "other ethnic groups". It would be impossible in the course of a short paper to deal adequately with the vast amount of historical and sociological research on English-French relations, French-Canadians, British-Canadians or native peoples. The history and present status of the dominant groups and native peoples also differ in many ways from other ethnic groups.

I History

The Pre-World War II Period

Research on non-British, non-French ethnic groups prior to World War II differs somewhat from research undertaken since the war. Books on other ethnic groups between the period of massive immigration at the turn of the century and the outbreak of World War II were marked by an attempt to understand the implications for Canada of immigration from a wide variety of ethnic, religious and national backgrounds. Who were these "strangers within our gates" and how could they be made part of Canadian society? The interest was primarily directed towards the formulation of social policy; there was little interest in the theoretical questions which many social scientists now bring to their study of ethnic groups.

Pre-war research and writing was done by people active in the institutions which were most concerned about the social issues raised by immigration— government, churches, schools, social welfare agencies and railway companies. Thus, prior to 1940, research on ethnic groups was carried out almost

167

entirely within the context of developing policies and promoting interest in the assimilation programmes of the institution concerned. The books written within this context include: J.A. Woodsworth's *Strangers Within Our Gates* (1908); C.A. Magrath's *Canada's Growth and Some Problems Affecting It* (1910); J.T.M. Anderson's *The Education of the New Canadian* (1918) W.G. Smith's *Building the Nation* (1922) and *A Study in Canadian Immigration* (1920); A. Fitzpatrick's *A Handbook for New Canadians* (1919); Kate Foster's *Our Canadian Mosaic* (1926); Dr. P.H. Bryce's, *The Value to Canada of the Continental Immigrant* (1928); Robert England's *The Central European Immigrant in Canada* (1929) and *The Colonization of Western Canada* (1936); and John Murray Gibbon's *Canadian Mosaic* (1938). While each of these books contains some factual material based on first-hand observation of various groups (along with a large dose of personal bias), all focus c Canadian immigration and social policy. The authors were concerned with formulating goals for Canadian society and determining how each ethnic group related to these goals. Virtually all of these writers (with perhaps the exception of Gibbon) believed that immigrants should be assimilated to a Canadian norm. But they differed in their view of how rapid assimilation should or could be and disagreed over the characteristics of the Canadian norm. Their primary concern was to determine the degree to which particular immigrant groups could be assimilated. Differences of opinion arose over Canada's ability to "digest" central and eastern Europeans and Orientals and, consequently, whether these groups should be allowed to enter Canada. Because these authors were writing for a mass audience, their styles were generally impressionistic and unanalytical: only rarely did they disassociate prescription from description.[1]

Probably the two most significant books of this era were those by J.S. Woodsworth, a Methodist minister who later became one of the principal founders of the C.C.F. movement, and Robert England, who was the superintendent in charge of continental Europeans for the Canadian Nationa Railways. At the time that he wrote *Strangers Within Our Gates,* Woodsworth was the director of the All Peoples' Mission in Winnipeg. This was one of the many home missions established in western Canadian immigrant centres at the turn of the century by Congregationalists, Methodists, Presbyterians and Baptists to Canadianize and protestantize eastern European and Oriental immigrants.[2] Woodsworth directed assimilation programmes at the mission and wrote and lectured on the immigration question to inform Canadians of the plight of the immigrant. His concern was stimulated by his belief in the social gospel.[3] Social gospellers believed that immigrant social problems like insanity, intemperance, illiteracy and crime were the result of social conditions, rather than individual failings. They believed that these problems could only be solved through a change in social conditions and the establishment of a truly Christian society. For Woodsworth, assimilation was not an inevitable process but one which required assistance.

In *Strangers Within Our Gates*[4] Woodsworth denounced indifference towards immigrants. He urged the adoption of programmes to improve their living and working conditions and educational opportunities in order to prevent social stratification, social disintegration, political corruption and the undermining of "British institutions". Unlike some other writers of the time, Woodsworth did not believe that immigrant social problems were the result of any inherent cultural or racial inferiority; he saw that the problems in large measure stemmed from generational conflict as the second generation became assimilated into Canadian society.[5] Even though he believed that some undesirable characteristics of different ethnic groups were genetically transmitted, he felt that these characteristics could be changed through a better social environment. In other words, he believed that acquired characteristics could overcome genetic problems and facilitate assimilation.

Woodsworth illustrated the difficulty of assimilation and the importance of assimilation programmes by comparing the ratio of immigrants to native-born population in the U.S. and Canada. Comparing Canada in 1900 to the U.S. in 1800, he calculated that Canada's immigration problem was thirty-seven times greater than that of America.[6]

Many social forces and institutions, such as neighborhood associations, commercial contacts, public schools, labour unions, the press, churches and intermarriage, acted to aid in the assimilation of immigrants. But Woodsworth pointed out that few agencies carried on the work of Canadianization. Although critical of a number of immigrant groups, particularly Orientals and Mormons, Woodsworth believed that Canada had something to gain from non-British immigrants. As a solution to what he perceived as the "immigration problem", he recommended that there by more careful screening of immigrants and that immigrants already in Canada should be subjected to an intensive assimilation campaign by the schools, social welfare agencies and labour unions.

Although basically of the same genre as *Strangers Within Our Gates,* Robert England's *The Central European Immigrant in Canada* was more sympathetic to the immigrant point of view. England was a graduate in Economics from Queen's and the University of Paris and had long and close experience with central and eastern Europeans in western Canada, first as a teacher in Ukrainian communities during World War I and later in his work for the C.N.R. He was the first to question the assumptions of Anglo conformity. *The Central European Immigrant in Canada* was written during the late 1920s, primarily as a defence against the verbal attacks on central and eastern European immigrants which were being made by nativist organization like the Ku Klux Klan, the Orange Order and the National Association of Canada.[7] The book attempted to defuse nativist arguments and mobilize public support for assimilation programmes.

In contrast to earlier writers like Woodsworth, England was uncertain about the desirability of assimilation. He had read widely in anthropological literature and was influenced by the cultural relativism of Franz Boas and other anthropologists. Their theories led him to ask himself whether British culture (or alternatively, urban industrial society) was really superior to immigrant cultures. England's book reflects an unresolved tension between admiration for peasant values, such as dedication to the land, industriousness and loyalty to the church and patriarchal family on the one hand and concern about the "social problems" of "ignorance, poverty and social degradation" on the other.[8] It was therefore difficult for him to resolve the ideological dilemma concerning the desirability of assimilation. Despite his concern for the decline in peasant values and the social disorganization which resulted from the breakdown of primary group relations in rural immigrant communities,[9] England finally opted for the melting pot vision of assimilation in which all groups lose their separate identities as they blend their cultures into a new Canadian type. Assimilation would alleviate the social problems in immigrant communities and overcome the lack of social solidarity in rural "bloc" settlements and in Canadian society as a whole. "We must incorporate the races who have come to us into *one* people: otherwise our dominion from sea to sea will perish in strife and anarchy."[10] But England also stressed the need for tolerance in the assimilation process and the right of immigrants to maintain their "ethnic individuality" in some attenuated form. As England saw it the major question with regard to assimilation was, "Can we achieve the transformation without injuring the best in the old-country heritage?"[11]

Even though England held some of the racial ideas of the nativists, he marshalled his arguments in defence of central and eastern Europeans. In his analysis of ethnic groups he used the commonly-accepted three-fold categorization of Europeans—Nordic, Alpine and Mediterranean[12]—and argued that racial qualities would remain despite intermarriage. But he believed that assimilation was possible because environment could modify "racial qualities, vices and instincts".[13] He dismissed notions of racial superiority and fears that racial intermarriage would lead to deterioration of the "stock". In fact he argued that a "blending of stocks" might produce a more tolerant Canadian culture. Although he accepted many of the assimilationist and racial premises of those who believed in restrictive immigration policies, he argued that central and eastern Europeans could be, and were being assimilated, making a restrictive immigration policy unnecessary.

The Depression marked a shift in the discussion of immigration and specific ethnic groups away from questions of their desirability as constituent elements within Canadian society—the social cost—to questions of their desirability as economic units—the financial cost. Academics replaced social activists as the prime investigators. Social scientists, especially economists, geographers and demographers, talked of labor conditions, business cycles, regional growth and rural-urban shifts with a wary eye on the possibly disruptive effects of immigration or cultural "deviance".[14] During the 1930s there was also increasing interest in Canadian immigration policy among Canadian, American and European historians.[15]

The earlier concern about the impact of culturally-divergent ethnic groups on Canadian society, reflected in the writing of Woodsworth and England, was still apparent in several sociological studies written during the 1930s. The Canadian National Committee for Mental Hygiene sponsored research by sociologists on two groups who were considered to be among the major ethnic problems facing Canada—the Japanese and the Ukrainians.[16] Both studies are still of considerable value because they contain a large amount of careful research on the migration and settlement patterns, economic and social conditions and the religious and secular institutions of these two communities. But one must not take these studies out of their context. Valuable though they are, both studies were concerned with examining the desirability of these groups in terms of the social problems which they created and their capacity for assimilation.

Although a more scholarly approach to ethnic research did not reach maturity until after the war, one pre-war example should be noted. In *Group Settlement* (1936) sociologist C.A. Dawson and his associates examined what was perceived by many Canadians to be a critical issue—the cohesive rural ethnic settlement. In dealing with Doukhobors, Mennonites, Mormons, German Catholics and French Canadians, the authors attempted to explain how group settlement aided in the adjustment process, and how, in spite of popular doubts, integration was proceeding in varying degrees within these groups. Even though Dawson was concerned to some extent with the seemingly inevitable questions of social policy, his book marked a significant departure in the study of ethnic groups in Canada. For the first time group characteristics were attributed to culture, rather than to biology. Dawson also guided a number of his students at McGill University into a study of the social organization of immigrant communities in Montreal, thus creating a small body of research relating to the urban ethnic experience.[17] One of Dawson's colleagues at McGill in the late 1930s, Everett C. Hughes, also promoted scholarly research and publishing in this field. His best-known work on the Canadian experience is *French Canada in Transition*, published after he moved to the University of Chicago. Hughes was also instrumental in laying the theoretical groundwork for later studies of ethnicity and intergroup relations.

The Post-War Period

Research on the other ethnic groups expanded tremendously after World War II. Renewed interest sparked by large-scale post-war migration was fanned by a steadily growing sociological profession which included newly-arrived European intellectuals, some of whom naturally turned to the study of their own ethnic group,[18] and an increasing number of minority group members in Canadian graduate schools who sought to study questions of identity which related to their own life experience. A wide variety of research approaches were used as university disciplines became increasingly specialized.

Research on ethnicity in the post-war period differed in a number of ways from the earlier works of people like Woodsworth. One of the most important differences was that ethnic minorities were no longer viewed primarily as "problem" groups which must be assimilated as quickly as possible. Some of the research done for graduate degrees in social work[19] and some research on the Doukhobors and on immigrant children in the public schools maintained this "problem" approach, but increasingly research took a more neutral approach to ethnic diversity. Some of it assumed that ethnic pluralism was a valuable aspect of Canadian society rather than a social problem.

This shift from the assimilationist to the pluralist viewpoint in the scholarly world was part of a larger shift in Canadian attitudes.[20] The changed climate was due in part to the impact of cultural relativism which undermined racist thinking and assimilationist assumptions. Emerging pluralist assumptions in the academic world also stemmed from the growing presence of second and third generation non-Anglo-Saxons and post-war immigrant scholars who often looked on the history and social conditions of their own ethnic group with different eyes than had their Anglo-Saxon predecessors. However ethnic tolerance and the abandoning of the "problem" approach were also the result of a decrease in ethnic differentiation in some parts of the country, particularly in the Prairie Provinces. Pre-World War II immigrants and their descendants were being assimilated, while the more highly educated post-war immigrants were not as culturally distinctive as the predominantly rural and working class pre-war, non-Anglo-Saxon immigrants. Concern about ethnic minorities as problems to be assimilated decreased as the importance of ethnicity as a basis of social differentiation decreased.

Two first-rate sociological studies which set the tone for the high level of sociological analysis in the post-war period were Forest La Violette's *The Canadian Japanese and World War II* (Toronto, 1948) and William Peterson's *Planned Migration* (Berkeley, 1955). Another significant indication of the advances in the study of ethnic minorities in Canada was the series on ethnic groups in Manitoba sponsored during the 1950s and 1960s by the Manitoba Historical Society. The series, which included books on Hutterites, Mennonites, Jews, Ukrainians and Poles,[21] was of almost uniformly high quality. However the book by sociologist E.K. Francis on the Mennonites, *In Search of Utopia,* stood in a class of its own as an outstanding synthesis of historical and sociological approaches.

In the 1950s and 1960s, as older and more established Canadian ethnic groups found time to look back at their past, there emerged a proliferation of historical works by the groups themselves which emphasized their contributions. Canada's Centennial gave considerable impetus to this impulse. The Centennial Commission funded a series of books entitled Canada Ethnica written by individuals involved in the life of ethnic organizations. The books were long on lists of individual immigrant's accomplishments and short on analysis.[22] Too often these works tended to be more filial-pietous than factual, glossing over areas of controversy, intra-group problems and generational friction. In spite of the significant amount of primary research which went into them, these defects limited their appeal. Another major weakness of the series was that the studies were not generally placed within the overall context of Canadian history.

The Royal Commission on Bilingualism and Biculturalism provided considerable stimulus to research on other ethnic groups during the late 1960s. The historical research was mainly of the "achievements" variety and of little value, but the sociological research was of generally high quality.[23] The volume summarizing and analyzing this research, Book IV of the Royal Commission on Bilingualism and Biculturalism, most of which was written by Jean Burnet, will remain a landmark of analysis in this field. The only other research published by the Royal Commission on other ethnic groups was the outstanding anthropological study by Jeremy Boissevain, *The Italians of Montreal.*

II Current State of Research

No attempt can be made here to list or assess the vast amount of research on ethnic groups in Canada which has appeared since 1945. Some indication of what has been done, however, can be given by assessing the major gaps in current research. There are three distinct types of research in which gaps appear: research on particular groups, research by particular disciplines and research on particular topics.[24]

Research on particular groups

Those groups which are the least culturally similar to the established Canadian norm have been most studied. Mennonites, Doukhobors, Hutterites, Ukrainians and blacks have received a good deal of attention. Three books by scholars of international reputation—Robin Winks on the blacks, John Bennett on the Hutterites and Woodcock and Avakumovic on the Doukhobors—are particularly outstanding.[25] Groups which are relatively invisible in Canadian society—Scandinavians, Dutch, Americans and Belgians— have received less attention. Interest in newly-arrived groups—Koreans, Filipinos, South Americans and West Indians—seems to be increasing, but little research has been published to date.[26]

Research by disciplines

Canadian sociologists have examined ethnicity from a variety of perspectives: race and ethnic relations, sociology of the family, sociology of religion demography, occupational sociology, social stratification, political sociology and the sociology of migration. Particularly outstanding contributions have been made by Frank Jones, Raymond Breton, Anthony Richmond and Jean Burnet through their own work and through the direction they have provided to countless graduate students. Breton's concept of "institutional completeness"[27] and Richmond's description of the type of internationally-mobile immigrant or "transient" are of considerable value. Although they have made the greatest contribution, sociologists have not been alone in the study of ethnic groups in Canada. Social psychologists are showing increasing interest in ethnic identity, ethnic stereotypes, bilingualism, political behaviour and the dynamics of family life within ethnic groups.[28] In 1975 three social psychologists, John Berry, Don Taylor and M.R. Kalin, began work on a large national study of majority attitudes toward multiculturalism and minority ethnic groups. Their work surveys such topics as stereotyping, prejudice and social distance. Geographers have done some research on ethnic minorities within the context of settlement geography, human geography and urban geography. Quantitative studies of ethnic residential patterns in cities are now in vogue and will contribute much to an overall understanding of ethnicity. Two major studies of Canadian immigration policy have been done by political scientists David Corbett and Freda Hawkins,[29] but political scientists in Canada have been relatively slow to do research on ethnic voting behaviour. Economists are just beginning to study the relationship between immigration and economic growth. In Linguistics, departments of Slavic Studies have led the way in research, and there is now a considerable body of research on Slavic languages in Canada. Departments of Slavic Studies have also led the way in analyzing Canadian ethnic literature. Although students of Canadian literature are now beginning to devote some attention to this literature, little research has as yet been published. No one has replaced Watson Kirkconnell who so diligently surveyed literature in languages other than French and English for the *University of Toronto Quarterly* from 1937 to 1965.

Although Anthropology is a relatively new social science in Canada, anthropologists have shown some interest in the country's other ethnic groups, particularly in the areas of linguistics[30] and the anthropology of religion. However research on native peoples has attracted most of their interest. The closely-related field of folklore is still in its infancy in Canada. The National Museum of Man has sponsored research on a wide range of ethnic groups and their folklore, but much of it is still in unpublished form. Mention should be made, however, of the pioneering work of Robert Klymasz on Ukrainian folklore in Canada. With the stimulus of the federal government's multicultural policy, the Center for Folk Culture Studies at the National Museum has increased its staff considerably, and some of the results of the research are beginning to appear in published form.[31]

Canadian historians generally have not interested themselves in research on other ethnic groups. The biases which have pervaded the documentation of Canadian history in the past—nationalism, politics, economics and biography—still predominate, as do white Anglo-Saxon Protestant or French-Canadian middle-class biases. This lack of interest on the part of early Canadian historians has resulted in a scarcity of factual information, making current research difficult and unappealing. Fortunately, due to the new emphasis on social history, research on immigration and ethnic history is growing. The main focus of current ethnic history is on immigration policy and the attitudes of native-Canadians toward minority ethnic groups, rather than on the history of the groups themselves.[32] The series of twenty-two ethnic histories which the Department of the Secretary of State is sponsoring under the federal government's multicultural programme should fill many of the gaps in Canadian historical writing. The growing collections in the Ethnic Archives division of the Public Archives, the National Library's attempts to collect ethnic newspapers and provincial archivists' growing interest in ethnic manuscript material and artifacts should further facilitate research on other ethnic groups.

Research on particular topics
An informal survey of research on ethnic groups in Canada indicates that most research has been done on historical background, settlement patterns, ethnic identity, assimilation and ethnic associations. Some research has been done on population trends, religion, values, occupations and social class, kinship, the ethnic press, intergroup relations, social control and group maintenance, but relatively little information has been compiled on language, mental health and deviance, the arts, recreation and political behaviour.[33] To give some idea of the range of topics available, let us consider five areas: economics, politics, religion, ethnic identity and language loyalty.

In economic history and occupational sociology there is a definite need for extensive research into the role of ethnic groups in industries such as mining, transportation, forestry, dairying, construction, manufacturing, sports, entertainment and the arts, as well as research on the overall effects of immigration on the economy. The reasons for occupational specialization among different ethnic groups need further study, and comparative studies of social mobility among different ethnic groups would provide useful information about value and family structure differences.

Labour and political historians have paid too little attention to ethnic factors.[34] Histories of the major parties and politicians fail to discuss ethnic differences in bases of support and how politicians perceived ethnic issues. There is virtually no research on the impact of non-British and non-French groups on Canadian foreign policy, however insignificant that impact might seem. More research should be done on political parties' attempts to gain support among various ethnic groups, as well as analyses of voting behaviour. Labour historians often discuss attitudes of organized labour toward immigration but seldom discuss ethnic factors in support of unions, aside from emphasizing the importance of British and American union organizers.[35]

There are a number of gaps in Canadian religious history and the sociology of religion as they relate to the other ethnic groups. There are a few studies of the Protestant Church's response to immigration, but no studies of the Roman Catholic response. There is some material on the role of churches in promoting and aiding immigration, but (with the exception of churches among Ukrainians) there is virtually no research on immigrant churches themselves. Hutterites, Doukhobors and Mennonites have been studied extensively, but nothing has been written on what is perhaps the most important component of their religions—their theology. The question of the modification of a group's religious beliefs in Canada has been largely ignored.

Assimilation and ethnic identification have been the focus for much of the research that has been done on ethnic groups in Canada. There has, however, been a transition from the debates over whether particular groups could be assimilated during the early part of the century to highly sophisticated analyses of the assimilation, integration and acculturation processes. Although these analyses enrich our understanding of sociological processes and the nature of Canadian society, they leave a number of gaps which should be filled.

While there are dangers in applying American models to Canadian situations, the sociological analyses of assimilation and ethnic identification by such Americans as Joshua Fishman, Milton Gordon and Will Herberg should be more carefully examined. Gordon's model of assimilation, which distinguishes between behavioral and structural assimilation, could provide the basis for comparative studies of Canadian ethnic groups.[36] And although they are somewhat less rigorous analytically, some of Joshua Fishman's ideas concerning ethnic identification in the United States might also provide the basis for a useful interchange between Canadian historians and sociologists concerning the nature and evolution of ethnic identification in Canadian society. According to Fishman most pre-World War I immigrants in the United States became conscious of their own ethnicity only after immigration. Group consciousness developed as immigrants attempted to adjust to the new world: they joined with fellow countrymen to solve common social problems, to fight discrimination and to establish an identity for themselves in a highly heterogeneous society.[37] The massive shifts in the size of various ethnic groups in Canadian census records between 1900 and 1920 suggest that the immigrant was confused about his ethnic identity (although it may also reflect the census officials' confusion). These data raise questions which demand further investigation.

Joshua Fishman and Vladimir Nahirny, following Marcus Lee Hansen's law of "third generation return" to ethnicity, suggest that fathers, sons and grandsons (and naturally, mothers, daughters and granddaughters) may differ not only in the degree, but also in the nature of their identification with their ethnic group.[38] For the first generation, ethnic identification was an inescapable reality. For the sons, ethnicity was not part of their pattern of daily life and was often despised. The grandsons neither rejected nor rushed to embrace the past. Because the third generation did not experience marginality like the second generation did, ethnicity became simply something about which to learn: it did not have much relevance to daily life. Although little research has been done on these theories in Canada, Hobart found similar modes of ethnic orientation in Alberta among Ukrainians,[39] and W.W. Isajiw has begun some interesting work prompted by the insights of Fishman and Nahirny.[40]

In his book, *Protestant, Catholic, Jew,* Will Herberg suggested that in the United States during the 1950s organized religion served as a substitute for ethnicity and that "ethnic" religions sacrificed language and ethnic maintenance when these were perceived as being in conflict with religious survival. My own research on the history of ethnic churches in Alberta seems to support this finding, and studies of residential segregation in Toronto and Alberta seem to give indirect evidence that religion is now more important as a basis of residential segregation than is ethnicity.[41] Findings in this area are still very tentative, however, and given that attitudes toward religion and ethnicity are changing, the relationship between these two factors may be changing too. In any case, the interrelationship between religion and ethnic identification needs to be examined both in the past and in contemporary society.

The relationship between ethnic identity, ethnic group solidarity, religious identity, religious solidarity and the maintenance of cultural symbols is very complex, and sociologists are just beginning to sort it out. Of particular current interest, given the federal government's desire to develop a policy on "non-official" languages, is the relationship between these variables and the knowledge and use of non-official languages. The non-official languages study, commissioned by the Department of the Secretary of State, which included in its sample ten of the largest ethnic groups in five metropolitan areas, provides a wealth of information on non-official language knowledge and use, the demand for non-official language retention (including the type and location of the demand) and the relationship between language retention and the retention of other distinctive social characteristics such as group identification, patterns of social interaction and observance of cultural traditions.[42]

Ethnic identification seems to vary depending on time of arrival, educational background and generation. The intensity of ethnic identification and language retention (or to put it the other way around, the degree of integration or assimilation) depends not only on the ethnic group involved, but on the individual involved—his or her age, generation, sex, time of arrival, socioeconomic status, length of residence and access to ethnic media. The difficult task now is to analyze the relative importance of these different factors. In conclusion let me suggest some important general avenues for ethnic studies. Much ethnocentrism can be overcome and new insights can be gained into social causation through comparative studies of two or more ethnic groups. Book IV of the *Report of the Royal Commission on Bilingualism and Biculturalism,* the Introduction to John Norris's *Strangers Entertained: A History of the Ethnic Groups of British Columbia*[43] and Stanford Lyman's article, "Contrasts in the Community Organization of Chinese and Japanese in North America",[44] all provide outstanding examples of the lessons that can be learned from comparative research. Needless to say, comparative studies of ethnic groups, both within Canada and in other countries, and studies of inter-ethnic relations require an interdisciplinary approach.

However comparative studies should not focus solely on ethnic groups at the national and provincial level. One of the real weaknesses of John Porter's *The Vertical Mosaic* is its failure to take into account regional and local differences in the "vertical mosaic". By community studies I mean not only studies of majority-minority group relationships, but also the question of relationships between different minority ethnic groups. Research on conflict and co-operation among Baltic, Scandinavian, Oriental, Slavic and Anabaptist groups would be particularly interesting.

There are also some geographical gaps in research. Manitoba, British Columbia, Alberta[45] and urban areas have been relatively well researched, but there is very little material on other ethnic groups in Saskatchewan, the Maritimes, in areas of Quebec outside of Montreal or in rural and frontier communities.[46]

Although there have been significant advances since World War II both in the quantity and quality of research on other ethnic groups in Canada, there are still a great number of research gaps. Further research on ethnicity in Canadian society can provide not only a better understanding of Canadian society, but insights useful in the development of theory in the social sciences. With the existence of the Canadian Ethnic Studies Association, the journal *Canadian Ethnic Studies* at the University of Calgary, the Ethnic Research programme at York University, begun under the able and energetic direction of Anthony Richmond, the Canadian Ethnic Studies Advisory Committee, under the sponsorship of the Department of the Secretary of State, and with considerable interest on the part of researchers and the availability of research money, the prospects for ethnic studies in Canada are bright.[47]

Howard Palmer is a professor of History at the University of Calgary and editor of Canadian Ethnic Studies.

NOTES

1 One partial exception was E. Bradwin's fascinating account of ethnic stratification in the construction camps in northern Canada in *Bunkhouse Man* (New York, 1928).

2 H. Palmer "Nativism and Ethnic Tolerance in Alberta: 1880-1920" (M.A. thesis, University of Alberta, 1971), pp. 158-165; George Emery, "Methodist Missions Among the Ukrainians", *Alberta Historical Review* (Spring, 1971), pp. 8-19.

3 Richard Allen, *The Social Passion* (Toronto, 1971).

4 For an excellent analysis of this book, see Marilyn Barber's Introduction to the reprinted edition (Toronto, 1972).

5 J.S. Woodsworth, *Strangers Within Our Gates* (Winnipeg, 1908), p. 165.

6 J.S. Woodsworth, "Canadians of Tomorrow", *Proceedings of the Canadian Club of Toronto* (Toronto, 1910), p. 142.

7 For an analysis of nativism during the 1920s see W. Calderwood, "The Rise and Fall of the Ku Klux Klan in Saskatchewan" (M.A. thesis, University of Saskatchewan, 1968); H. Palmer, "Nativism and Ethnic Tolerance in Alberta, 1920-1972" (Ph.D. diss. York University, 1972), chapter 2.

8 Robert England, *The Central European Immigrant in Canada* (Toronto, 1929), p. 103.

9 *Ibid.,* p. 163.

10 *Ibid.,* p. 173.

11 Robert England, *Central European,* pp. 169, 176.

12 For a brief discussion of the origins of this classification, see John Higham, *Strangers in the Land* (New York, 1967), chapter 6.

13 *Ibid.,* p. 175.

14 A.R.M. Lower, "The Case Against Immigration", *Queen's Quarterly* (Summer, 1930); W.B. Hurd, The Case for a Quota", *Queen's Quarterly* (January, 1928); "The Relation of Origins of Immigrants to the Settlement of the Country", *Papers and Proceedings of the Canadian Political Science Association* (1930).

15 Paul W. Gates, "Official Encouragement to Immigration by the Provinces of Canada", *Canadian Historical Review* (March, 1934); A. Marchbin, "The Origins of Migration from South-Eastern Europe to Canada", *CHAR* (1934), pp. 110-120; Edwin Guillet, *The Great Migration* (Toronto, 1937); Helen Cowan, *British Emigration to British North America* (Toronto, 1928); Heinz Lehmann, *Das Deutschum in West Kanada* (Berlin, 1939); Helge Nelson, *The Swedes and Swedish Settlement in North America* (Lund, Sweden, 1943); M. Hansen and J.B. Brebner, *The Mingling of the Canadian and American Peoples* (New Haven, 1943).

16 Charles Young and Helen R. Reid, *The Japanese Canadians* (Toronto, 1938); Charles Young, *The Ukrainian Canadians* (Toronto, 1931).

17 C.M. Bayley, "The Social Structure of the Italian and Ukrainian Immigrant Communities in Montreal" (M.A. thesis, McGill, 1939); L.G. Reynolds, *The British Immigrant* (Toronto, 1935); Jean Schwab, "Migration between Canada and the United States with particular reference to Professional and Intellectual Classes" (M.A. thesis, McGill, 1932); H.A. Gibbard, "The Means and Modes of Living of European Immigrants in Montreal" (M.A. thesis, McGill, 1935); Wilfrid Israel, "Montreal Negro Community" (M.A. thesis, McGill, 1928); A. Moelimann, "The Germans in Canada: Occupational and Social Adjustment of German Immigrants in Canada" (M.A. thesis, McGill, 1935).

18 J.M. Kirschbaum, *Slovaks in Canada* (Toronto, 1967); Victor Turek, *Poles in Manitoba* (Toronto, 1967).

19 For a listing of Masters of Social Work theses on immigrants and ethnic groups completed at the University of Toronto see "Minority Group Research in Ontario", *Ontario Human Rights Commission*, 1969.

20 Howard Palmer, "Mosaic vs. Melting Pot: Some Comparative Observations on Ethnicity in Canada and the United States", *International Journal* (Summer, 1975).

21 Victor Peters, *All Things Common* (Minneapolis, 1965); E.K. Francis, *In Search of Utopia* (Glencoe, Illinois, 1955); Arthur Chiel, *Jews in Manitoba* (Toronto, 1961); Paul Yuzyk, *Ukrainians in Manitoba* (Toronto, 1953); Victor Turek, *Poles in Manitoba* (Toronto, 1967).

22 W.J. Lindal, *The Icelanders in Canada*; Ludwick Kos-Rabiewicz Zubkowski, *The Poles in Canada*; A Spada, *The Italians in Canada*; P.R. Gaida, *The Lithuanians in Canada*; Ol' ha Woycenko, *The Ukrainians in Canada*. The study of the Ukrainians was far superior to the other books in the series.

23 The following studies were prepared for the Royal Commission on Bilingualism and Biculturalism: R.F. Adie, "The Ethnic Press"; R. Choulguine, "La contribution culturelle des Ukrainiens au Canada"; H.W. Debor, "The Cultural Contribution of the German Ethnic Group to Canada"; J.A. Diening, "Contributions of the Dutch to the Cultural Enrichment of Canada"; M.S. Donnelly, "Ethnic Participation in Municipal Government—Winnipeg, St. Boniface, and the Metropolitan Corporation of Greater Winnipeg"; Foon Sien, "The Chinese in Canada"; Saul Frankel, "Political Orientation and Ethnicity in a Bicultural Society"; C.W. Hobart, "Italian Immigrants in Edmonton: Adjustment and Integration"; P. Kellner, "Hungarian Participation in Canadian Culture"; T. Krukowski and P. McKellar, "The Other Ethnic Groups and Education"; W.J. Lindal, "The Contribution Made by the Scandinavian Ethnic Groups to the Cultural Enrichment of Canada"; H.H. Potter and D.G. Hill, "Negro Settlement in Canada, 1628-1965; A Survey"; C. Romalis, "The Attitudes of the Montreal Jewish Community toward French-Canadian Nationalism and Separatism"; Norma E. Walmsley, "Some Aspects of Canada's Immigration Policy"; R.R. Wisse, "Jewish Participation in Canadian Culture"; O. Woycenko, "Ukrainian Contributions to Canada's Cultural Life".

24 Based on a survey of materials contained in the following bibliographies and bibliographic surveys: Andrew Gregorvich, *Canadian Ethnic Groups Bibliography* (Toronto, 1972); *Citizenship, Immigration and Ethnic Groups in Canada: A Bibliography of Research, 1920-1958* (Ottawa, 1960) with supplements covering 1959-1961, 1962-1964, 1964-1968; *Canadian Ethnic Studies* Vol. I, No. I (June, 1970); Howard Palmer, *Land of the Second Chance* (Lethbridge, 1972), pp. 260-265; R.C. Harris, "Historical Geography in Canada", *Canadian Geographer* (1967), pp. 235-245; John Berry and G.J.S. Wilde, *Social Psychology of Canada: An Annotated Bibliography* (Kingston, 1971), pp. 41-55.

25 Robin Winks, *The Blacks in Canada* (New Haven, 1971); John Bennett, *Hutterian Brethren* (Stanford, 1967); G. Woodcock and Ivan Avakumovic *The Doukhobors* (Toronto, 1968).

26 One exception is the study by Eleanor Laqvian, *A Study of Filipino Immigration to Canada, 1962-72* (Ottawa, 1972).

27 Raymond Breton, "Institutional Completeness of Ethnic Communities and the Personal Relations of Immigrants" in B. Blishen et. al. (eds.), *Canadian Society: Sociological Perspectives* (Toronto, 1968); Anthony Richmond, "Sociology of Migration in Industrial and Post-industrial Societies", *Sociological Studies* (1969).

28 John Berry and G.J.S. Wilde, *Social Psychology of Canada: An Annotated Bibliography* (Kingston, 1971), pp. 41-55.

29 D. Corbett, *Canada's Immigration Policy: A Critique* (Toronto, 1957); Freda Hawkins, *Canada and Immigration* (Montreal, 1972).

30 Regna Darnell, *Linguistic Diversity in Canadian Society* (Edmonton, 1971).

31 Some of the publications of the staff of the National Museum are: *Ethno-Musicology*, Vol. XVI, No. 3 (September, 1972); Robert B. Klymasz *An Introduction to the Ukrainian-Canadian Immigrant Folksong Cycle*, National Museums of Canada Bulletin No. 234, Folklore Series 8 (Ottawa, 1970) and *The Ukrainian Winter*

Folksong Cycle in Canada, National Museums of Canada Bulletin No. 236, Folklore Series 9, (Ottawa, 1970) and *Folk Narrative among the Ukrainian Canadians in Western Canada,* Mercury Series, Canadian Centre for Folk Culture Studies, (Ottawa, 1973); Kenneth Peacock, *A Garland of Rue,* National Museum of Man Publications in Folk Culture, No. 2 (Ottawa, 1971); Jan Perowski, *Vampires, Dwarves, and Witches Among the Ontario Kashubs,* Mercury Series, Canadian Centre for Folk Culture Studies Paper No. 1 (Ottawa, 1972). See also *Canadian Ethnic Studies,* Vol. VII, No. 2 (1975).

32 Patricia Roy, "The Oriental 'Menace' in British Columbia" in S.M. Trofimenkoff (ed.), *The Twenties in Western Canada* (Ottawa, 1972) pp. 243-58; Introduction to Hilda Glynn-Ward, *The Writing on the Wall* (Toronto, 1974); "Educating the 'East'; British Columbia and the Oriental Question in the Inter-War Years", *B.C. Within Our Gates* (Toronto, 1972); Donald Avery, "Canadian Immigration Policy, the Anglo-Canadian Perspective" (Ph.D. diss., University of Western Ontario, 1973); "Canadian Immigration Policy and the 'Foreign' Navvy, 1896-1914", *CHAR* (1972), pp. 135-156; Claudette Begin-Wolff, "L'Opinion Publique Québécoise Face á l'Immigration, 1906-1913" (M.A. theses, Université de Montréal, 1970); W.E. Calderwood, "The Rise and Fall of the Ku Klux Klan in Saskatchewan" (M.A. thesis, University of Saskatchewan, 1968); Norman Macdonald, *"Canada: Immigration and Colonization 1841-1903* (Toronto, 1966). Moris Mott, "The Foreign Peril, Nativism in Winnipeg, 1916-1923" (M.A. thesis, University of Manitoba, 1970); H. Palmer, "Responses to Foreign Immigration: Nativism and Ethnic Tolerance in Alberta 1880-1920" (M.A. thesis, University of Alberta 1971); "Anti-Oriental Sentiment in Alberta, 1880-1920", *Canadian Ethnic Studies* (December, 1970), pp. 31-58; "Nativism and Ethnic Tolerance in Alberta, 1920-1972" (Ph.D. diss., York University, 1973); Harold Troper, *Only Farmers Need Apply* (Toronto, 1972); W.P. Ward, "The Oriental Immigrant and Canada's Protestant Clergy, 1855-1925", *B.C. Studies* (Summer, 1974), pp. 40-55.

33 For a similar assessment by topic of priority areas of research on ethnicity in the United States see Richard Kolm, "Ethnicity and Ethnic Groups: Research Needs" *International Migration Review* Vol. VIII, No. 1 (Spring, 1974), pp. 59-67.

34 Interesting exceptions are studies of the relationship of ethnicity to the working class and political parties at the Lakehead. Jean Morrison, "Community and Conflict: The Working Class and its relationships at the Canadian Lakehead, 1903-1913" (M.A. thesis, Lakehead University, 1974) and A.W. Rasporich, "Faction and Class in Modern Lakehead Politics", *Lakehead Review* (Summer, 1974).

35 Labour historian Irving Abella is presently studying the Jewish role in the Canadian labour movement. For an analysis of immigrant labour radicalism in the Alberta coal fields prior to 1920, see Don Avery, "Foreign Workers and Labour Radicalism in the Western Canadian Mining Industry, 1900-1919" (Paper delivered at the Western Canadian Urban Conference, University of Winnipeg, October, 1974).

36 Milton Gordon, *Assimilation in American Life* (New York, 1964).

37 Joshua Fishman, *Language Loyalty in the United States* (The Hague, 1966); see also Andrew Greeley, *Ethnicity in the United States* (New York, 1974).

38 Fishman and Nahirny, "American Immigrant Groups: Ethnic Identification and the Problem of Generations", *Social Review* (1965).

39 C.W. Hobart, "Adjustment of Ukrainians in Alberta: Alienation and Integration", *Slavs in Canada* Vol. 1 (Edmonton, 1966), pp. 69-85.

40 "The Process of Maintenance of Ethnic Identity" in Paul Migus (ed.), *Sounds Canadian: Languages and Cultures in Multi-Ethnic Society* (Toronto, 1975).

41 A.H. Richmond, *Ethnic Residential Segregation in Metropolitan Toronto* (Toronto: Institute of Behavioural Research, York University, 1972); Harry Hiller, "Religion, Populism, and Social Credit in Alberta" (Ph.D. diss., McMaster University, 1972).

42 K.G. O'Bryan, J. Reitz and O. Kuplowsky, "Non-Official Languages: A Study in Canadian Multiculturalism", Department of the Secretary of State (Ottawa, 1974).

43 Vancouver, 1971.

44 *Canadian Review of Sociology and Anthropology,* Vol. 5, No. 2 (May, 1968), pp. 51-67.

45 See John Norris, *Strangers Entertained*; Howard Palmer, *Land of the Second Chance* (Lethbridge, 1972).

46 The exceptions to the last statement are the studies of ethnic groups in Saskatchewan by Alan Anderson, "Assimilation in the Bloc Settlement of North-Central Saskatchewan" (Ph.D. diss., University of Saskatchewan, 1972) and the studies on blacks in Nova Scotia by D. Clairmont and D. Magill, *Nova Scotian Blacks; An Historical and Structural Overview* (Halifax, 1970), and D. Magill, *Africville* (Toronto, 1974).

47 There are two major questions concerning Canadian ethnic studies which I have not dealt with in this paper because of the limitation of space and because I have discussed them elsewhere. The first question is why French-Canadian scholars have shown little interest in other ethnic groups and the other concerns the relationship of the study of ethnicity to the perpetuation of ethnic identification. Some people who promote ethnic studies see it as a means of fostering ethnicity, while other people have some doubts about the value of ethnic studies because they doubt the value of the perpetuation of ethnicity. However ethnic studies need not be concerned either with fostering or eliminating ethnic diversity: it can concern itself primarily with understanding Canadian social reality.

Research on Ethnicity in Australia and Canada
Jerzy Zubrzycki

I have been asked to comment on the two papers presented in this section from the viewpoint of a social scientist who is studying ethnic relations in a Commonwealth country with an immigration programme comparable in size and intensity to that of Canada. In the twenty-five year period between 1947 and 1971 immigration to Australia totalled 3.75 million and to Canada, 3.54 million.

Since the end of World War II, Australia has experienced the largest sustained migration in its history. For many scholars interest in this movement is economic, social and cultural: they study the number of newcomers entering different branches of the work-force; problems of health, housing and education; the introduction of new customs; the formation of immigrant communities. Others are deeply interested in problems of personal adjustment—the way in which individual migrants and families adapt to new conditions or, in some cases, break down under stress.

Behind all these matters, however, lies the general demographic background of migration. It is this aspect which has received most attention from the social scientists who pioneered research into immigration and ethnicity in the Research School of Social Sciences at the Australian National University (ANU) in Canberra. The studies undertaken by W.D. Borrie, Charles Price, R.T. Appleyard, Egon Kunz, I.H. Burnely and J. Zubrzycki have resulted in a substantial volume of demographic analyses of the size and structure of the new immigrant population and its relationship to the pre-war population. Comparable research on the demographic aspect of ethnicity and migration in Canada is limited. There was an inordinate delay in the publication of W.B. Hurd's 1941 census monograph[1] followed five years later by W.E. Kalbach's 1961 census monograph, *The Impact of Immigration on Canada's Population.*[2]

Two types of demographic analyses of Australian immigration should be mentioned here because, until recently, there were no counterparts in Canada: the analysis of residential distribution of Australia's ethnic population and the study of ethnic intermarriage. Zubrzycki developed measures of ethnic concentration and segregation in the major cities of Australia,[3] while Jones included a chapter on residential patterns of the major immigrant groups in his study of the social areas of Melbourne.[4] This work is being continued by I.H. Burnley.[5] The only comparable study in Canada is Anthony Richmond's monograph on ethnic segregation in Toronto.[6]

The Toronto study by Richmond has touched on one significant aspect of the pattern of ethnic settlement which received special attention in the work of Charles Price in Australia, namely the significance of chain migration. In his definitive study of southern Europeans in Australia Price has has shown that only a small proportion of the total inflow of southern European settlers came to Australia outside the chain process.[7] The majority came out privately, usually sponsored by relatives or friends who undertook to provide them with accommodation and jobs and quite often advanced some or all of the passage money.

In the immediate post-war years sponsors were usually pre-war settlers. Subsequently, however, "later arrivals wrote letters home, or paid short visits home, urging their friends left behind them to come and join them; these in their turn did the same".

> This 'chain-letter' system, or 'chain migration' as it is usually called . . . has often resulted in chain settlements, that is, immigrant communities made up of families from the same village or district of origin. Sometimes these exist alone in the general Australian environment: sometimes they are mixed with chain groups from other districts in the same region or from other regions in the same country.[8]

This distinct mode of chain migration has important consequences on the process of settlement of Italians and Greeks in Australian cities and also in Canada as Price observed during his field work in Toronto.[9] The basis of chain migration is the force of kinship ties. Families tend to live in close physical proximity, and ties of kinship seem to dominate patterns of visiting as well as membership in small informal associations of settlers from a common village or region. In such conditions there is a marked tendency to mix with families from the same region, to preserve the customs of the district or region of origin, in short to perpetuate *companilismo*—"a loyalty to that which falls within the range of the village bell tower".[10] There seem to be many parallels between Australian work on cohesive ethnic settlements and the research on rural settlements pioneered by C.A. Dawson and other Canadian scholars noted in Dr. Palmer's paper.

The study of ethnic intermarriage is the second type of demographic analysis which engaged the attention of ANU researchers. In a series of papers Price and Zubrzycki explored patterns of exogamy and endogamy among first and second generation settlers and linked the degree of in-marriage to the incidence of chain migration and the residential concentration of particular ethnic groups.[11]

The wide range of historical studies of immigrant groups in Canada cited in Dr. Palmer's paper have no parallel in Australia. Several scholarly studies of non-European migration by Willard, Palfreeman and Yarwood[12] have been published but there has been no comprehensive study of British immigration, nor is there a single study of the origin and pattern of the large movement of displaced persons which marked the beginning of the post-World War II immigration programme in 1957. No study comparable to Price's *Southern Europeans in Australia* has been undertaken for other countries of origin, for example, the Dutch, the Germans, etc. For the remaining groups, Kunz's *Blood and Gold,*[13] a history of Hungarians in Australia, is about the only study which encompasses the fortunes of one minority from the beginning of the nineteenth century to the present.

Finally, it seems apparent that in both countries there is a shortage of solid research on the political behaviour of ethnic groups. Some gaps in this area were recently filled by Jean Martin's studies of refugee groups,[14] but more systematic research should be undertaken by political scientists and labour historians. It may well be that a significant contribution to the study of political socialization will be made by a group of social psychologists at the University of Western Australia under the guidance of Ronald A. Taft and Allan Richardson. Taft's principal contribution, summarized in his book *From Stranger to Citizen,*[15] is an attempt to put forward a fundamentally psychological theory of immigrant adjustment which follows a simple sequence: knowledge of the host culture; change of attitude toward the host and ethnic culture; assumption of roles within host culture; and entry into host society's primary and secondary group. The final stage of this process is convergence of the immigrant's norms of behaviour and those of the host society. Richardson's theory of adjustment[16] stresses that members of minority groups must reach a certain level of satisfaction before they can identify with the host society. A high level of identification leads to the convergence of norms, including the norms of political behaviour.

This brief review of selected areas of ethnic studies in Australia and Canada has stressed several points of difference as well as similarity. It seems that researchers in both countries have experienced much the same problems of access to data, research facilities and publication outlets. In addition both countries have been equally reticent to spell out the priorities and foci of research. In Australia the role of a co-ordinating centre for ethnic research was assumed first by the Research School of Social Sciences at ANU and later by the Project on Immigration of the Academy of Social Sciences in Australia.[17] There has, therefore, been a sense of direction in the activities of many Australian scholars. But the time may have come when we would profit from the formation of a scholarly body similar to the Canadian Ethnic Studies Association. If such a body is founded in

Australia we shall no doubt profit from the experience and the activities of your Association. I wish you well.

Jerzy Zubrzycki is the head of the Department of Sociology at the Australian National University.

NOTES

1 *Ethnic Origin and Nativity of the Canadian People,* 1941 Census Monograph, (Ottawa: Queen's Printer, 1965).

2 (Ottawa: Queen's Printer, 1970).

3 Jerzy Zubrzycki, *Immigrants in Australia: A Demographic Survey Based Upon the 1954 Census* (Melbourne: Melbourne University Press, 1960); *Immigrants in Australia: Statistical Supplement* (Canberra: Australian National University Press, 1960); "Ethnic Segregation in Australian Cities" in L. Henry and W. Winkler (eds.), *International Population Conference, Vienna 1959* (Vienna: International Union for the Scientific Study of Population, 1959), pp. 610-616; "Immigration" in *Atlas of Australian Resources* (Canberra, 1960).

4 F. Lancaster Jones, *Dimensions of Urban Social Structure* (Canberra: Australian National University Press, 1969).

5 I.H. Burnley, "Immigrants in Australian Cities", *The Australian Quarterly,* Vol. 43, No. 4 (December, 1971) pp. 57-69; "European Immigration Settlement Patterns in Metropolitan Sydney, 1947-1966", *Australian Geographical Studies,* Vol. 10 (1972), pp. 61-78.

6 Anthony H. Richmond, *Ethnic Residential Segregation in Metropolitan Toronto* (Toronto: Institute of Behavioural Research, York University, 1972).

7 *Southern Europeans in Australia* (Melbourne: Oxford University Press, 1963), p. 109.

8 C.A. Price, "Post-war migration: Demographic background" in Alan Stoller (ed.), *New Faces: Immigration and Family Life in Australia* (Melbourne: F.W. Cheshire, 1966), p. 22.

9 *Southern Europeans in Australia,* pp. 314-23.

10 R.M. Foerster, *The Italian Emigration of Our Time* (Cambridge, Mass, 1919) p. 432.

11 C.A. Price and J. Zubrzycki, "The use of intermarriage statistics as an index of assimilation", *Population Studies,* Vol. XVI, No. 1 (July, 1962), pp. 58-69 and "Immigrant marriage patterns in Australia", Vol. XVI, No. 2 (November, 1962), pp. 123-133.

12 Myra Willard, *History of the White Australia Policy to 1920* (Melbourne: Melbourne University Press, 1967); A.C. Palfseeman, *The Administration of the White Australia Policy* (Melbourne: Melbourne University Press, 1967); A.T. Yarwood, *Asian Migration to Australia: the Background to Exclusion, 1896-1923* (Melbourne: Melbourne University Press, 1964).

13 E.F. Kunz, *Blood and Gold: Hungarians in Australia* (Melbourne: F.W. Cheshire, 1969).

14 Jean I. Martin, *Refugee Settlers: A Study of Displaced Persons in Australia* (Canberra: Australian National University Press, 1965).

15 Ronald A. Taft, *From Stranger to Citizen: A Survey of Studies of Immigrant Assimilation in Western Australia* (London: Tavistock, 1966).

16 "A theory and method for the psychological study of assimilation", *International Migration Review,* vol. 2 (Fall, 1967), pp. 3-30.

17 A systematic evaluation of research on ethnicity and immigration in Australia can be found in C.A. Price (ed.) *Australian Immigration: A Bibliography and Digest* (Canberra: Australian National University Press), No. 1 (1966) and No. 2 (1970).

6 Canadian Culture and Ethnic Groups: an Analysis

Raymond Breton, 191 **The Impact of Ethnic Groups on**
Jean Burnet, **Canadian Society: Research Issues**
Norbert Hartmann,
Wsevolod W. Isajiw and
Jos Lennards

The Impact of Ethnic Groups on Canadian Society: Research Issues

Raymond Breton, Jean Burnet,
Norbert Hartmann, Wsevolod Isajiw, Jos Lennards

Conferences are meant to be opportunities to reflect on certain questions. Issues are raised, concepts discussed, models of analysis proposed and so on. On the occasion of the conference on Canadian Culture and Ethnic Groups in Canada, we decided to try to systematize our reflections with the objective of spelling out the issues raised that seemed to us to need research. Perhaps, we reasoned, the conference contained an implicit research programme. The following pages constitute the result of our discussions organized under five major headings: immigrants and ethnic groups in relation to the structure of opportunities in Canada, ethnicity in its expressive dimensions and dynamics, the models of intergroup relations that have been proposed and institutionalized, the forces underlying the existing institutionalized models of intergroup relations, and the consequences of these patterns for ethnicity in both its instrumental and its expressive dimensions.

This article constitutes neither a theoretical statement on these questions nor a summary of the conference or of the literature. Rather, it is a survey of some of the research needed concerning ethnicity in Canadian society and culture as suggested by reflection on the conference.

I Ethnicity and Stratification

In Canada, as in most culturally plural societies, one's ethnic identity affects one's position in the stratification hierarchy. Since this fact was not documented until recently, an understanding of the relationship between ethnicity and stratification is only beginning to emerge. While the relationship was not systematically explored at the conference, several areas of potentially fruitful investigation were identified, and the need to expand our research into the sources and consequences of variations in ethnic status was made clear.

Class and ethnic affiliation

It is generally agreed that group status is a function of the quality of participation in the economic, social and legal orders of society. Yet our knowledge of the connection between ethnicity, especially among members of the non-charter groups, and opportunity in each of these contexts is still rudimentary.

Take for example the class distribution of the various ethnic groups in Canada. The tendency has been to account for variations along this dimension by the concept of entrance status. Clearly this is important, for immigration policies have been instrumental in shaping the Canadian stratification system. The policy in force influenced the language fluency, education, occupational training and capital resources with which members of the various ethnic groups confronted the host society and attained their initial position. Thus work such as Donald Avery's, documenting the influence of Anglo-Canadian industrialists on entrance status through their ability to gain relaxation of federal immigration policies and create an industrial proletariat of central and eastern Europeans, is a welcome addition to the field. Much more work needs to be undertaken for other historical periods.

Entrance status, however, only describes the initial conditions under which an ethnic group confronts the host society. The immigrant experience is but one phase of the ethnic experience. With the exception of Italians, Hungarians and Chinese, no major ethnic group has more than 50 percent of its members in the immigrant category. Approximately three-quarters of the members of such groups as the Germans, Japanese, Russians, Scandinavians and Ukrainians are native-born. As immigration declines as a major contributor to the occupational composition of Canadian ethnic groups, evaluations of the effect of ethnic affiliation on economic opportunity must be undertaken. In fact, whether there are differences attributable to ethnicity rather than entrance status is one of the most important empirical questions that must be tackled by those interested in developing theories of ethnic stratification.

There is some evidence that this will prove a fruitful avenue of research. Once the stage has been set by entrance status, changes in class position are a matter of the degree of mobility. While we have no conclusive studies of intergenerational mobility among ethnic groups, we do know that not all faced similar impediments to economic mobility. The low economic position of those of central and eastern European origin, for instance, can be attributed not only to their entrance status but also to their ethnicity. As a result of the hostilities of 1914, they were considered enemy aliens. As Avery notes, large numbers were dismissed from their jobs at the outbreak of the war; later, even more were dismissed in order to provide employment for returning soldiers. Fear of a connection between ethnic affiliation and socialist or anarchist activity aggravated the situation. Apparently discrimination in employment opportunities against members of certain ethnic groups lasted well into the following decade: the average period of unemployment for Ukrainian workers in 1930 was twenty weeks, for British-born workers only nine weeks. We now know that not only Chinese, Japanese, Doukhobors, Indians and Eskimos but also a number of groups of European origin suffered from employment restrictions.

This observation raises many further questions. For example, did all central and eastern European groups suffer equally from such policies? Was the intensity of discrimination equally severe in all parts of the country? Was the seemingly more equitable class distribution among pre-World War II immigrants of central and eastern European origin in Quebec and the Atlantic Provinces a function not only of numbers, but also of a less-pronounced restriction of opportunity along ethnic lines? To what extent did the policies outlined by Avery hinder long-term occupational mobility? Did the existence of restrictive employment policies and practices offer a competitive edge to immigrants who were not of central and eastern European origin? Policies of harassment and intimidation seem to have returned with the outbreak of World War II. We are partially aware of the effect these had on Canadians of Japanese origin. But what effect, if any, did the Nazi scare of the late thirties and forties have on the mobility of those of Germanic descent? Did fears concerning their loyalty or of public reaction to institutions or corporations that might employ them prevent them from moving into certain occupational categories?

The importance of studying restrictive employment practices and policies lies not only in documenting the effect of discrimination on economic security or mobility or both, but also in ascertaining whether they were a factor in the various patterns of occupational specialization characteristic of ethnic groups in Canada. The patterns may have been created by our immigration policies but maintained by certain discriminatory practices.

One vehicle for the improvement of economic position has been the union movement. The relationship between ethnicity, unionism and economic security is one that deserves special attention. Continental Europeans were preferred by some employers because they were seen to present an obstacle to the formation of unions and because they were prepared to work for wages and in conditions that would not be tolerated by native Canadian or British workers. Although Avery questions whether this was actually the case, we do not know how willing members of various ethnic groups were to participate in union activity or how effectively they could use this weapon to secure their economic welfare. British workers utilizing this lever could be characterized only as radicals, members of ethnic minorities both as radicals and as threats to the Canadian way of life. Union policies toward ethnic recruitment must also be investigated.

We were also reminded by a number of participants that much of the

English-French confrontation needs to be understood as a struggle for control of resources and those institutions which allocate and reallocate them. The ideal of "maitre chez nous" has a significant instrumental component. It is to some extent an attempt to expand the internal opportunities available to the Québécois. Differences in group opportunity structures are not limited to the English-French axis. Investigations of the extent to which various other groups provide differential opportunities for mobility also need to be undertaken. Such research would test Porter's hypothesis that the ethnic mosaic impedes social mobility. Groups immigrating in sizable numbers and tending to regional and residential concentration may create opportunities for their members that might have been more difficult to realize otherwise. In personally sensitive areas and those requiring intercultural contact people are prone to wish to deal with "persons like themselves". Thus demands for ethnic doctors, bank officials, priests, real-estate agents, life-insurance salesmen, journalists and the like may have been created. Does ethnic cohesiveness have a relation to the degree of structural assimilation? Do different settlement patterns and different desires to maintain identity mean different possibilities to capitalize on ethnic affiliation and create varying in-group stratification spans?

Class position is a matter not only of the structure of opportunities made available, but also of the extent to which those afforded are utilized. Much more research is needed in this area. Not all ethnic groups, for example, use schools to the same extent and in the same manner. What accounts for this? Different views of the role of the school? Different occupational preferences? Different abilities to cope with the scholastic environment? The level of achievement motivation also contributes to the uses made of opportunities. Yet little is known of inter-ethnic variations in this area. Some have speculated that culturally-induced variations in cognitive style may further effect the ability to use the opportunity structure. This possibility has not yet been explored among ethnic groups other than the British and French.

Ethnicity and prestige

Status is also a function of the quality of participation in the social and cultural sphere. The prestige accorded a group is, in part, a function of the contributions it is seen to make to the public good and to societal welfare. Little is known, however, of the extent to which the status accorded to ethnic groups depends on such evaluations. Some material potentially relevant to developing research into the subjective aspects of ethnic status also emerged from the conference.

Much, for instance, was made of the expressive role of the ethnic artist. But there is a sense in which the artist must be seen in instrumental terms. He can become a representative of the ethnic group's potential for social and cultural achievement to other groups in the community. The same is, of course, true for scientists, intellectuals, politicians, sportsmen and other figures who contribute either to the national welfare or to the international prestige of a country. One must know, therefore, the extent to which there is ethnic diversity in the social and cultural sphere and the factors which generate it. Further, one must know whether their accomplishments are seen as those of Canadians or those of *ethnic* Canadians. Are Mordecai Richler and Leonard Cohen, for example, considered Jewish Canadians? Do their accomplishments and failures reflect on the group from which they originate? What opportunities have the various ethnic groups to gain access to positions that allow societally significant achievements? What is the relationship between the availability of such opportunities and government policies? What effect, for example, will the policy of multiculturalism have on the visibility of the various ethnic communities? What is the role of galleries and other "gatekeepers" in the extension or restriction of entry along ethnic lines?

It is also vital to examine the impact of the official image-makers of the society: the historians, the publicists and the mass media. Through their patterns of selectivity certain conceptions of the contributions made by the various ethnic groups are generated. The history taught in the schools has been written, as Jaenen noted, largely from the political perspective and tends to emphasize the contributions of the English and French. What effect has this had on the prestige accorded the ethnic communities in Canada? Would a social history, which could scarcely ignore the contributions of ethnic minorities, have had a different impact on ethnic status? Have the scholars' approaches to the ethnic question in the past reinforced the doctrine of Anglo-conformity and thus aided in the maintenance of a differential prestige hierarchy?

Since prestige is partly a function of the kind of information made available, the role of newspapers, magazines, radio and television in the formation of ethnic status must be determined. Styles of news presentation, feature selection and editorial policy on ethnic minorities have no doubt varied according to group, time, region and between the various media. What has been the nature and effect of this variation?

Ethnic pluralism and system maintenance

Research into the factors generating ethnic status was but one of the issues related to stratification raised at the conference. The need to determine whether ethnic pluralism was a significant mechanism for the perpetuation of the infrastructure upon which class divisions are based also emerged.

The superordinate/subordinate cleavage based on cultural differences seems to have introduced a number of additional mechanisms for system maintenance. Avery's data suggest that the responsiveness of the economic system to potentially disruptive forces was heightened by ethnic diversity. It may, for instance, have helped stave off threats to the system by impeding the development of worker solidarity. When threats to the legitimacy of economic arrangements did come, they could be reinterpreted and promulgated by the elite as a cultural and ideological attack, a threat to the Canadian way of life from a foreign element. This interpretation would have been much more difficult had the unions and elite been culturally homogeneous. When the economic system could no longer absorb the thousands of returning soldiers, the problem could be defined as an extra-systemic rather than an economic one—too many foreigners. Since, as Bosnitch noted, members of ethnic minorities, especially immigrants, possess little or no political power, industrialists were able to use the legal system to attain their ends. When alien workers were required, they could get anti-loafing laws enacted; to curb the growth of worker solidarity the foreign-language press was suppressed, and so forth.

Many questions need to be asked. How much fragmentation of opposition was introduced by ethnic diversity? How long did it last? What role did Old World prejudices and hatreds play? Under what conditions did they break down and solidarity emerge? To what extent is it easier to exploit and control persons who lack the knowledge and skills to deal with the culture than those who, though disadvantaged, are of the same cultural group?

Furthermore, immigrants are not all of the same type. Some, we know, came to Canada only as a stopover on their way elsewhere: does the "sojourner" present different systemic problems and potentials than the future citizen? Some immigrants came as political refugees, others as economic entrepreneurs: did these different types differ in their willingness to endure exploitive situations?

To the sociologist interested in the question of elite control and system maintenance these questions should open an interesting and vital avenue of research. Their answers should be of extreme interest to the students of ethnic stratification.

II Ethnic Identity and Ethnic Boundaries

To be meaningful, ethnic boundaries should be related to the problem of ethnic identity. Differential life chances form only one dimension of ethnic boundaries. Other dimensions are the subjective processes of membership exclusion and inclusion. William Kurelek implicitly referred to these processes when he said that he first became conscious of being "ethnic" at the age of seven, when a teacher shamed him for speaking Ukrainian. If ethnic boundaries are a result of membership exclusion, then ethnic identity can be seen to be a result of membership inclusion. The relationship between these two processes becomes the frontier of intergroup relations. Hubert Guindon, for example, pointed out that unwritten codes may exist on language frontiers, such as one prescribing that when an English speaker walks in, all French speakers switch to English.

Most sociologists study ethnic identity as an independent variable. Little work has been done on it as a dependent variable. Yet for many immigrants ethnic identity may develop within, rather than outside of the host society. Likewise, under some conditions increased social mobility may stimulate rather than diminish ethnic consciousness. In this section ethnic identity will be seen in relation to the factors of generation, public policy, and ethnic and inter-ethnic organizations as they relate to inter-ethnic relations and institutionalization. All these issues, which the conference papers raised either directly or indirectly, have to do with the exclusion and inclusion by which ethnic identity comes to be defined.

Ethnic identity and ethnic generations

The relationship between ethnicity and assimilation has often been assumed to be unilinear. That is, as the second or third immigrant generation becomes assimilated, ethnicity disappears. Marcus Lee Hansen, with his hypothesis of third generation return, saw that this was not necessarily so, but even today we have no systematic research on the subject. Eli Mandel makes a sharp distinction between community culture and ethnicity. "An integrated community," he suggests, "will not see itself in ethnic terms but as an authentic culture." Ethnicity presents itself as a problem of self-definition, that is, of identity. In this sense cultural assimilation may create rather than eliminate the problem of ethnic identity. According to Mandel, the ethnic voice in literature, written in English as it is, is hard pressed to articulate a doubleness which it can resolve only by remaking itself, by becoming a reconstructed universal—man, unnatural man, a monster.

We may rephrase the problem sociologically by modifying and reconceptualizing Hansen's hypothesis. There is no reason to assume that ethnic identity is one and the same thing for everybody. On the contrary, one may develop various patterns of identity maintenance in relation to one's ethnic origin. Scrupulously preserving the culture of the ancestral group seems to be the pattern prevalent among the first immigrant generation. For the second generation identity may be linked with rebellion against ethnic ancestry, to which, nevertheless, because of the early socialization process it remains inexorably tied. To resolve this doubleness a person may overidentify with society at large, becoming, in a sense, more Canadian than the Canadians. Or he may strongly identify with movements which stand for such goals as universal justice or love. Then again, the culturally assimilated person may "rediscover" his ethnic origin, not in the sense of returning to the old culture, but in finding aspects of it meaningful to his present pattern of life. Whether or not these patterns of identity maintenance correspond to specific ethnic generations, distinction between some such patterns is necessary if ethnicity is to be understood as a phenomenon involving several generations.

Ethnic status and immigrant status

A further important distinction to be made in connection with the question of generations is that between ethnic status and immigrant status. An ethnic group does not exist as such unless, in addition to the immigrant generation, there is at least one generation born to it in the host society. Although historically immigrant status provides the basis for the group's ethnic status, the problems of ethnic status go far beyond those of immigrant status. The immigrant generation's problem of adjustment is not the problem that later generations face. The policy of multiculturalism, for example, is much more relevant for the second or third generation than for the immigrant generation. Yet an unsuccessful solution to the immigrant problem may have consequences for the second or other generations. Bosnitch pointed out that the immigrants' ineffectiveness and lack of a power base for the first five to seven years may reduce their political effectiveness as an ethnic group later on. We can say that any act of membership exclusion is implicitly a political act and, as such, a determinant of positions of advantage or disadvantage.

Usually ethnic social mobility has been studied as simply the social mobility of persons of specific ethnic backgrounds and examined within the accepted system of social stratification. It is seldom seen as a change of status of an ethnic group vis-à-vis other ethnic groups. If status is also seen as involving stereotypical aspects as determinants of positions of advantage and disadvantage, then change of ethnic status is a question of, not simply mobility into better paying, higher status jobs, but rather mobility into strategic occupations that allow direct influence on wider sectors of society, influence which goes beyond the job environment.

Ethnicity as expressive and as instrumental reality and public policy

Another set of issues is posed by the question: to what extent is ethnicity an instrumental or an expressive reality? As a source of identity ethnicity is an expressive phenomenon, but an ethnic community may or may not be a source of various economic or political opportunities. The multicultural policies of the federal government have approached ethnicity primarily as expressive and have emphasized ethnic cultures. The policy of bilingualism, however, has been more instrumentally oriented in providing opportunities to the French-Canadian community. Nevertheless, multicultural policies may have indirect instrumental consequences, just as bilingual policies have symbolic, expressive effects. What needs further study are the variations among ethnic situations in this regard. Frank Vallee showed that there are regional variations in language patterns and patterns of inter-ethnic relations that may necessitate regional variations in policies regarding language and culture. In Zone II, the "bilingual belt", bilingualism may be a realistic policy, but in Zone III, the ethnically-mixed English Canada, multiculturalism would probably be more effective.

The relationship between public policies and the subsectors of society that take advantage of them should be studied systematically. The same policy may be utilized in different ways by different subsectors and may have unintended consequences. The relationship between intended and unintended consequences is often difficult to assess. Avery pointed out that the railroad and other industrialists in Winnipeg at the turn of the century profited by Sifton's immigration policies by employing immigrants as cheap labour. Yet Sifton's policies were essentially population development policies intended to settle the prairies. McKenna, commenting on Avery's paper, raised the issue of whether the industrialists were simply taking advantage of government policies or were also helping to formulate them to an extent not yet revealed in available historical records. Similarly the manifest intention of the policy of multiculturalism has been to encourage and assist the preservation of cultural differences. Many members of various ethnic groups, however, especially the white minority groups, see the policy as a way in which they can gain public recognition of their diverse subcultures, not as foreign, but as Canadian. On the psychological level this may serve to integrate ethnic identity with Canadian identity. Yet probably few members of the Anglo-Saxon group would perceive the policy in this way.

Ethnic organizations and intergroup conflict

An important question which was not adequately discussed at the conference is why some ethnic groups develop more instrumental organizations than others, why some develop more expressive organizations, and why still others develop few organizations of any kind. How do the various types of ethnic organizations function to create ethnic boundaries and to manage inter-ethnic conflict?

There appears to be virtually no research on voluntary organizations with an inter-ethnic, rather than simply an ethnic social base. They may play a significant role in intergroup relations. In the United States such organizations as NAACP and CORE have involved both blacks and whites and, in their own manner, they seem to have helped to effect changes in the discriminatory laws. The function of such organizations is perhaps not so much to increase understanding of the issues involved in the interracial or inter-ethnic conflict, but to suggest and articulate techniques of effecting social change acceptable to the conflicting parties.

In Canada there have been few national organizations composed of both English and French members dedicated to the solution of the long-standing conflict. It may be that the Canadian approach to intergroup conflict resolution has traditionally put more stress on the participation of public bodies than that of private voluntary organizations. But if there is a Canadian model of conflict resolution, it can only be known through comparison with other societies. In this context Baker's three-way comparative study of intergroup conflict is significant.

The problem of institutionalization of ethnic boundaries

Finally, an important issue connected with ethnic identity and ethnic boundaries has to do with the way in which ethnic identity is objectified and institutionalized in society as a whole. A definitive method of institutionalization is legal support. When ethnic boundaries become legal boundaries, group rights can be invoked. Expressive elements acquire instrumental value; in their own right they can be used as an instrumental resource. Yet legal definitions of ethnic boundaries may be a double-edged sword: they may serve as a basis for claiming rights as well as a means of containing them. The Canadian Indians and the debate over the Indian Act, discussed by Weaver, present the issue of a double support for the Indian identity—legal and territorial. Legal recognition of territorial claims may give the Indians a citizen plus status and thus special recognition and support for their ethnic identity. In this respect the Quebec situation is analogous. Weaver, however, suggests that excessive dependence on the legal boundaries may weaken the historically-developed community boundaries upon which those ethnic groups which have no grounds for legal claims have relied. In-depth investigation is needed to assess to what extent and under what conditions reliance on legal boundaries may strengthen or weaken ethnic community boundaries.

III Models of Intergroup Relations in Canadian Society

A number of models of intergroup relations were set forth as having been either proposed or institutionalized. Most of them focused on the dominant group and one type of minority group. Several papers raised questions concerning the relationship of the models to time, social class and to region. Underlying many were questions concerning Canadian identity and the relationship between ethnicity and culture.

The most explicit discussion of models was by Baker. He proposed that Canada was a plural society, with an English dominant group and three types of minorities: non-whites, including indigenous and non-indigenous groups, immigrant white groups, and a white siege culture, the French-Canadian. His classification provides a framework for analysis, although of the non-white groups only the native Indian received attention during the conference. The others, the Inuit and the Asian and black groups, are likely to be of increasing interest: the Inuit because their isolation, like that of the Indian peoples, is being broken down at present; and the Asian and black groups because of the recent marked increase in their numbers.

For Baker the dominant group was English; for others it was Anglo-Canadian, Anglo-Celtic, English-Canadian or WASP. In certain contexts, however, it was necessary to distinguish between Anglo-Canadians in western and in eastern (or central) Canada, Canadian-born and British immigrants, and radicals or socialist workers on the one hand and industrialists and politicians on the other. The dominant group, then, was far from homogeneous and Anglo-conformity far from simple. Further explorations of what it involved seems indicated.

Anglo-conformity

In relation to white immigrant ethnic groups, Anglo-conformity was held as an ideal until the 1930s and institutionalized for several decades longer.

Avery indicated that in the period 1896-1930 white immigrants were considered cheap and docile labour for agriculture and industry. Recruited for agriculture, in many cases they worked on the railroad or in mining. They were fired from jobs in industry when Anglo-Canadians were available and jailed or deported, sometimes with little regard for legal niceties, if they earned the label of hostile aliens or alien radicals, as some did at the time of the Winnipeg General Strike. Although the vocabulary of racism was employe with reference to them, most were considered assimilable or at least their children were. The ending of bilingual schools in Manitoba in 1916 was intended, according to J.E. Rea, to hasten the adoption of the English language and English-Canadian values by immigrants as well as by French Canadians. English-Canadian culture was seen as superior to the cultures of the immigrants; it seems also to have been seen as extremely vulnerable, especially during wartime.

The ideal of Anglo-conformity was apparently transformed, and eventually western Canadian institutions also changed to afford a pluralist or multicultural base from which the Royal Commission on Bilingualism and Biculturalism could be attacked in the 1960s. Just how this occurred should be a fruitful topic for research. The part played in the attacks by east-west differences among Anglo-Canadians, how the westerners viewed multiculturalism and in particular how they viewed the relation of multiculturalism to language and to Canadian identity were among the issues raised but not resolved. Both historical and sociological research is clearly needed.

The French-Canadian siege culture

Baker described the French-Canadian as a "white siege culture", the extinction of which was feared because of encounters with the dominant Anglo-Canadian culture. It is under siege, presumably, in what Vallee (following Richard Joy) characterized as Zone II, "the bilingual belt", since in Zone I, French Canada, there is assimilation to French rather than English and in Zone III, English Canada, assimilation to English seems accepted, except by local French elites. Guindon's criticism of the Report of the Royal Commission on Bilingualism and Biculturalism for basing its recommendations on institutions rather than territory, and his challenge that research be done on changing codes regarding language use are consonant with Vallee's analysis. Historically, according to Réjean Landry, the French Canadians have defended their position by a succession of bargaining negotiations in which assimilation was staved off and dualism secured. The analysis of other situations involving ethnic contact in terms of such negotiations would be interesting. The development of political dualism into bilingualism and biculturalism and the projected alternative of independence was related to the imbalance between the French and the English zones. The model of intergroup relations held by French Canadians regarding immigrant ethnic groups and native Indians and Inuit was not set forth. Again, research is called for. If, as seems likely, the implicit model is Franco-conformity, under what political conditions it would persist would be a topic worthy of examination.

Non-white minorities

The recent proposal to terminate the Indian Act indicates that adaptation might be delayed by isolation. The response of the Indians in calling for continued special status citizenship plus rather than a minority position raises questions concerning their model of society and its compatibility with multiculturalism which stresses equal status for all ethnic groups. The consolidation of the Indian peoples was presented as a by-product of the Indian Act and of opposition to the government proposal to rescind it. The relation between consolidation and the urbanization of Indians, and the trend to urbanization and its significance were not discussed. As the trend continues, comparison of Indians to other urban immigrants may become fruitful. To what extent do the recent activities of Indian groups represent borrowing from immigrant ethnic groups and from other minority groups. There can be little doubt that native Indians, like other Canadians, have been much influenced by American examples.

The indigenous non-white population raises the question of racism. Nonindigenous non-white groups have hitherto been small. Efforts were made to exclude them or at least to restrict severely the number admitted, presumably because they were considered unassimilable. The changed immigration regulations of the 1960s suggest that the multicultural model may well accommodate non-whites in a way the Anglo-conformist model could not, by the premium it places on diversity.

Multiculturalism

Multiculturalism as such was little discussed, either as to its meaning, its origins or its implications. There was no probing of the relation between bilingualism and multiculturalism, a subject that has occasioned heated debate in Quebec and in western Canada: the significance of the fact that the federal government's policy was proclaimed to be multiculturalism within a bilingual framework was not explored. All of these areas hold promise for research. As has been indicated, problems more difficult for the social scientist but potentially worthwhile were poignantly posed by the artists, Istvan Inhalt, Eli Mandel and William Kurelek. Other participants in the conference touched on the relation of culture to ethnicity, to dual identity and to Canadian ident ity only fleetingly. Both conceptual clarification and empirical research in these areas are called for.

IV Social Forces Underlying Existing Models of Intergroup Relations

To a large extent, the existing patterns of intergroup relations—based either on assimilationist, pluralist or mixed models—emerge as a partly anticipated, partly unanticipated result of steps taken by people who control sizable amounts of resources. In order to attain their goals and deal with the problems and obstacles encountered, controlling elites mobilize economic, political and military or police resources, establish organizational structures and thus, over time, shape the patterns of intergroup relations in a society. Interesting issues were raised and material provided at the conference in relation to two general objectives—rapid economic development and nation-building. Patterns of inter-ethnic relations also emerge from interaction between ethnic groups and their elites. This was seen by a number of authors as involving more or less formal bargaining processes. This section will examine some of the questions raised about how the pursuit of economic development, the attempts at nation-building and the bargaining between groups have contributed to the shaping of the institutional patterns of inter-ethnic relations in Canada.

The pursuit of economic development

One of the main economic goals pursued was rapid development through capital accumulation. Such a goal tended to lead to certain kinds of manpower policies. Indeed, since labour costs were seen as the main obstacle to be overcome, one of the manpower requirements that has been defined was the procuring and maintaining a supply of cheap labour. This requirement led to several different policies and practices with regard to the recruitment of labour, the control of workers and public relations. It also led to pressures toward certain structures and policies in other institutions, particularly political structures and schools.

Even though the recruitment of labour was oriented toward costs, it was subject to cultural constraints—that is, as indicated by Avery, standards of cultural and racial acceptability. The reasons for cultural constraints should be explored further. They may have been related in part to problems of nation-building (as shall be discussed later); they may have been simply a matter of cultural homophily. But acceptance of cultural constraints on recruitment may also have been economically motivated: it is possible that entrepreneurs thought that a racially-mixed labour force would entail many tensions and hostilities and thus reduce productivity. Further research should deal with non-cultural hypotheses, such as those pertaining to the costs of recruitment in different parts of the world and the pressures exerted by governments of countries with an excess supply of labour.

Rapid economic expansion was defined as requiring not only the recruitment of cheap labour, but also the development of means of social control to keep it inexpensive. This seems to have involved at least four kinds of processes: 1) preventing worker solidarity and the formation of unions, 2) preventing disruption of work and keeping as rapid a pace as possible, 3) preventing alien workers from thinking that they were entitled to better treatment and 4) preventing the establishment or the application of various kinds of regulations such as safety standards.

A certain amount of material was presented at the conference regarding these processes. For instance, there appears to be evidence that employers deliberately counted on ethnic differences as an impediment to worker solidarity. Illiteracy was also considered to be an asset because illiterates were seen as easier to control and as maintaining low aspirations. There is also evidence that managers tried to avoid costly safety measures and that government inspectors were frequently willing to collaborate in this regard.

The possibility of a cross-class convergence of interests, especially in the Anglo-Saxon group, is also relevant to the issue of class solidarity. Rapid economic development, for instance, was profitable not only for capitalists but also for certain segments of the labour force who saw in industrial growth opportunities for their own upward mobility, provided that other people were found for the hard, unskilled and poorly paying labour. The ethnic cleavages in the working class brought about by such social forces do not have the same dynamics and perhaps not the same long-term consequences as those fostered by employers.

Additional research on these questions would be extremely useful in throwing light on the impact of ethnic differences on class solidarity.

The accumulation of capital also involves the formation and control of financial institutions. Patterns of inter-ethnic relations emerge in part from the role played by different ethnic groups in the structuring and control of such institutions. But this issue was not dealt with at the conference, even though it is probably crucial in shaping the character of ethnic diversity in Canada.

The pursuit of nation-building

Related to processes of economic development were those of nation-building—that is, the definition of a political culture and the establishment and control of political institutions. Economic development and nation-building were related both because the political integration of the society required an economic basis and because economic activities needed government support. Political and economic goals also became interrelated by the fact that, to a substantial degree, the same people (or members of the same social circles) were involved in both domains.

Much research is needed on those issues. Indeed, even though we know that English settlers in Canada, in conjuction with the metropolitan British government, "manipulated political and economic institutions to retain power" and thus determined "both the types of cultural integration and how other groups would be structually incorporated" (Baker), much still has to be learned about how this has taken place historically.

Moreover, it cannot be argued that there was always convergence between the political and economic elites or that the activities of one never created problems for the other. Compromises may have had to have been worked out. For instance, did the cheap labour policies mentioned above add to the problems of achieving societal integration and of maintaining English political control, even if employers accepted certain constraints of cultural and racial acceptability? Were the restrictions placed on the recruitment of Orientals a sacrifice for employers? Also, when the rise of socialist organizations and the involvement of immigrants of certain ethnic origins in them became significant, "even the Canadian Manufacturers' Association, the long-time advocate of the 'open door' immigration policy, endorsed the exclusion of continental European immigrants. Temporarily, at least, the ethnic, cultural and ideological objections of these immigrants had become more important than their economic worth" (Avery). To what extent was the CMA's endorsement due to fears of socialism and to what extent a concern with the growing numbers of less assimilable immigrants?

From a certain point of view the requirements of industrial expansion and those of political integration and of English political hegemony were contradictory. These at least apparent contradictions constitute rather difficult research problems. But their study and the analysis of the processes they brought about could throw light on several issues. One that has been discussed is the issue of assimilation. Ethnic diversity may have been profitable, but it had to be contained. Bilingualism and multiculturalism were seen as threats to the social order and had to be dealt with. And, as Rea has shown in the case of Manitoba, the educational system was shaped for assimilation-ist purposes. How successful the educational system was in this regard still has to be established, since there were other assimilationist forces operating in the society. The basic point is that the ethnic diversity resulting from in-dustrial expansion brought about other institutional activities—political, educational, religious—that contributed to the present patterns of inter-ethnic relations in Canada.

Intergroup bargaining

Institutionalized patterns in intergroup relations also emerge from a some-times formal but frequently informal social bargaining process. Such a pro-cess involves conflicts of interest and more or less reluctantly accepted com-promises. Once two or more groups share an environment, they become obstacles to each other, but they can also be useful and even necessary to each other. As several authors have pointed out, a crucial factor in the con-frontations and in the exchange relationships is the amount and kind of re-sources available to each of the groups.

Power confrontations represent "contests for control of resources and for control of the institutions through which are allocated or reallocated the resources, power and privilege" (Baker). It is important to emphasize here that the institutions themselves are the object of confrontations and bargaining, because institutional arrangements are an important factor in the distribution of power and access to resources. Referring to political institutions, Landry mentioned that they "are the outcomes of inter-ethnic bargaining negotiations as well as the framework within which these bargain-ing negotiations take place. But these political institutions, in turn, have consequences for the course of the ongoing bargaining negotiations."

The conference, then, raised important issues which require a consider-able amount of further research. One of the research difficulties, of course, is that most of the bargaining between ethnic groups does not go on around conference tables, and when meetings do take place, they are usually the culmination of long processes of group interaction. We need to know much more about the character of such interactions, about their content as well as the social mechanisms through which they occur. Research should be done not only on how much influence and power groups exert, but also on how these are exerted. Empirical studies of the sort undertaken by Landry would be extremely useful in this regard. Such studies should examine the processes and the contents of the interactions, as well as the institutional structures, if any, in which they occur. In this connection an examination of the effect of different institutional arrangements upon intergroup bargaining negotiations and conflict regulation, and an analysis of the absence of any such formal institutional structures would be quite enlightening. Another set of issues concerns the types of resources available to each group and their mobilization. An area not sufficiently researched is the role of intellectuals and artists in Canada in the creation of symbolic resources and in the mobilization of emotions and commitment. The study of variations among ethnic groups in this regard would be revealing.

The case of Canadian Indians is striking with respect to resources and their mobilization, largely because it represents an extreme situation. As indicated earlier, one of the main features of that situation is that boundary-maintaining and adaptive mechanisms were imposed by external agencies. As a result, the population has come to depend on external protection rather than developing its own means of coping with external forces (Weaver). The means available for mobilization as well as the constraints that have to be overcome constitute an important area of research on which much still needs to be done in the Canadian context.

IV Ethnic Policy and its Consequences

The models governing the relationship between the different ethnic groupings in Canada and their sources have been discussed above. In this section we intend to raise some questions about the social consequences of ethnic policy. Several papers addressed themselves to this issue either directly or indirectly.

Indian policy

Only one paper was presented on Canada's indigenous ethnic group. It assessed the costs and benefits of an equal rights versus a special status approach for the Indian population. Weaver's main argument was that the Indian Act secured a land base to the Indians and provided special economic and social protection against intrusion into this territory by whites but, in doing so, removed the opportunity and the incentive for Indians to come to terms with their ethnicity. As a result of a lack of internally-generated boundary-maintaining mechanisms, Indian communities can only survive if they are given special status. Although convincing in its analysis of the detrimental effects of reliance on external sources of support, the conclusion that in spite of its high costs there is no alternative to continuing this policy at present needs to be critically examined.

The distinction between an equal rights versus a special status approach corresponds to the difference between a strategy aimed at encouraging individual mobility and a policy aimed at promoting collective mobility. Phrased in these terms, the questions raised concern the relative merit of each of these approaches in dealing with the Indian population.

A major postulate underlying the White Paper of 1969, now withdrawn, seemed to be that the Indian experience has not been sufficiently different from that of other ethnic groups to warrant the continuation of a special policy. The aim was to make the Indian into a member of a multicultural society, assimilated into the Canadian social structure but free to express his cultural identity in the private sphere. The mobility of Indians was seen to have been impeded in the past by obstacles to participation in the institutional activities of the larger society. It was assumed that once these obstacles were removed the Indians would be able to avail themselves of opportunities in the same way as newcomers to Canadian society had done.

The main thrust of Weaver's paper is to question the validity of such assumptions on the ground that they fail to take into account the distinctive nature of the Indian problem. The disintegration of the Indian community imposes on the Indians special handicaps not faced by other groups in their struggle for self-advancement and identity formation. To put the Indians on an equal footing with these groups requires, therefore, a policy aimed at strengthening the collective life of the Indians as a first priority.

In pointing to the internal organization of the ethnic community as a resource base for ethnic identity and mobility, Weaver raises an issue of considerable empirical and practical importance. There is a tendency to view the existence of ethnic communities as an impediment to social advancement. The successful member of an ethnic group is one who has severed his particularistic ties, thereby avoiding the dangers of ethnic mobility traps (Wiley) or overprotection (Vallee). This view of the importance of individual self-reliance and of the dangers inherent in the self-containment of ethnic groups deserves to be critically examined. Particularly in those situations where the permeability of the political and economic institutions is low—as a result, for example, of discrimination based on race or language— the cohesiveness of an ethnic group might be its most important mobility resource, providing political strength and economic and cultural support. To ascertain the exact role played by individual as against collective factors in determining ethnic success in Canada we need to undertake studies comparing mobility rates both between and within ethnic groups (controlling for time of arrival) and relating mobility to the nature and the extent of ethnic group involvement. In the absence of such studies, the view that the road to equality lies in structural assimilation and individual mobility deserves to be treated with caution.

In the case of the Indians it seems clear that at present they lack the solidarity required for the successful mobilization of power or for the establishment of effective patterns of self-help. Their problem is compounded by the fact that they are invited to enter the mainstream of society at a time when the demand for unskilled labour is decreasing. Under these circumstances, a policy aimed at encouraging individual mobility might in practice mean that a small number of Indians will be successfully absorbed into the institutional network of the larger society, leaving those who are unassimilable behind. Also, a policy of extending equal opportunities to those unequally equipped to take advantage of these opportunities might serve to put the blame for failure on the shoulders of the recipients, thereby increasing the burden of social prejudice under which the Indians labour. A final issue deserving attention is whether the identity problem faced by Indians is the same as that for other ethnic groups. Those who have been colonized probably have a different, more ambivalent basis of identification with the larger society than those who came to Canada as a result of voluntary migration. At the same time, the absence of a host society which can serve as a cultural model and the lack of vitality of the Indian culture itself make it more difficult for Indians to establish a firm sense of their own identity. In view of these considerations we need more research on how, in the absence of a communal base, the Indians come to terms with their identity, on the kinds of ideological and behavioural responses arising in this situation, and on the distribution of these responses among the different strata of the Indian population. Such investigations can throw light on the nature of the adjustment process and the effectiveness of the multicultural policy in this area.

Before concluding our comments on Weaver's paper some mention should be made of the political difficulties involved in shifting from an approach centred on individual mobility to one centred on collective mobility. It may well be that the very actions required for group mobilization are the ones least acceptable to the rest of society. For instance, while leaders espousing militant ideologies might fulfil an important function in mobilizing group energies, political authorities and the public at large tend to prefer leaders who try to prevent overt confrontation. It would be worth undertaking a study to examine which Indian leaders are given official status as spokesmen for the Indian cause and the grounds on which this selection is based. Such study can help to illuminate the nature of the policy restraints operating in the present situation.

Policy regarding immigrants

Of the three major types of ethnic groups in Canada the immigrant population received most attention during the conference. Of the many papers presented, one in particular deserves comment because of the questions it raised about the policy of multiculturalism. According to Bosnitch, multiculturalism required a policy, not of structural assimilation, but of structural pluralism. The logical end-point of multiculturalism is a polyethnic society in which ethnicity forms the basis for interest articulation and group representation.

To evaluate Bosnitch's argument it is important to explicate the major assumptions on which his analysis is based. The polyethnic model assumes the existence of a society in which ethnicity is the major source of social cleavage and the major determinant of a person's social stratification prospects. In such a situation a balkanization of the society along ethnic lines may well be the appropriate strategy for bringing about social equality. The general issue raised by Bosnitch's paper, then, concerns the societal conditions required for making multiculturalism work within its intended framework.

Commitment to a policy of structural assimilation in the instrumental area of life carries with it the obligation to ensure that the economic and political opportunity structure of the larger society is readily accessible to all ethnic groups. To the extent that the official institutions are unable or unwilling to accommodate the legitimate interests and aspirations of the ethnic populations, a policy of discouraging political group formation along ethnic lines might work against the welfare of the parties concerned.

In much of the discussion about multiculturalism an instrumental component tends to be neglected. Certainly at the conference the expressive function of multiculturalism received most attention. For this reason, Bosnitch's paper made a valuable contribution. It fostered an awareness of the structural underpinnings required by a policy aimed at achieving equality through assimilation. It also raised the questions as to whether multiculturalism is equally relevant to all ethnic groups and whether there are differences among ethnic groups in the importance attached to each of the components of this policy. Does the expressive aspect of the policy draw support mainly from those ethnic groups who have successfully established themselves in Canada and whose interest in maintaining their ethnic identity derives from the fact that they are "refugee cultures"? Does multiculturalism have the same function for those groups who have recently arrived in Canada or are they motivated by more instrumental concerns, such as the need for mutual support? What is the value of a multicultural policy for groups who have made their way into the mainstream of Canadian society and who have no extra reason for wanting to preserve their cultural heritage?

Policy regarding charter groups

The status of Canada's two charter groups within the ethnic mosaic is circumscribed in the Official Languages Act. The purpose of the bilingual policy is two-fold: to define the linguistic boundaries within which the other ethnic groups have to operate and to establish an "equal partnership" between the majority and minority charter group. During the conference only the latter aspect was discussed.

Vallee, in his research on French-language groups in Canada, found that the willingness of the English-speaking and French-speaking groups to accord equal language rights to the other varied depending on the language belt in which they were located. Following Joy, Vallee identified three language zones: French Canada, "the bilingual belt" and English Canada. In the first and third zones assimilation to the language of the majority tended to be taken for granted: only in the second was the prevailing orientation dualistic and the policy of bilingualism accepted. These important findings raise questions about the basis for the contextual effects. It would be advisable to undertake detailed studies within each language belt to identify those who are the proponents and the opponents of bilingualism and to ascertain whether there are systematic differences between these two groups in terms of such factors as their economic prospects and cultural attachment to their own ethnic group.

Another fruitful starting point for analysis was proposed by Guindon, who argued that people will make an effort to become or stay bilingual only when they can perceive a pay-off for doing so. Necessity is the key to understanding language behaviour. The effectiveness of any language policy will, therefore, depend on the extent to which it affects language frontiers.

The hypothesis proposed by Guindon needs sharpening before it can be fruitfully used as a tool for research. The key variable, necessity, has a number of different dimensions that should be clearly differentiated. Language frontiers may be created by economic, political or moral necessities or by a combination of these. The potential impact of each of these necessities on language behaviour needs to be explored systematically.

Much is to be learned from studying people who have decided to learn a second language. What was the major motivational force behind this decision? How did these people become aware of the existence of a language frontier? By what kind of formal and informal mechanisms are language expectations communicated and enforced? Studies along these lines are necessary in order to increase our understanding of how language behaviour is influenced by social conditions.

Raymond Breton is a professor of Sociology at the University of Toronto. Jean Burnet is a professor of Sociology at Glendon College, York University. Norbert Hartmann is a Research Associate for the Metropolitan Separate School Board of Toronto. Wsevolod Isajiw is an associate professor of Sociology at the University of Toronto. Jos Lennards is an assistant professor of Sociology at Glendon College, York University.

Publications of the Canadian Ethnic Studies Association*

Other volumes in the series:

Slavs in Canada, Volume I (Toronto: Inter-University Committee on Canadian Slavs, 1967).

Slavs in Canada, Volume II (Toronto: Inter-University Committee on Canadian Slavs, 1968). Available from Peter Martin Associates.

Slavs in Canada, Volume III (Toronto: Inter-University Committee on Canadian Slavs, 1971).

Sounds Canadian: Languages and Cultures in Multi-Ethnic Society, Volume IV. Edited by Paul Migus (Toronto: Peter Martin Associates, 1975).

Journals:

Canadian Ethnic Studies / Études Ethniques du Canada

Canadian Ethnic Studies Bulletin / Bulletin Société Canadienne d'Études Ethniques

*formerly the Inter-University Committee on Canadian Slavs.

Index

A

Acadia, xii
Acculturation, 133, 135, 136, 140
l'Action Libérale Nationale, 85n.
Africa, 109; *see also* South Africa
Akhmatova, 66
Alberta, 51, 53, 178, 179; immigrant
    labour in, 18, 24; immigration to,
    16
All People's Mission, 12, 168
Almazoff, Moses, 27
American Revolution, xvi, 74, 75
Anderson, J.T.M., 168
Andrews, A.J., 26-27
Anerca, 41
"Anti-loafing Law", 21
Apartheid, 114
Appleyard, R.T., 184
The Apprenticeship of Duddy Kravitz,
    60
Art, ethnicity in, 46-56
Articles of Capitulation (1759), xiii
Ashdown, J.H., 20, 20n.
Asia, 109
Assimilation, 202, 212; and ethnicity,
    197-198; and structural incorpora-
    tion, 116; as form of cultural integra-
    tion, 110n., 111, 115; behavioural,
    177; church as agent of, 10; cultural,
    110n., 117, 124; in New France, xii,
    xiv, xvi; in South Africa, 119-121; in
    United States, 115-116; of Amerin-
    dians, xii, 155-156; of Canadian
    Indians, 155; of French Canadians, 72,
    73, 77, 121-122; of immigrants in Can-
    ada, 15, 117, 168-172, 173, 176; of
    immigrants in Manitoba, 3-10; of seige
    cultures, 118-126; public school as
    agent of, 9-10, 12; structural, 110n.,
    177, 194, 211; studies of, 167-172
Atwood, Margaret, 41, 57, 58, 59
Australasia, 5
Australia, 43; ethnicity research in, 184-
    187
Australian National University, 184, 185,
    186
Austria, 8
Austro-Hungarian Empire, 19
Avakumovic, Ivan, 174

B

"Baal Shem Tov", 65
Baldwin, James, 67
Barbeau, Raymond, 103
Beautiful Losers, 61, 62
Beckwith, John, 40-41
Bennett, John, 174
Berio, Luciano, 43
Berry, John, 174
Bhagavad Gita, 43

Bilingualism, xv, 80-81, 203, 212; in
    Manitoba public schools, 3-10,
    11-14
Bill of Rights, 158, 159, 160
Blake, William, 58
Blood and Gold, 186
Blumenberg, Sam, 25, 27
Boas, Franz, 170
Boissevain, Jeremy, 173
Borden, Robert, 15, 17, 21, 22, 23, 33
Borrie, W.D., 184
Borwitsi (Ukraine), 55
Bourassa, Henri, 6
Bourassa, Robert, 82
Bourgault, Pierre, 90, 96, 97, 101, 102
Bradwin, E., 168n.
Brandon (Manitoba), 5
Breton, Raymond, 174
Britain, xv, 28, 111; and inter-ethnic
    group bargaining in Quebec, 72-77
British Columbia, xvi, 179; aboriginal
    land claims in, 159, 160; immigrant
    labour in, 19, 20, 22, 24
British Columbia Employers' Association,
    24
British Columbia Loggers' Association, 24
British Columbia Manufacturers' Associa-
    tion, 24
British Empire, xiv, 8
British North America, 78
British North America Act (1867), 81,
    77-79, 154
Browning, Robert, 64
Bryce, P.H., 168
Building the Nation, 168
Bunkhouse Man, 168n.
Burnely, I.H., 184
Burnet, Jean, 173, 174
Burroughs, William, 62
Butler, Samuel, 48

C

Cage, John, 39, 43
Cahan, C.H., 22, 23, 24
Canada Dot — Canada Dash, 40
*Canada's Growth and Some Problems
    Affecting It,* 168
Canadian Ethnic Studies, 179
Canadian Ethnic Studies Association, 179,
    186
Canada Ethica Series, 173
Canadian Finnish Organization, 25
Canadian identification index, 133-150
The Canadian Japanese and World War II,
    173
Canadian Manufacturers' Association, 28,
    206
Canadian Mosaic, 168
Canadian National Committee for Mental
    Hygiene, 171

Canadian National Railways, 168
Canadian Northern Railways, 17
Canadian Pacific Railway (CPR), xvi, 34
Canadian Registration Board, 21
Canadian Society, 109
Canadian Studies, and ethnic studies, xi-xvii
Canberra (Australia), 184
Cannon, Helen, 51
Caouette, Réal, 89, 93, 97
Cardinal, Harold, 158
Carleton, Guy, 74
Cartier, George-Etienne, 78
Cento, 45
The Central European Immigrant in Canada, 168, 169, 170
Centre for Folk Culture Studies (National Museum of Man), 175
Chaput, Marcel, 90, 95, 102
Charitinoff, Michael, 23, 27
Children of Peace, 41
China, 39
Choosing a Path, 157
Citizens' Committee of One Thousand, 26
Clements, H.S., 21
Cohen, Leonard, 59, 61-62
Colbert, Minister of Finance, xiii
The Colonization of Western Canada, 168
Comparative Ethnic Relations, 109
Confederation, xvi, 4, 79
Confusions, 65
Connor, Ralph, 3, 6, 10
Constitutional Act (1791), 75-76, 77, 81
Co-operative Commonwealth Federation (CCF), 168
Corbett, David, 175
Cornwall, xvi
Côté-Mercier, Gilbert, 89, 93
Créditiste Movement (Quebec), 85-107
Crow's Nest Pass, 17, 20
Cultural Integration, and inter-ethnic relations, 109-126; and structural incorporation, 109-110, 110n., 111-110; comparison of, in Canada, United States and South Africa, 109-126; forms of, 110n., 111, 115; of Canadian Indians, xii-xiii, 154-160; of immigrants, 115-117, 125; of non-whites, 112-114, 124-125; of seige cultures, 118-126
Cultural Pluralism, 110n., 115, 117, 140; in New France, xii, xvi; in South Africa, 116-117; research, 172-179
Cultural Segmentation, as form of cultural integration, 110n., 111, 115
Culture, and ethnicity, 123-126; economic development as determinant of, 123-126; power as determinant of, 123-126.

D

Dafoe, John W., 5-6, 9, 10

d'Allemagne, André, 90, 95, 102
Dawson, C.A., 171-172, 185
"Dead End", 40
Debussy, Claude, 43
Department of Indian Affairs, xiii, 157
Department of Justice, 23, 26
Department of Secretary of State, 175 178, 179
Dion, Léon, 81, 82
Dorion, Antoine-Aimé, 79
Douglas, Major, 89, 94
Dream Passage, 43
Drumheller (Alberta), 24
Drybones Case, 158
Duplessis, Maurice, 79, 85n.
Dupuis, Yvon, 94, 95, 97
Durham, Lord, 76, 120
Durham Report, 76

E

Edict of Nantes (1685), xiv
Edmonton, immigrant labourers in, 20
Education, as agent of assimilation in Manitoba, 3-10
The Education of the New Canadian, 168
Elliott Lake, xvi
The Energy of Slaves, 62
England, 49, 50
England, Robert, 169-170, 171
Ethnic Groups, xi, 162, 171; Afrikaners, 110-126; American white southerners, 110-126; Amerindians, xii, xvi; Anglo-Canadians, 16, 23; Anglo-Saxons, 18, 20; Austro-Hungarians, 23; Canadian Indians, vi, 73, 154-160, 162; continental Europeans, 18; cultural integration of, *see* Cultural Integration; Doukhobors, 35, 171, 172; English Canadians, 71; Finns, 28; French, 162; French Canadians, 71-84, 110-126, 171; Germans, 23, 171; Hutterites, 160; in Manitoba, 3-10; inter-ethnic relations, *see* Inter-ethnic Relations; Japanese, 171; Mennonites, 9, 13, 160, 171; Mormons, 171; Poles, 163; research on, 167-179; Russians, 28; Ukrainians, 28, 35, 162, 163
Ethnic Identity, research issues on, 197-200
Ethnic Press, 13, 162
Ethnic Studies, American, 177-178; as part of Canadian Studies, xi-xvii; Australian, 184-187; Canadian, 162, 167-173
Ethnicity, xvi, 164, 211; and assimilation, 197-198; and culture, 123-126; and cultural identities, 58-59; and history, xi; and religion, 139-140; economic development as determinant of, 123-126; in art, 46-56; in Canadian writing, 57-67; in music, 39-45; power as determinant of, 123-126; research on, 167-179, 184-187, 191-196, 199-200

Europe, xii, 5, 15, 17, 21, 26, 28, 33, 35, 43, 48
Even, Louis, 89, 92
"Experiments in Didactic Art", 50
Expo '67, 40

F

Fellegi, Dr. Ivan, 133n.
Fernie, 25
Ferretti, Andrée, 95, 97, 101
Finnish Social Democratic Party, 19, 22, 22n.
Fishman, Joshua, 177, 178
Fitzpatrick, A., 28, 168
Fletcher, Robert F., 8
Foci, 44
The Foreigner, 3, 5
Fort William, immigrant labourers in, 20
Foster, Kate, 168
France, xiv, 73, 121
Francis, E.K., 173
French Canada in Transition, 172
Freud, Sigmund, 43
From Stranger to Citizen, 186
From the Tibetan Book of the Dead, 43
Frontenac, Comte de, xiii
Frye, Northrop, 65

G

Galicia (Austria), 19
Garant, Serge, 41-42
Gas, 40
Gendron Report, xvi
Germany, 8
Gibbon, John Murray, 168
Gingras, François-Pierre, 97n., 99
Gita, 43
Goldman, Emma, 20, 20n.
Gordon, Milton, 177
Gouin, Paul, 85n.
Grand Council of the Cree (Quebec), 159
Grand Trunk Railway, 17
Greene, Victor, 18
Greenway, 5
Gregoire, Gilles, 93
Group Settlement, 171
Grove, F.P., 59, 63-65
Guevara, Ché, 42
Gwatkin, Major General, 25

H

A Handbook for New Canadians, 168
Hansen, Marcus Lee, 177
Hartford (Connecticut), 36
Hartz, Louis, 109
Hawkins, Freda, 175
Heidegger, Martin, 58
Henderson, William, 24
Herberg, Will, 177, 178
Hobart, C.W., 178
Hoffman, E.T.A., 43
Hudson's Bay Company, xv

Hughes, Everett C., 172
Hughes, J.E., 40
Hunyadi, Sandor, 29
Hurd, W.B., 184

I

Icons, 44
Illinois, xii
"An Immigrant Farms in Western Canada", 51, 52
Immigrants, xi; acculturation of, 133; adaptation of, to new culture, 132-150; and anti-alien agitation, 22-28; Anglo-American, xiv; Asian, 134; as unskilled labour, 33, 15-29; Austrian, 21, 26; Basque, xiv; Black, 134; Bolshevist, 16; Catholic, 139, 140; central, 33, 169-170; continental European, 15, 16; cultural integration of, 115-117, 125; Doukhobor, 117; eastern European, 13, 33, 169-170; Eastern Orthodox, 139; English-speaking, 134-135, 136, 137, 139, 140, 162; European, 29; Finnish, 19, 22; French, xiii; German, xiv, 5, 24, 24n., 26; Greek, 134; Hutterite, 117; Icelandic, 13; identification of, with Canada, 132-150, 162; in New France, xi, xiii-xiv; in South Africa, 115-117, 125; in United States, 115-117, 125; intimidation of, 23-29; involvement of, in socialist organizations, 19, 22; involvement of, in trade unions, 18-19; Irish, xiv; Italian, xiv, 133n., 134; Jewish, xiv, 13, 133n., 134, 134n., 139, 140; Lithuanian, 18; Loyalist, xv, 75; Mennonite, 13; Mormon, 169; non-British, 169; non-English speaking, 136, 139; non-white, 134; Oriental, 15, 169; Polish, 5, 18, 27; Portuguese, 134; Protestant, 139; Russian, 22, 26, 27; Ruthenian, 27; Scandinavian, 18; Scottish, xiv; Slavic, xvi, 18, 19, 35, 117, 133n., 134; Slavic-speaking, 139, 140; Ukrainian, xvi, 5, 16, 17, 18, 22, 24, 29, 117; white European, 113, 125
Immigration, xv; Laurier-Sifton (1896-1914), xvi; to Eastern Canada (1815-1850), xvi; to Manitoba, 4-5; to Western Canada, xvi, 16
Immigration Act (Section 41), 27, 28
Immigration Deportation Board, 28
The Impact of Immigration on Canada's Population, 184
Indépendantiste Movement (Quebec), 86-103
India, 43
Indian Act, 154-160, 163, 203, 208
In Search of Utopia, 173
In Search of Zoroaster, 43
Institute of Political Action, 89
Integration, cultural, *see* Cultural Integration; social, 133, 140

Inter-ethnic relations, xii, xv, 15; and anti-alien agitation in Western Canada, 22-28; and inter-ethnic bargaining in Quebec, 71-84, 207-208; in New France, xii-xv; in South Africa, 109-126; in United States, 109-126; in Western Canada, 15-29; Indian Act as instrument in, 157-158; research issues in, 201-204; role of economic development and power in, 109-126, 204-205.
Intergroup Relations, *see* Inter-ethnic Relations
International Nickel Company, 24
International Workers of the World (IWW), 20
Iran, 43
Isaacs, Av, 51
Isaacs Gallery (Toronto), 50, 51, 53
Isajiw, W.W., 178
The Italians of Montreal, 173
Italy, 8

J

James, Henry, 64
James Bay, hydro electric development, xvi, 159
Janeway, Elizabeth, 57
Japan, 113
Joachim, Otto, 39
Johns, Jasper, 39
Johnson, Daniel, 85n.
Jones, Frank, 174
Jonsson, Einar Pall, 66
Joyce, James, 48
Jung, Carl, 43

K

Kalbach, W.E., 184
Kalin, M.R., 174
Kapuskasing (Ontario), 22
Kapuskasing Internment Camp, 27
Kasemets, Udo, 39
Kiev, 53
Kirby, Edmund, 18
Kirkconnell, Watson, 175
Klein, A.M., 65
Klymasz, Robert, 175
KolianKiwsky, Mykola, 53
KolianKiwsky, Olga, 53
Kreisel, Henry, 65
Kroetsch, Robert, 59
Ku Klux Klan, 47, 170
Kunitz, Stanley, 66
Kunz, Egon, 184, 186
Kyrie, 42

L

Ladysmith, 20
Lafontaine, Louis, 77
Laing, R.D., 58
La Ligue du Crédit Social, 93

Lamphier, Michael, 133n.
Lapalme, Georges, 93n.
"The Laundress", 66
Laurier, Sir Wilfrid, 5, 15, 17, 33, 35
Laurier-Greenway Compromise (1897), 4, 5, 6, 12
Lautt, M.L., 57
La Violette, Forest, 173
Layton, Irving, 59, 62-63
Leach, Edmund R., 61
Le Devoir, 6
Legault, Laurent, 93
Lemieux, Vincent, 85
Lévesque, René, 91, 95, 96, 97, 102
Levi-Strauss, Claude, 61
Lewis, John L., 19
Lichtenstein, Roy, 39
The Line Across, 40
Lipset, Seymour, 109
"Literary Criticism", 66
Literature, ethnicity in Canadian, 57-67
London (England), 77
Louisiana, xii
Louis Riel, 42
Lower Canada, 75, 76, 77, 79, 121
Ludwig, Jack, 65
Lust for Life, 48
Lutoslawski, Witold 43
Lyman, Stanford, 179

M

McClung, Nellie, 14
Macdonald, Hugh John, 23, 27
Macdonald, John A., xvi
McGill University, 172
Machaut, Guillaume de, 43
Mackenzie Pipeline, 159
Magrath, C.A., 168
Manitoba, xv, xvi, 121, 173, 179; assimilation in, 3-10; bilingualism in, 11-14; ethnic minority groups in, 3-10; immigration to, 4-5, 16; Legislative Act of 1916, 12, 13; multiculturalism in, 6; public education in, 3-10
Manitoba Educational Association, 8
Manitoba Free Press, 5, 12
Manitoba Historical Society, 7, 173
Manitoba Public Schools Act, 4, 5, 8
Manitoba School Trustees Association, 9
Manitoba Schools Question, xvi, 4
Mann, Thomas, 58
Marlyn, John, 29, 59, 65, 67
Marteau Sans Maitre, 41
Martin, Jean, 186
Mayewsky, Father, 47, 48
Meighen, Arthur, 21, 27
Melbourne (Australia), 184
"Memories of Farm and Bush Life", 50
Mercier, Honoré, 79, 85n.
Mexico, 48
Milner, Alfred, 120

Minority Groups, xi-xii, xvii, 3; French Canadians, 110, 118, 121-122, 126; Huguenot, xii; in Manitoba, 3, 5; in New France, xii, xiii-xv; in South Africa, 110-126; in United States, 110-126
Mobility, economic, 33, 34; social, 15, 34
Monteverdi, Claudio, 43
Montreal, 40, 42, 86, 94, 98, 172, 179
Morin, Claude, 96
Morton, W.L., 4
Mountain Lumber Manufacturers' Association, 21
Mouvement Souveraineté Association, 95
Multiculturalism, xii, 6, 163, 203, 211
Murray, James, 72
Musée Rath, 45
Music, ethnicity in, 39-45

N

Nagasaki (Japan), 44
Nahirny, Vladimir, 177, 178
National Association of Canada, 170
National Film Board, 52
National Museum of Man, 175
The National Policy, xvi, 5
Neumann, Brigitte, 133n.
New Brunswick Schools Question, xvi
Newcombe, Charles K., 7, 8, 14
Newcombe Report 7, 8, 12
Newfoundland, French colonies in, xii
New France, xii, 74; assimilation of non-French in, xiv; cultural pluralism in, xii; French/aboriginal relations in, xiii-xiv; minority groups in, xiii-xv
Niagara Falls (Ontario), 53
Nishga Tribal Council (British Columbia), 159
Norris, John, 179
Norris, T.C., 7, 8, 14
North West Company, xv
North West Mounted Police, 26, 27
Northwest Territories, 4, 158, 160; Supreme Court of, 159
Nova Scotia, United Mine Workers Strike (1909) in, 20

O

"Ode to Ecology", 40
Odyssey, 44
Official Languages Act, 212
Official Languages Bill, 10
Oliver, Frank, 20n.
One Big Union, 23
Onley, Gloria, 58
Ontario, 4, 10, 40, 121, 159; immigrant labour in, 17, 18, 19, 22, 24, 25
Option Québec, 96
Ossenberg, Richard, 109
Ostenso, Martha, 65
Ottawa, 80
Our Canadian Mosaic, 168

P

Pacific Scandal, xvi
Palfreeman, A.C., 185
Parizeau, Jacques, 96
Parti Créditiste du Quebec, 82, 87
Parti Crédit Social du Québec, 87
Parti Nationaliste, 85n.
Parti Québécois, 82, 83, 85, 87, 90, 96, 102n., 103
Peace Shall Destroy Many, 65
Pelletier, Réjean, 99, 102n.
Peterson, William, 173
Phrases II, 42
Picasso, Pablo, 58
Planned Migration, 173
Pluralism, cultural, *see* Cultural Pluralism
Plural Society Theory, 109, 110
The Polish Peasant in Europe and America, 162
Poole, I.R., 21
Port Arthur, 25
Porter, John, 15, 34, 179
Portrait of the Artist as a Young Man, 48
"Portraits of Minyan", 65
Potato Eaters, 53
Potsdam Conference (1945), 44
Pound, Ezra, 43
Prairie Provinces, 5, 11; immigration to, 16, 35
Price, Charles, 184, 185, 186
Protestant, Catholic, Jew, 178
Public Archives (Ethnic Archives division), 176

Q

Quand Nous Serons Vraiment Chez Nous, 90
Quebec, xv, xvi, 3, 40, 159, 160, 179; contemporary political movements in, 85-103; independence for, 81-84; political development of, 71-84; special status for, 80-81; *see also* New France
Quebec Act (1774), 74, 81, 121
Quebec City, 86, 98

R

Radicalism, alien, 22-23, 24, 25, 34
Ralliement des Créditistes, 85, 89, 93, 94, 94n.
Rassemblement pour l'Independance Nationale (RIN), 90, 95, 97, 98, 101, 102, 102n.
The Raw and the Cooked, 61
Rebellion of 1837-38, 76, 121
The Red Flag, 19
Red River, 4
Red River Rising (1869-70), xv
Registrar of Alien Enemies, 22
Religion, and Ethnicity, 139-140
Requiems for the Party Girl, 43
Richardson, Allan, 186

Richler, Mordecai, 59-61, 62
The Rich Man, 65
Richmond, Anthony, 133n., 174, 179, 184, 185
Riel, Louis, xv, 121
Rilke, Rainer, 60
Roblin, Sir Rodmond, 7, 14
Roman Catholic Church, xii, 73, 80
Rosthern (Saskatchewan), 16
Rouyn-Noranda (Quebec), 94
Royal Commission on Bilingualism and Biculturalism, 3, 10, 13, 14, 65, 167, 173; Report of, 11, 179, 202
Royal Commission on Industrial Relations, 24
Royal Proclamation (1763), 72, 81
Russia, 8, 22, 25
Russian Empire, 19
Russian Revolution, 16
Russian Social Democratic Party, 19, 22
Russian Workers' Union, 25
Ruthenian Training School, 5
Rutherford, Brent, 135n.
Ryan, Claude, 90

S

The Sacrifice, 65
Salverson, Laura, 65
Samson, Camil, 94
Sartre, Jean-Paul, 59
Saskatchewan, 179; immigration to, 16
Schafer, Murray, 43-44
Schermerhorn, R.A., 109
Schoppelerie, Oscar, 27, 28
A Search for America, 63, 64
The Second Scroll, 65
Seige Culture, 118-126; Afrikaner, 124-126; American white southern, 118-119, 126; Boer-Afrikaner, 119-121; French-Canadian, 118, 121-122, 126, 202-203
Segmentation, cultural, *see* Cultural Segmentation
Sharon (Ontario), 41
Sharon Fragments, 41
Siberia, 23
Sifton, Clifford, 5, 35
Sims, John, 51
Smith, Margaret, 49
Smith, W.G., 168
Social Democratic Party, Finnish, 22, 22n.; Russian, 22; Ukrainian, 22
Socialist Organizations, 23, 24, 27; involvement of immigrant labourers in, 19-20
Somers, Harry, 42-43
Son of a Smaller Hero, 60
South Africa, cultural integration in, 109-126; immigrants in, 115-117, 125; non-white ethnic groups in, 112-114; seige culture in, 119-121, 125
South Indian Lake, xvi
Southern Europeans in Australia, 186

Spettigue, Douglas, 64
Steiner, George, 67
Stockhausen, Karlheinz, 43
Stone, Irving, 48
Strangers Entertained, 179
Strangers Within Our Gates, 168, 169
Structural Incorporation, 109, 110n., 111, 116, 122-123, 124, 125
A Study in Canadian Immigration, 168
Sudbury (Ontario), 19, 25
Supreme Court of Canada, 158, 160
Survival, 58
Sweden, 90
Sydney (Nova Scotia), 24

T

Tachereau, Alexandre, 79
Taft, Ronald A., 186
Tallman, Warren, 63
Talon, Jean, xiii
Tanguily, Jean, 39
Tanguy, Yves, 39
Taylor, Don, 174
Terrebonne, 77
Thorton, R.S., 7, 8, 9, 10, 12, 14
Threnody, 43
The Toiling People, 19, 23
"Toi-Loving", 43
Toronto, 133n., 178, 184, 185; adaptation of immigrants in, 133-150
12 Miniatures, 42
Trades and Labor Congress (1915 Convention), 21
Trade Union Movement, and immigrant labour, 18-20, 24, 36
The Trumpets of Summer, 41
Turkey, 43

U

Ukraine, 9, 47, 52
Ukrainian Labour Temple Association, 25, 27
Ukrainian Social Democratic Party, 22; Lviv branch of, 19; Winnipeg branch of, 19
Ukrainian Women's Committee of Canada, 52
Under the Ribs of Death, 29, 65, 69
Union Act (1840), 76-77
United Mine Workers of America (UMWA), 18, 20, 22
Union Nationale, 82, 85, 85n., 86, 93n.
United (Province of) Canada, 76, 77, 79
United States, 17, 19, 21, 22, 35, 36, 44, 78, 79, 109; cultural integration in, 109-126; ethnic studies research in, 177-178; immigrants in, 115-117, 125; non-white ethnic groups in, 112-114, 124-125; seige culture in, 118-119
University of Calgary, 179
University of Chicago, 172

University of Toronto Quarterly, 175
University of Western Australia, 186
Upper Canada, 75, 76, 77, 156

V

Vallance Coal Company, 21
The Value to Canada of the Continental Immigrant, 168
Vancouver, 25
Vancouver Island, United Mine Workers Strike (1913) on, 20
Van Dyck, Anthony, 53
Van Gogh, Vincent, 53
Vapaus (Liberty), 19
Varèse, Edgard, 39
Vasyl Stephanyk (Ukraine), 53
Vers Demain, 93
The Vertical Mosaic, 15, 179
Victoria (British Columbia), 24
Volvox, 66

W

War Eagle Mine (British Columbia), 18
War of 1812, xv
Washington, D.C., 36
The Way of All Flesh, 48
Western Labor News, 26
Western School Journal, 9
Wiebe, Rudy, 65

Willard, Myra, 185
Willson, David, 41
Winks, Robin, 174
Winnipeg (Manitoba), 3, 5, 14, 22, 23, 25, 26, 47, 53, 54, 168; immigrant labourers in, 20
Winnipeg *Free Press,* 34
Winnipeg General Strike, xvi, 26, 27
Winnipeg Telegram, 23, 26
Winnipeg Trades and Labor Council, 25, 27
Wiseman, Adele, 65
Wood, W.A., 21
Woodcock, George, 59, 60, 174
Woodsworth, J.S., 12, 14, 168-169, 170, 171, 172
World War I, xvi, 3, 6, 15, 16, 20, 21, 23, 35, 102, 119, 170
World War II, 102, 113, 114, 117, 167, 179, 184

Y

Yarwood, A.T., 185
York University, 179
Yukon Territory, 160

Z

Zend, Robert, 66
Zubrzycki, J., 184, 185